GEORGE BUSH AT WAR . . .

"Saddam Hussein should have read *Flight of the Avenger* . . . The book . . . is of value precisely because George Bush is President and a president who has been willing to use American military power and risk American lives . . . Bush has seen men die and faced death himself."
—*Chicago Tribune*

. . . AND IN LOVE

"The best account this reviewer has seen on how Bush met, courted, and married Barbara Pierce."
—*Sunday Journal* (Flint, MI)

FLIGHT OF THE AVENGER

"Sheds new light on a period of the President's life unfamiliar to many Americans."
—*The State* (Columbia, SC)

"Written by an experienced reporter, *Flight of the Avenger* reveals the character and personality of George Bush at war . . . [and] the love story of George Bush and Barbara Pierce. Based on 'old-fashioned' and familial values, it reveals much about both personalities then and now."
—*Newport News Daily Press*

"The dramatic story of President Bush's days as a Navy bomber pilot and the heartwarming tale of his courtship and marriage . . . Hyams catches the full drama."
—*Extension Magazine*

FLIGHT
OF THE
AVENGER

GEORGE BUSH AT WAR

JOE HYAMS

B

BERKLEY BOOKS, NEW YORK

Excerpts first appeared in *U.S. News and World Report*, December 31, 1990/January 7, 1991 issue.

All photographs reproduced courtesy of the White House.

This Berkley book contains the complete text of the original hardcover edition. It has been completely reset in a typeface designed for easy reading, and was printed from new film.

FLIGHT OF THE AVENGER

A Berkley Book / published by arrangement with Harcourt Brace Jovanovich, Publishers

PRINTING HISTORY
Harcourt Brace Jovanovich edition published 1991
Berkley edition / October 1992

ISBN: 0-425-13466-0

A BERKLEY BOOK ® TM 757,375
Berkley Books are published by
The Berkley Publishing Group,
200 Madison Avenue, New York, New York 10016.
The name "BERKLEY" and the "B" logo
are trademarks belonging to Berkley Publishing Corporation.

PRINTED IN THE UNITED STATES OF AMERICA

10 9 8 7 6 5 4 3 2 1

Dedicated to the men of VT-51*

Ilie Amici, ARM 3/c

Hyman Atun, ARM 2/c

Andrew C. Barbera,
AMM 2/c

Paul B. Bensman,
AOM 2/c

Howard G. Boren, Lt.
(jg)

Richard L. Burdette,
Jr., ARM 3/c

Thomas W. Burns,
ARM 2/c

George H. W. Bush, Lt.
(jg)

Stanley P. Butchart,
Lt. (jg)

Charles Y. Bynum,
AMM 3/c

Ervin O. Carlson,
AMM 3/c

Howard Cramer, ACRM

James J. Cullen, CAMM

Forrest H. Daniels, Lt.
(jg)

John L. Delaney,
ARM 2/c

William K. Fenger,
ARM 3/c

Joseph L. Foshee,
AMM 2/c

Harold Fuchs, S 1/c

John L. Gallagher,
ARM 3/c

Donald Gaylien, ARM
3/c

Richard P. Gorman,
ARM 3/c

Lou J. Grab, Lt. (jg)

George A. Griffith,
ART 1/c

Jack O. Guy, Lt. (jg)

Charles L. Haggard,
ARM 3/c

Warren C. Heddy,

ACEM

Legare R. Hole, Lt.

Arthur L. Horan,
ARM 3/c

Roland R. Houle, Lt.

William M. Hutton,
ARM 3/c

Otis E. Ingram, ACOM

William R. Joyce,
AMM 2/c

Martin E. Kilpatrick,
Lt.

Richard O. Kolstad,
ARM 3/c

Albert W. Maxwell,
ACMM

William M. McCarter,
Lt. (jg)

George C. McJilton,
AOM 2/c

Samuel Melton, ARM 1/c

Donald J. Melvin,
Lt. Commander

Chester J. Mierzejewski,
AOM 1/c

Walter E. Mintus,
ARM 3/c

Milton G. Moore, Lt. (jg)

Lawrence L. Mueller,
AOM 2/c

Fred D. Myers, AMM 2/c

Leo W. Nadeau, AOM 2/c

Milan M. Nemsak, Ens.

Harold F. Nunnally,
ARM 3/c

Ralph E. Paulson,
AM 1/c

Charles Peter, Jr.,
AOM 2/c

Richard B. Playstead,
Lt. (jg)

John J. Raquepau,
Lt. (jg)

Joseph H. Reichert,
ARM 1/c

John H. Richards,
AMM 2/c

Denzel A. Rybolt,
AMM 1/c

Joseph S. Smith, Jr.,
AMM 2/c

George L. Stoudt,
AMM 3/c

Bryon E. Teer, AMM 1/c

Wendell M. Tomes,
ARM 2/c

Jerrold R. Ward,
ARM 3/c

Francis M. Waters,
Lt. (jg)

Douglas H. West, Lt. (jg)

Robert E. Whalen,
AMM 1/c

William G. White,
   Lt. (jg)
Roy W. Whitman, YM 1/c

Carl H. Woie, Ens.
James J. Wykes, Ens.

---

*Navy rating code for WWII

ACEM: Aviation Chief
   Electrician's Mate
ACOM: Aviation Chief
   Ordnance Man
ACRM: Aviation Chief
   Radio Man
ACMM: Aviation Chief
   Machinist Mate
AM: Aviation Metalsmith
AMM: Aviation Machinist Mate

AOM: Aviation Ordnance
   Man
ARM: Aviation Radio-
   man
ART: Aviation Radio
   Technician
Ens.: Ensign
Lt.: Lieutenant
Lt. (jg): Lieutenant,
   junior grade
S: Seaman
Y: Yeoman

Prologue

The first warnings of what was to come arrived from distant corners of the world, from faraway places unknown to most Americans. There was the Manchurian incident—the name now given to Japan's 1931 invasion of Manchuria—and beginning in 1937 there was the so-called Sino-Japanese War, which meant Japan had invaded China. Cities were bombed, civilians slaughtered. From their seats in movie houses or sitting at home reading the evening paper, Americans learned of the madness beyond the oceans. Watching newsreels, Americans laughed at Italy's Mussolini: dressed in an elaborate uniform, he waved his arms and shouted. Then in 1935 the Italians invaded Ethiopia, and more cities were bombed, more civilians were killed. Hitler, too, was in Europe. Dressed in his own snappy getup, he waved his arms and shouted. In 1936 Germany remilitarized the Rhineland and then in 1938 annexed Austria and Czechoslova-

kia's Sudetenland. Then Italy invaded Albania.
And there was the Spanish Civil War.

The Europeans signed pacts and made
pledges. They all declared themselves for peace,
and then, early in the morning of September 1,
1939—without declaring war—German soldiers invaded Poland. Something terrible had
begun.

War again in Europe: remembering World
War I, most Americans wanted nothing of this
new conflict. Feeling themselves safe between
the two broad oceans, they looked on as the
fighting spread. And it spread with flames,
with spectacular and terrifying destruction
made possible by new weapons that changed
forever the nature of war. Battlefields covered
enormous areas—eventually continents—and
the fighting was not between rival armies but
between entire nations, with as many civilians
killed as uniformed soldiers. Americans learned
new words: Blitzkrieg and Messerschmitt, Stuka
and Panzer. And as they watched, the flames
spread closer.

The world war came to the United States on
December 7, 1941: Pearl Harbor was attacked,
as were American bases on Wake and Midway
islands farther off in the Pacific. The Japanese
Empire, using aircraft carriers within three
hundred miles of Pearl Harbor, launched wave
after wave of torpedo bombers, dive bombers, and
fighters against soldiers, sailors, and airmen who
had just started their Sunday morning routines.

The surprise attack caught not only the military personnel and civilians but also the navy fleet in the harbor totally unprepared. Within two hours 2,000 navy men were killed and 710 wounded, while the army and Marines lost 327 killed and 433 wounded; and eighteen ships of the fleet were destroyed.

The nation reacted with horror, and four days later, declaring Sunday, December 7, "a date which will live in infamy," President Roosevelt asked Congress to declare war on Japan. Congress complied, and war was declared six and one-half minutes later. On that same day Germany and Italy declared war on the United States.

The declarations of war were followed by outrage and a surge of patriotism unparalleled in American history. Despite the fact that draft evasion for this war reached unparalleled heights, it seemed that every American wanted to avenge the country's honor. Enlistments in the armed services shot up; youths under seventeen lied about their age and falsified birth certificates so they could join up; within months after Pearl Harbor any male of draft age who was not in the service was embarrassed to be seen on the streets, afraid of being charged with not doing his share in the war effort.

The country was united, and the war was no longer far away. It was now truly a global conflict, involving thirty-eight nations. Ameri-

cans suddenly found themselves fighting on nearly all the world's continents and all its oceans—in particular, in the 70 million square miles of the Pacific.

On the home front Americans worked together for victory. Isolationism had ended with Pearl Harbor, and the "arsenal of democracy" swung into high gear, supplying the Allies with the materials of war—and of survival. The war brought prosperity, an end to the Depression, but few Americans found joy in that, for few American families were unaffected by the war, as fathers and sons left home. Suddenly women became an important part of the work force— some 3.5 million American women took jobs on factory assembly lines, in stores and offices, taking over jobs traditionally held by men, particularly in defense plants. Rosie the Riveter (real name: Rosina D. Bonavita) became a new national image, and for working women, trousers became a "badge of honor."

Pearl Harbor was only the first in what seemed an endless series of defeats for America and her allies. The Japanese conquered the Philippines, Malaya, most of Burma, Indonesia, Singapore, many more Pacific islands, even parts of the Aleutians and New Guinea. The Allies were losing the war throughout the world, and late summer of 1942 was their darkest moment. The eastern boundary of the Empire of the Rising Sun then ran from the Aleutians down past Wake Island in the central

Pacific to the Gilberts on the equator; in the west it extended from the Manchurian border through eastern China to Burma and on to India; to the south it included Sumatra, Java, Timor, half of New Guinea, and all of the Solomons. In North Africa the Germans and Italians were driving into Egypt, in Russia they had penetrated the Caucasus and launched a massive attack on Stalingrad, and German submarines were sinking Allied ships in the Atlantic right up to the Gulf of Mexico and the shores of the United States—ships were sunk in New York Harbor. Then the tide began to turn, and on continent after continent, in battle after battle, the Allies moved from defeat toward ultimate victory: North Africa, Sicily, the mainland of Italy, and then Normandy.

In 1943 the war, especially the one being fought in the Pacific, was beginning to change. After the battles of the Coral Sea and Midway, the Japanese navy no longer dominated the Pacific. General Douglas MacArthur and Admirals Nimitz and Halsey, facing an enemy spread across the enormous ocean, designed a technique of island hopping, attacking certain Japanese bases and leaving others stranded and helpless without supplies. Their overall strategy involved two broad thrusts: one from Guadalcanal up the Solomon Islands toward New Guinea and on to the Philippines; the other toward the Marshall and Gilbert islands and then on to the Marianas and the Philippines. The war against the Japanese became a list of names: islands attacked, one after another, first by bombers and naval guns, then by amphibious landings of Marines and army infantry. Each of the islands—Guadalcanal, Tarawa, Palau, Eniwetok, Kwajalein—pitted Americans against Japanese defenders determined to die rather than surrender.

By the summer of 1944 German submarines were losing the struggle in the Atlantic and the Allies controlled the skies over Europe: massed bombers struck at cities deep in Germany. To the east the Russians had counterattacked and, pushing back the Germans, were making their way toward Berlin.

The Allies were making headway in the Pacific, too. They had secured all the outer-island strongholds from the Solomons to the Aleutians. In June 1944, while the Allies in Europe were breaking out of their Normandy beachheads, American forces attacked the Japanese on Saipan and Guam. The Japanese sent a fleet to aid the base: historians call the ensuing encounter the battle of the Philippine Sea; the men who took part in it dubbed it the Marianas Turkey Shoot.

American aircraft made long-range attacks on Japanese-held islands, sometimes cutting off supply lines, sometimes destroying radio transmitters or airfields. On the last day of August, planes from carrier-based Pacific squadrons began a three-day attack on the Japanese installations on Iwo Jima and the Bonin Islands.

Among the planes used in these attacks was a new bomber with a powerful design created to meet the needs of the new and aggressive war. Since the prototype had been approved on December 15, 1941, just eight days after the Japanese attack on Pearl Harbor, it had been christened the Avenger.

Chapter One

September 1, 1944.

Don Melvin, commander of Torpedo Bombing Squadron Fifty-one (VT-51) stood alongside the blackboard in the ready room of the fast aircraft carrier USS *San Jacinto* and looked out at the thirteen pilots and thirty-two enlisted men in his squadron as they were being briefed on that morning's assignment by Lt. M. E. "Buster" Kilpatrick, the air combat intelligence (ACI) officer. The carrier was only fourteen thousand tons—three thousand tons less than the standard carriers—and thus the compartment in which the men were being briefed was small. She had been built hurriedly after Pearl Harbor on the hull of a light cruiser, but she was fast and effective.

In his heavy Georgia drawl Kilpatrick told the men their mission was a bomber strike on the radio tower transmitter atop Mount Yoake Peak on Chichi Jima, one of three islands in

the Bonin chain, which also included Iwo Jima.
For a time the Japanese on the tiny island had
been intercepting U.S. military radio transmissions and warning Tokyo and occupied enemy
islands of impending American air strikes. Also a
key supply center, the Bonins were only six
hundred miles south of Tokyo, and the Japanese
had dug in for a protracted fight.

As Kilpatrick continued his explanation of the
day's mission, Melvin studied the men in his
squadron. Today, like every other day, he was
concerned about them: he had already lost six
pilots, and he considered each man as family. He
himself had but one mission in life: to get all of
them back home safely.

Sitting at the far end of the first row of
seated pilots was the next-to-oldest member of
the squadron, twenty-seven-year-old Legare
"Gar" Hole, the squadron executive officer. A
New Yorker and the father of an infant son,
Hole had been an instructor at the navy flight
school in Pensacola and had spent the previous
nine months flying observation planes over
Cuba. Melvin had recently recommended him
for a Navy Cross. Seated next to Hole was wiry,
twenty-two-year-old Stanley "Butch" Butchart
from Spokane, Washington. Butchart could fix
anything mechanical on a plane. He was also
the best natural flier Melvin had ever known.
Then there was Milton Moore, one of the
squadron's youngest. Moore had loved airplanes since his childhood in a New York

suburb and had enlisted in the navy on his eighteenth birthday. Not only was he steady and dependable, but he was also an excellent flier.

Seated next to Moore was Jack O. Guy, a tall, easygoing Southerner who had been a bank clerk in Atlanta before enlisting in the navy. Guy had received a Navy Cross for action against the Japanese fleet in the first battle of the Philippine Sea in June of that year. And next to Guy was George Herbert Walker Bush, who, at six feet two inches, was the tallest and the youngest pilot in the squadron.

Melvin knew all the facts in Bush's records. He had enlisted in the navy's flight training program on his eighteenth birthday and had become one of the youngest commissioned pilots in the U.S. Navy when he won his wings.

The lanky boy from Connecticut had blue eyes, a thatch of brown hair, and a wacky sense of humor; he had given nicknames to almost every pilot in the squadron. He was the best at playing Twenty Questions, the game pilots played on the flight deck to while away boredom between flights. Only the day before, Bush had correctly deduced from the clues that the right answer to a tough question was "George Washington's right eyebrow."

Melvin could also have compiled a long list of things George Bush did not do. He didn't cuss, drink, smoke, or talk about women. Melvin had heard that the young pilot came from a wealthy

Eastern family, but Bush never spoke about them. Bush had good manners and spoke with a correctness rare even among officers. The young pilot kept his own counsel, wrote a lot of letters, and read voraciously. He was a good athlete, the man to have on your side in a volleyball game on the hangar deck. He wasn't a natural flier like Butchart, who flew by the seat of his pants, but he was capable and, when given an order, carried it out without griping or questioning. He was a kid doing a man's work, and Melvin was glad to have him aboard.

The pilots wore sweat-stained khaki flight suits and sat in leather chairs held by brackets to the constantly rolling deck. In between sips of steaming coffee from heavy white mugs they plotted the day's course on navigation chart boards held on their laps. The enlisted men who were their crews—gunners and radio operator–gunners—sat or stood in the back of the room. The air was choked with cigarette smoke and clammy with drafts from air-conditioning vents that were better at making noise than ventilating.

The pilots listened intently. Although they knew that some of them might not make it back to the carrier, after several days of inactivity they were eager to see action. It was their responsibility to fly the enormous single-engine TBF (Torpedo-Bomber by Grumman) Avenger planes to Chichi Jima and drop their four five-hundred-pound bombs on the target.

Kilpatrick, who had been a successful lawyer in Atlanta, Georgia, before enlisting, told the men only that their target was an essential link in Japanese transpacific communications. It was important that they not know too much, in the event that they were shot down, captured, and tortured.

He said that, according to intelligence reports, the Japanese had concealed their defensive cannons in hundreds of ridges and terraces and underground pillboxes connected by subterranean tunnels and covered with eight to twelve feet of solid concrete. The pilots could expect heavy antiaircraft fire but little activity from enemy aircraft—the landing strip had already been bombed. Any pilots shot down or forced to abandon their planes should head out to sea, where a U.S. submarine would be circling to pick them up. "Look for the periscope," he said. The men had small maps of the Bonin Islands made of waterproofed silk, which they carried in their flying suits. Those maps indicated the strength of the water currents and prevailing winds so that, if shot down, the men would have some idea of what to consider when navigating to safety.

When Kilpatrick finished his briefing, Melvin took over. A broad-shouldered man, five feet eleven inches and 175 pounds, Melvin had been in the navy for five years before the United States entered the war, and already had been awarded a Navy Cross. Most of his squadron considered him an old man because he was thirty-three and they were in their twenties. His age showed in his thinning brown hair, but he had the merry blue eyes of a kid and a smile made boyish by two protruding buck teeth. Behind his back the pilots affectionately referred to their skipper as Mortimer, after the ventriloquist's dummy Mortimer Snerd.

All his life Don Melvin had dreamed of being a pilot. As a boy growing up in New Jersey, the youngest of three brothers, he had a bedroom filled with balsa wood models of airplanes painstakingly carved after school. When his family moved to Los Angeles, he spent Saturdays at the airport watching the planes land and take off. He got his pilot's license in 1929 at the age of eighteen and his navy wings of gold in 1937, the same year he married his "Honey," a petite (five-foot-one-half-inch) brunette named Catherine.

Melvin had shouldered responsibility quickly as a young husband and father, and now he felt responsible for the lives of the men who sat facing him. All of them had been with the squadron since it was commissioned as a torpedo bomber group in September 1943 in Norfolk, Virginia. Since then most of his pilots had flown more than fifty missions each, but they were always vying with one another to see who could get in the most. They were long overdue for rotation back to the States, and Melvin knew that each time they went on a strike the odds against their safe return increased.

He told the men that he would be leading them in and that they should maintain radio silence until over the target area. He handed each pilot a map of Chichi Jima with the coordinates of the transmitter, a pinpoint on the tiny island, which is only five miles by three, about double the size of New York's Central Park.

"If I have my way, we'll probably go up to nine thousand feet; then we'll try to approach the target from the sun, and we'll come out of the sun at them, and then we'll retire out here," Melvin said, pointing with his pencil to an area of the wall map behind him.

It was overcast at 0530 hours that morning with a thin cloud layer at around one thousand feet. It was always overcast in the morning, although Melvin promised the skies would be clear by dawn. "Perfect flying weather," he said.

He gave the plan of attack. Bush and two other pilots from the squadron would attempt to bomb the transmitter, during a strike on Futami Harbor by torpedo and dive-bombers from the heavy carrier *Enterprise*.

His instructions were brief. "The radio station is your primary target," he said. "The dock is your secondary. Don't waste your bombs. If you can't hit the primary, go for the secondary."

There was no joking around at the briefing session, which was all business.

"One last thing," Melvin said before dismissing his pilots. "If you're on target while making a dive-bombing run, drop your bombs and get the hell out of there. There's no point in getting yourself shot up."

After the dawn briefing, Bush and his fellow pilots ate a breakfast of powdered eggs, bacon, sausage, dehydrated fried potatoes, and toast while the ship's ordnance crew brought up the bombs and ammunition for their planes by elevator from four decks below. The guns were loaded and the bombs put in racks in the bomb bay. All the planes that were to be used in the strike were warmed up by the plane captains, enlisted men in charge of servicing and maintaining the carrier's aircraft.

Melvin had been right. Within half an hour of the scheduled strike the weather cleared. On board the carrier, fifty miles east of Chichi Jima, the morning was warm and humid. The San Jacinto was churning along at twenty-two knots, waiting for Adm. Marc Mitscher, commander of Task Force Fifty-eight, which comprised nine aircraft carriers, to give the order for all ships to turn into the wind so that the planes could be launched. When the command was given by semaphore (a system of signaling by the use of two flags, one held in each hand), the carriers turned into the northwest breeze, which brought the wind along the flight deck of the San Jacinto to a steady thirty to thirty-two knots.

A minute into sunrise a metallic voice over

the squawk box in the ready room announced, "Pilots, man your planes!" Pilots and crews ran out to their planes on the flight deck. There was no small talk or kidding among the fliers now. They all knew it was going to be a rough mission.

Tall as he was, George Bush was dwarfed by his aircraft. The TBF Avenger of World War II was the largest single-engine carrier-based plane in the world. The standard joke among the pilots was that weighing eight tons loaded, it could fall faster than it could fly. The forty-foot-long Avenger towered almost eighteen feet over the carrier's deck. It had a fifty-four-foot wingspan (reduced to nineteen when the wings were folded). Like all navy planes, it was painted dark blue on top fading to white on the bottom of the fuselage and wings. A large 2 was stenciled aft of the wings of Bush's plane, and 2X was painted on the rudder. Just under the cockpit, his gunner, twenty-year-old Leo "Lee" Nadeau, in contravention of navy practice, had long ago painted *Barbara*, the name of Bush's fiancée. No one in the squadron knew that Lee had gotten married five days before the ship left the States, but he had painted *Ginny*, his wife's name, under his turret.

Bush wore a yellow Mae West (inflatable vest) over his lightweight flight suit. On his chest the gold navy wings had faded from a worn leather namepatch. In a shoulder holster under the jacket he carried a short-barreled .38 Smith & Wesson revolver, standard issue for the navy.

The earflaps of his sweat-stained cotton helmet smacked in the wind. He put his feet fully into the footholds inset in the plane's armored fuselage and gripped the recessed hand-grips tightly as he pulled himself up into the cockpit, using the bar that halved the open canopy for purchase. Frank Paoletti, his plane captain, who was standing on the wing, helped him into his shoulder harness, which was hooked to the chute strap. The seat pack contained a parachute, some survival gear, and a cushion on top. Bush settled uncomfortably on the pack, wriggling as he tried to maneuver the small cans of water in the seat pack so they would not dig into him.

He studied the navigational chart again so that he could orient himself to the contours of the island as it would look from the air. The chart also had a grid, on which he indicated wind direction, the location of the carrier, and the direction from ship to target. With the variables of longitude and latitude, he would be able to know where he was at any time, especially in the event that he was forced down. Satisfied that he was familiar with all he needed to know, he stored the chart board under the instrument panel and began his instrument check.

Lee Nadeau crawled into the plane through

the radio operator's hatch in the lower fuselage. He pulled himself up through a narrow opening into the aft-facing Plexiglas ball turret directly behind Bush and secured an armor plate underneath his seat. His chest chute hung outside the turret in the radioman-gunner's compartment below. The turret was so small that Lee could not wear a chute. If he had to bail out he would go below into the turret, where the radioman would assist him into his chute and they would both exit through the starboard-side fuselage hatch. Both men were experienced at this procedure from many drills.

As Lee was checking out the rotation of his .50 caliber machine gun, John "Del" Delaney, the radioman, closed the fuselage hatch. Del, a cheerful, blue-eyed Irishman from Rhode Island and the old man of the crew—he was twenty-three—also manned the aft-facing .30 caliber machine gun, or "stinger," just forward of the rudder at the belly of the fuselage.

Bush checked his fuel gauge: the plane had been topped off. He then connected the plug to his helmet earphones, switched on his microphone, and tested the intercom to be certain he was in contact with each member of his crew.

On the bridge Lt. Comdr. A. B. Cahn, the flight director, shouted through the loud hailer, "Start engines!" As the engines started, they sputtered, coughed, backfired, belched flame from the exhaust stacks, and then settled into a deep, throaty roar. Specialized flight-deck crewmen wearing distinguishing colors rushed from plane to plane in a carefully controlled frenzy of activity, coaching each airplane into position. Bush got a thumbs-up sign from the brown-shirted plane captain on the flight deck. Two purple-shirted chock-men pulled the chocks out from under the wheels. Following hand signals, he taxied forward as fire fighters in red got out of the way through a cacophony of engines, loudspeakers, and prop wash. The plane rocked as he tested his brakes. He was passed by hand signals from one red-shirted taximan to another, spreading his wings out on a signal as he went. Two blue-shirted and helmeted plane-handlers darted under the wings to make sure they were locked in place. Satisfied, they gave him a thumbs-up. Green-shirted catapult crewmen hooked the plane by cables from the landing gear to the hydraulic catapult.

The order "Launch aircraft!" came from Cahn on the bridge. Melvin was the first to be catapulted from the carrier. Then it was Bush's turn. The catapult officer gave him a signal to rev up. He stayed at full throttle until the ship's deck tilted upward and the catapult officer crossed his arms over his chest—the ready signal. Released, the catapult pulled the huge plane down the flight deck, accelerating it from 0 to 150 knots (172 mph) in 120 feet, slamming Bush and his crew back into their seats as they were hurled with a thrust of eight G's into the void beyond the flight deck.

The deck disappeared in a flash of light, replaced by the blue waves of the ocean. Bush breathed a sigh of relief as he felt the plane airborne: although he had made more than one hundred carrier takeoffs, he was never sure whether the gargantuan plane would gain altitude or just plop down into the water under the carrier's bow. He tucked up his landing gear, milked up his flaps, closed the canopy cover, and gained altitude to reach Melvin, who was circling at fifteen hundred feet forward of the carrier waiting for his squadron to join him.

The skies were light-blue with scattered clouds. High in the distance, to the west, Bush could see eight F-6 Hellcats from the *Enterprise* slowly weaving back and forth, waiting for the even slower Avengers. Other planes would bomb and strafe the island while Melvin's squadron went for the transmitter. The Hellcat fighters would escort them all, providing protection against any attacking Japanese aircraft.

The four Avengers were soon flying in diamond formation at around 150 knots with the Hellcats flying in a thatch weave pattern, crisscrossing overhead to provide protection. Within half an hour they were at their assigned altitude of nine thousand feet, and Bush could make out the jagged peaks of Chichi Jima off in the distance. He pulled out the chart board and glanced from the map out to the island; there was the harbor, and rising above it the mountain with his primary target. The other squadrons began to dive on Futami Harbor. Their attack caught several enemy vessels out in the harbor, and as Bush watched, he could see one of the fighters dive low to strafe a small cargo ship.

Melvin peeled off and in a steadily accelerating glide headed straight for the radio tower perched on the slope of Mount Yoake. Tracers rising from the ground like Roman candles probed the squadron leader's aircraft as he released his bombs. Seconds later Bush saw the buildings surrounding the tower explode in orange flame. The skipper made a wide, gentle turn toward the ocean and gained altitude. He would wait for the other planes in his squadron to join him and then head for home.

Suddenly Bush saw and felt the pounding jolt of black shellbursts from Japanese antiaircraft guns, the heaviest flak he could recall. Realizing that the Japanese gunners had him in a crossfire, he tried to maneuver his plane to make himself a difficult target. He rolled the huge Avenger nearly over, pulling the plane's nose onto the target from an inverted position. As the plane dove, his weight was no longer on his back and seat but forward against the seat harness, his feet pressed on the rudder pedals. As the earth raced toward him, he fought to keep the plane on target while holding the dive.

The sudden drop in altitude hurt his ears, and he shouted to relieve the pressure. He glanced at his altimeter: the thin, black needle was dropping swiftly. He kicked the plane onto target and looked down into the stream of tracer bullets streaking over the cockpit. Had the Japanese gunner down there on the island moved his barrel a fraction of an inch, the Avenger would have been hit.

On target, Bush pressed the electrical switch that opened his bomb bay doors. As he hit the button on the bomb release, an explosion just off his wing rocked the aircraft. But it was too late to make a correction. He continued the dive and pulled up only two or three hundred feet above the water.

He was so occupied with managing the plane that it was moments before he reacted to Lee's frantic voice on the radio: "Gunner to pilot. Are you all right?"

"Pilot to gunner," he replied. "I'm okay, but I had to drop low. They were right on us and I was busy."

Bush made a sharp turn to the left and poured on the power. It was time to rendezvous with the rest of the squadron and head home. But Bush's heart was heavy. Because of the mass of flak, he knew that he had missed the transmitter. From what he had seen, none of the other Avengers had scored direct hits, either.

At the debriefing session after the flight,

Bush learned that VT-51 was going to have to strike Chichi Jima again the next day. The future president of the United States had no idea that that day—September 2, 1944—would be one of the longest and saddest in his life.

Chapter Two

The future of George Herbert Walker Bush, along with all the hopes his family had for him, was manifested in his name. His parents had often discussed what to call their second child and had agreed that if the child was a boy, he would be named after his maternal grandfather, George Herbert Walker. The choice was apt: Grandfather Walker, a fourth-generation American whose ancestors had come from England in the seventeenth century, embodied the best aspects of a certain portion of American society. A devoutly religious man—he himself was named for the seventeenth-century English religious poet George Herbert—he was also a successful businessman, founder of his own investment firm, and an avid sportsman: not only a champion polo player but also the founder of the Walker Cup for international golfing competition. After establishing himself in St. Louis, he had built a family summer-house on a rockbound promontory in Kennebunkport, Maine, which he named Walkers Point. He loved the sea and sailing. Family was important to him, work was important to him, but above all he was active in his community, using his position and his power for the benefit of others.

Prescott Sheldon Bush, George's father, was a third-generation American who could trace his family's roots back to England's King Henry III, making George a thirteenth cousin, twice removed, of Queen Elizabeth II. An imposing six foot four, with deep-set blue-gray eyes and a resonant voice, Prescott was a natural athlete and expert at most sports. A successful investment broker, he was also a community leader and, later in life, a United States senator.

The Bush family had been listed in each edition of *Dau's Blue Book* from its first publication in 1907 until it was discontinued three decades later. Thus, at birth George inherited more than a name. He came into a long and proud family history with the accompanying traditions and emotional supports. He also inherited a good chance for success in the world of business; and he was probably destined to love sports and to excel at whichever he chose. Born into a tight-knit family, he formed a strong desire to have a large family of his own. But most of all, George Bush was born to serve—serve his country and the American people. That is part of what the name he was given entailed, that is what his parents hoped for him, that is what he himself planned. Public service was a responsibility and an obligation passed down to him from his ancestors: it was an integral part of his family tradition and an important aspect of his life from his earliest days.

George's father, Prescott Sheldon Bush, was born in Columbus, Ohio, in 1896 and attended St. George's School in Newport, Rhode Island. In 1913 he entered Yale, where he was inducted into the prestigious secret society Skull and Bones. He was also captain of the baseball team. Prescott graduated from Yale with a B.A. degree just after the United States entered World War I and immediately enlisted in the army. After training at Fort Sill, Oklahoma, he spent a year serving with the field artillery in the American Expeditionary Force in Europe, rising to the rank of captain.

After his discharge from the army he started his business career with Simmons Hardware and Wholesale Company of St. Louis, Missouri. The company soon realized that Prescott had a sharp mind for accounting, and put him in charge of a leather plant making saddles and bridles in Kingsport, Tennessee, which had been operating in the red. Given the opportunity to settle the plant's affairs, Prescott's advice to the home office was "Sell it." Prescott's advice was taken, and his reputation as an administrator was established.

Two years later, in 1921, Prescott married Dorothy Walker at the Episcopal Church of St. Ann in Kennebunkport, Maine. The tall, athletic Prescott and the lithe, beautiful, vivacious Dorothy made a handsome couple. He was a strict and hardworking man; she had an incisive wit that delighted her young husband.

After the hardware company was bought by the Winchester Repeating Arms Company, Prescott returned to Columbus to help his father, Samuel, who was president of the Buckeye Castings Company of Columbus, but the business failed within the year.

Prescott was then offered a job by the creditors of the Hupp Products Company, a floor-covering firm, to straighten out its financial affairs. Prescott quickly located the source of the company's problems—illegal profit skimming—and soon found himself facing the ire of Mr. Hupp, who had reason to take the matter seriously. The situation became so touchy that Prescott found it expedient to keep a loaded gun in his desk drawer. When Hupp was convicted of swindling, his creditors asked Prescott to stay on and run the small firm. He did, successfully, until after a series of mergers it became part of the United States Rubber Company.

For the first few years of their marriage the Bushes moved often. A first son, Prescott, Jr., nicknamed Pres, was born in Maine. George was born almost two years later on June 12, 1924, in Milton, Massachusetts. After Prescott and George, a daughter, Nancy, was born. Then came Jonathan and William Henry Trotter. (William, fourteen years younger than George, was named after a family friend whose nickname was Bucky, and so young William was also called Bucky.)

In 1926 Prescott accepted a job with W. A. Harriman Company, a prestigious and influential Wall Street brokerage house: Averell Harriman and E. Roland Harriman were Yale alumni as well as fellow members of the Skull and Bones. In 1931 the company was merged with Brown Brothers. Thanks to his diligence and charisma, Prescott was soon made a managing partner of Brown Brothers, Harriman.

The Bushes moved to a small house on Stanwick Road in Greenwich, Connecticut, a fashionable and exclusive bedroom community for New York City. Prescott's income enabled his growing family to live well, and they soon moved again, this time to a big, comfortable, dark-shingled house with a broad veranda on Grove Lane in Greenwich. There they were attended by four servants: a cook, two maids, and a chauffeur.

Pres's and George's lives were charted from birth. Their father had determined that his sons would be educated at Phillips Academy in Andover, Massachusetts, and then go on to

Yale. They would be educated and trained to be members of America's elite: they would be made into leaders.

Pres, who had been born with a weak leg and a blind eye from a congenital cataract, was enrolled at the Greenwich Country Day School, an exclusive all-male academy for youngsters slated for private secondary schools. When George was five, he, too, was enrolled at Greenwich, a year earlier than most others in his class so that he could be with his older brother and not be left alone at home. George carried around a weighty landmark of a name—George Herbert Walker Bush—but he himself was rather small—was, in fact, the shortest youngster in his class at school.

Alec, the family chauffeur, drove the two boys to school every morning after dropping Prescott, Sr., at the railroad station for the morning commute to Manhattan. The Depression was nowhere in evidence as the boys glided in the family's black Oldsmobile past the stone fences, stables, and swimming pools of one of the wealthiest communities in America.

Prescott Bush was a thrifty man who daily impressed on his children the value of a dollar and encouraged frugality and saving. He had no sympathy for the nouveaux riches who flaunted their wealth—they were without class, he said. As a sage and strictly honest businessman, he had often turned failing companies around, making them profitable again, and he had scorn for people who went bankrupt because they mismanaged their money.

Prescott's lessons were absorbed by young George, who very early on learned to seek value for every dollar spent and do without rather than get in debt.

He also learned fair measure, learned to ask for no more than what was due him. Although not the school's leading student, his report cards were good, and his mother was particularly pleased that he was always graded "excellent" in one category she thought of great importance: "Claims no more than his fair share of time and attention." This consistent ranking led to a little family joke—George always did best in "Claims no more."

He was not a selfish child, did not even display the innocent possessiveness common to most children. Until he was a little over two years old, he had no new toys of his own and had to make do with the hand-me-downs from Pres, who was just twenty-one months older. Young George did not complain, but his parents finally decided it was time he had a new toy of his own: they bought him a pedal car, a large toy car that could be made to move with foot pedals.

Older and wiser, Pres knew just how to work the pedals and had soon commandeered the small car. George ran over, grabbed the wheel, and told Pres he could "have half," meaning he was willing to share half of his new possession with his brother. He repeated his offer many times—"Have half, have half"—and for a while his parents called him "Have Half."

The early nickname that stuck, however, was an unusual one for a child: "Poppy." Since Dorothy Bush called her father "Pop," it made a certain family sense that his namesake should be dubbed "Little Pop." This was sometimes shortened to "Poppy." George's father was afraid the name—as undignified for a grown man as it was inappropriate for a child—might stick for life. It didn't; George eventually grew out of it.

Every summer the Bush family journeyed to Walkers Point and a cottage next door to Grandfather Walker's three-story dark-green shingle house on the Atlantic in Kennebunkport. It was there, at the cottage Grandfather Walker had given to his daughter as a wedding present, that the Bush children passed their school vacations with sports and relaxation. Bush had remarked that for him as a boy, "Maine in the summer was the best of all possible adventures." There were picnics by the seashore, tennis, and sailing in the cold Atlantic waters off the Maine coast. Grandfather Walker taught young George how to handle and dock a boat, sparking George's enduring love affair with motorboats and the sea.

George also enjoyed fishing and approached it with his characteristic unselfishness. When he caught a fish, he would not revel in his feat and rush around to show it off. Instead, he would immediately sit down on the end of the dock and clean the fish, an unpleasant chore that he would not leave to someone else. Only when he had finished would he parade his catch past family and friends. His mother appreciated his extra effort and saw it as a dimension of his character.

The Bushes were a remarkably close-knit family. Although competitive, they all stuck together. The family had a wonderful spirit, a powerful sense of togetherness, that was tangible to others. Their friends sensed it, were always struck by it, and to this day remember it. Hope Lincoln Coombe, a neighbor of the Bushes in Greenwich, remembers George as "a very attractive little boy" and thinks back on the afternoons her family spent with the Bushes. The two families often went on picnics together. "They were a nice, happy family, the kind everyone hopes for," she recalls. "Whatever they did, be it sports or entertaining, they did well and with style." Anne Sloane Morrison, a childhood friend of George's—she still remembers him as "Poppy"—has fond memories of the idealistic and beautiful life they all led. "It was great to be around them," she says.

Even the two brothers George and Pres were happier when together, which is not always the case with brothers. Their sister, Nancy, who was twenty-one months younger than George, recalls that she was always trying to get in with her two older brothers. "I adored George and Pres, but they were always slamming the door and saying I couldn't come in or play. They had each other and didn't need me. To try to please them, I'd make fudge on Sunday afternoons and bring it out to them while they were playing baseball. They'd eat the fudge and then ignore me. The only time they ever got me into a game with them is when they needed someone to run bases and there was no other friend around."

One year Dorothy Bush attended a series of lectures in Greenwich given by a child psychologist. She was impressed when the psychologist explained that the most important thing parents could do for their children was give them each their own room. The opportunity presented itself when the family moved into a bigger house that had two back rooms. For three months the two brothers lived apart in their separate rooms, but around November, when the family was beginning to think of Christmas, they came to their father and said, "Do you know what we want for Christmas? It won't cost you anything, but we'd like to tell you now." What they wanted was to go back to sharing the same room. So much for child psychology: they happily shared a room until they grew up.

At home their education was steady and strict, its emphasis on self-discipline and good habits. The Bush family was religious. At breakfast every morning a lesson was read from the Bible, and parables applicable to daily life were pointed out and emphasized. There was, for instance, the good Samaritan, who had bandaged the wounds of a stranger and demonstrated the meaning of being a good neighbor. The Bush children were taught to be good neighbors, to not walk past a neighbor in distress.

"I taught my children to be kind, and I taught them the golden rule: 'Do unto others as you would have them do unto you,'" says Dorothy Bush. She and Prescott read together in the morning and then again in the evening. One of their favorite books was *A Diary of Private Prayers*, by John Bailey.

Dorothy was the center of the family, and George remembers that she exuded a warm, cheerful spirit at all times. "She was very much the inspiration of our family," says George, who was amazed when one of his friends in the eighth grade told him he wished he had a mother like his. "I just thought everybody loved their own mother as we Bush kids did."

It was Prescott Bush, however, who was the single greatest influence in young George's life. He was a strict father but a just one. Prescott was a towering man who invited no argument and brandished a belt to punish his children. Even today George admits that his father was "pretty scary," and his brother Jonathan recalls, "We were all terrified of Dad as boys." Prescott presided over a breakfast table where children were to be seen and not heard. At dinner the boys were required to wear jackets and ties.

Prescott was well aware that his children were privileged. To offset this, he impressed on them the importance of being responsible citizens, instilling in them early on the awareness that they had to fulfill certain obligations to society. And he set an example for his children. After returning home from a long day at the office in New York, Prescott would go directly to chair the town meeting of Greenwich, or the hospital board, or the church board. Dorothy Bush recalls that her husband didn't enjoy business that much and rarely talked about it. Politics was his real love. (Many years later, when he was fifty-seven years old, he became a United States senator from Connecticut.) Prescott taught his sons to be kind, serve their country, and give something back.

Prescott Bush engendered a love of sports in his children. Dorothy, too, was competitive, always exhorting her offspring in games, "You can do it, you'll get it." She was a good athlete, a match for anyone in the family, and its fastest runner. Her favorite sport was tennis, the one game that was a major family recreation. George, who was a left-hander, learned to play serving left-handed and then switching the racket to his right hand for ground strokes. Later he changed to an unorthodox right-handed serve, something he still regrets.

Even today George recalls that when he was eight years old he came home from tennis and told his mother he'd been "off his game." With uncharacteristic anger she snapped, "You don't have a game. Get out and work harder and maybe someday you will."

When George was about ten, his parents gave him a new tennis racket for Christmas. "It was a Wright & Ditson with a wooden handle," he recalls. "A cousin-in-law of my mother borrowed my racket for a friend, but it didn't fit his hand, so he carved the grip down with a knife. I had never before felt such anger and rage."

Like many young boys at the time, George collected baseball cards with pictures of Lou Gehrig and Babe Ruth, his idols. "The fact is, all the big-league baseball players were my heroes," he recalls. "I knew the average of every batter and pitcher in the various leagues." But, probably because of his family's interest in tennis, his real ambition was to be a tennis bum, "except my family wouldn't hear of it."

The Bush family competed at anything that measured one person against another—golf, tennis, backgammon, blackjack, bridge, anagrams. "Theirs was a very competitive family, but they all stuck together," Anne Morrison recalls. "They had such a wonderful spirit."

Christmas was a particularly exciting time for the Bush clan. In mid-December they would all board a Pullman train and head for South

Carolina and Duncannon, a shooting lodge owned by Grandfather Walker. Life at Duncannon, near Barnwell in the northwestern part of the state, was gracious, like that of an old Southern plantation, a throwback to the previous century. "The boys were shooting all day long," Nancy recalls. "They shot doves at dawn, clay pigeons at noon, and then they would go out into the fields on horseback to hunt quail." George soon developed into a fine marksman.

Nancy also recalls real touches of luxury such as the trimmed edges of grapefruit at breakfast and the fact that the family members were waited on by servants, who would come into their bedrooms early in the morning and light crackling pinewood fires to take the chill off the morning cold.

After Greenwich Country Day School, George, then twelve years old, went to join his brother Pres at Phillips Academy—also called Andover, after the Massachusetts town where it is located twenty miles north of Boston. Sometime during the tenth grade George suddenly began to grow up into the person demanded by his name, becoming one of the tallest boys in his class.

Then as now, Andover is one of New England's top preparatory schools. Somewhat ironically, it was during the Thirties, the years of the Great Depression and on the eve of World War II, that New England private schools like Andover, Exeter, and Groton were at their peak. Their graduates dominated the major Eastern colleges, especially the so-called Ivy League, which included Harvard, Brown, Cornell, Princeton, and Yale. Prescott's boys were on the right track: their destination was Yale.

The Bush brothers were on their way and on their own. George was given an allowance of ten dollars a month, which was to cover all of his expenses, including dry cleaning, postage, and extras. He and Pres mailed their dirty clothing home each week in a hard container; it was returned clean and neatly folded the following week.

It was at Andover that George discovered the joy of reading: Ernest Hemingway's *For Whom the Bell Tolls* and A. J. Cronin's *The Keys of the Kingdom* were then best-sellers and suggested reading for the students.

During Christmas vacation in 1941, George, just seventeen years old, went to a cotillion at the Round Hill Country Club in Greenwich, Connecticut. It was a social affair attended by upcoming debutantes and acceptable young men: the boys wore tuxedos, and the girls were in long formal dresses.

The band was playing a Glenn Miller tune when George noticed a girl wearing a green-and-red off-the-shoulder dress. She instantly caught his attention. She was everything he liked: attractive, brunette, and tall (five feet ten inches in heels), with an athletic build and good posture. "She radiated joy and warmth," he recalled recently. George pointed her out to Jack Wozencraft, a friend with whom he occasionally played tennis.

Wozencraft not only knew the girl but could also tell George quite a bit about her. "Her name is Barbara Pierce," he said. "She's sixteen, lives in Rye, and is home for the holidays from her school, Ashley Hall in Charleston, South Carolina."

Wozencraft made the introductions. Barbara, who had likewise noticed George, recalls him as "the most attractive man I had ever seen; I could hardly breathe when he was in the room."

George asked Barbara to dance, but just as the music started, her brother Jim cut in to ask George if he was Poppy Bush. George acknowledged that he was. "Why don't you go over and stand by the side while I get rid of her?" Jim said, gesturing toward his sister. "I was just furious with my brother," Barbara recalled.

Jim wanted George, who was number six on the Andover basketball team, to play in a YMCA game. George accepted the invitation. "I saw this as a way to use my hook shot and impress my future wife," Bush said recently.

By the time George located Barbara on the dance floor again, the band leader had decided to change tempos to a waltz. Since George didn't waltz, he and Barbara sat the dance out.

And several more after that, talking and getting to know each other.

Before the evening was over, George had asked Barbara if he could see her again and told her about the basketball game a few nights later. He asked if she'd like to come and if he could take her home after the game. She accepted.

They had come to the dance with their own friends. George was with some chums from Greenwich, Barbara with girlfriends from Rye. Although they had grown up just a few miles apart and their fathers took the same club car on the daily commute by train to Manhattan, the two teenagers had never met.

The youngsters were apparently smitten with each other. Dorothy Bush heard about Barbara that night when George came home and reported that he had met "the niftiest girl at the dance." And when Barbara got home that night, she told her mother that she had met "the most terrific person. I slept until eleven the following morning, and by the time I went down for breakfast my mother already knew about George. Jim had been spreading the word."

The entire Pierce family was at the basketball game, ostensibly to see Jim play, but, as Barbara recalls, "They were really there to have a look at George."

Concerned that he and Barbara might not have much to say to each other after the game,

George had begged for permission to borrow the family car, which had a radio in it. If he came up short on conversation, he could always turn the radio on. Even now, so many years after the event, it is a standing joke with the Bushes that he needn't have bothered: Barbara started talking that night and, Bush claims, hasn't stopped since.

Soon after that first date, which concluded with an ice cream soda, Barbara and George grew "serious" and even met each other's families and friends. Anne Morrison remembers the first time she met Barbara: "She had a beautiful face and a glowing smile with very dark and curly brunette hair. She was slim and athletic, as was George, who was very good-looking. They were a handsome young couple."

Nancy, who was then at Farmington, a girls' school in Connecticut, remembers how all her friends there were dying to visit her at home so they could meet her handsome brothers. "But George was never home, he was always in Rye with Barbara. It was obvious to all of us in the family that he was 'interested in her.'"

At the end of the Christmas holidays Barbara returned to Ashley Hall and George to Andover. Barbara had a lot to talk about with her friends and roommates, and they soon realized that the boy with the odd name of Poppy was, for her, something more than an ordinary crush.

Later generations of separated young lovers

have closed the distance with the telephone; George and Barbara stayed in touch with letters. He wrote to her almost every day, and she did the same. Following the unwritten code of roommates, she read aloud to her friends from his letters but skipped over the more romantic parts, stuck to the straightforward news, and absolutely never let any of her friends actually hold a letter in her hands. When not writing letters to George, she sat on her bed knitting him Argyle socks, then the rage with prep-school boys.

It was to be months before they could see each other again: on the one day when their spring vacations overlapped. They went out on a double date to the movies with George's pal George "Red Dog" Warren and a school friend of Barbara's. They saw *Citizen Kane*, the movie that marked the Hollywood debut of Orson Welles as producer, director, and star. Afterward they had a soda and discussed the thinly disguised film portrait of press tycoon William Randolph Hearst. George walked Barbara to the door of her house and shyly kissed her good-night, thus becoming in Barbara's words "the only boy I had ever kissed."

If it sounds unlikely by today's standards that a sixteen-year-old girl had never been kissed, consider this: Barbara was a very proper young lady attending an all-female prep school where girls were forbidden to wear makeup or leave campus without hats, dates were chaperoned, and neglecting to wear white gloves was virtually a punishable offense.

Like George, she came from a religious family and was close to her father, who strongly influenced her. Barbara's background, though not quite so aristocratic as George's, was also socially impressive in a day when Society was defined by breeding rather than wealth. Her father, Marvin Pierce, was a distant nephew of President Franklin Pierce (1853–57), the only incumbent president whose party failed to renominate him. Barbara's mother, Pauline Robinson, born in 1896 in Marysville, Ohio, was one of four children. Her father was an Ohio Supreme Court justice. Pauline attended Oxford College in Oxford, Ohio, where as the campus beauty she met Marvin Pierce, the campus hero at nearby Miami University.

Marvin was born in 1893 in Sharpsville, Pennsylvania. His father was a member of a wealthy family who owned an iron foundry. But the iron market was soon to crash, and Marvin had to delay college to help out with the family finances. He entered Miami University in 1912, where he was a pitcher on the baseball team, a top tennis player, and captain of the football team. He graduated from college summa cum laude and married Pauline in 1918.

Marvin went on to MIT and Harvard, earning degrees in civil and architectural engineering. During World War I he joined the U.S.

Army Corps of Engineers and was sent to Europe, arriving just before the war ended. After working as an engineer for a time, he got a job as a clerk at the company that published *McCall's* magazine. He eventually worked his way up to chairman of the board of the McCall Corporation.

Barbara, born on June 8, 1925, in the prosperous suburb of Rye, New York, on Long Island Sound, had been the baby of her family for five years when a fourth child, a son named Scott, was born. When Scott was just two years old, the Pierces learned that he had a serious problem with the bone marrow of his shoulder. For the next seven years Scott, accompanied by Pauline, was in and out of specialists' offices and various New York hospitals for painful surgical procedures, including bone scrapings and grafts. His mother was with him much of the time. "Scott was the best little kid I ever knew," Barbara recalls. "He never complained. He was a saint. I know he hates to hear that, but it's true. I was always part of his life."

Nevertheless, as a child Barbara never quite understood the strain her brother's illness had placed on Pauline. "My mother, I'm sure, was always tired, and I didn't understand it at the time. But I guess I felt neglected, that she didn't spend as much time on me. She had this enormous responsibility, which I was never sympathetic about. Now, as a mother and grandmother, I realize what she was going through. She was a very good mother, but I did not have a great relationship with her. She was not perfect, but I always think the world was more beautiful because my mother was there. She taught us all a lot of good lessons.

"Actually, I was much closer to my father and probably the child least close to my mother. My father believed there were only three things parents could give their children: a fine education, a good example, and all the love in the world. My father used to say that children should be given lots of love and be shown good examples, in addition to being taught honesty and to follow the work ethic."

During her adolescence Barbara was taller and chubbier than most of her peers. Although a very happy child, by the age of twelve she weighed 148 pounds and believed she looked like Porky Pig. Her mother would say to her older sister, "Eat up, Martha," and then turn to Barbara and say, "Not you." Asked at what age she blossomed out into a trim young woman, Barbara said, "Around fourteen, fifteen, or sixteen, I guess." Then she laughed, "As a matter of fact I'm not sure I ever did."

At the time George and Barbara met, the Pierce family lived in the three-story, five-bedroom brick house on Onondage Street in Rye where Barbara had grown up. Like the Bush family, Barbara's was also well-to-do, which meant extra help around the house; the Pierce household included a three-member Filipino family. The Pierce children attended private schools and played golf and tennis.

Like George, Barbara was a good athlete. She was the Ashley Hall champion at swimming under water (two and a half times across the pool). She had developed her talents at knitting and was the record holder at speed knitting. For the Drama Club's 1941 Christmas pageant she took the part of the Speaking Angel. It was during an after-church rehearsal that the headmistress, Mary Vardrine McBee, announced the news of the Japanese attack on Pearl Harbor. "We were all frightened," Barbara recalls.

On that Sunday, December 7, 1941, George was walking across the campus with a friend when he heard about Pearl Harbor. "My reaction was one of shock, almost disbelief," he recalls. "I didn't fully comprehend world affairs. My interests were our undefeated soccer season just finished, basketball—baseball just coming up. Christmas vacation was only a couple of weeks away and then graduation. Then I guess that was followed by the typical American reaction that we had better do something about this. I remember the country's instant coming together for a common purpose, and my own gut feeling was the same as that of many young Americans—we wanted to fight for our country." On that day George decided to enlist.

The next day Dr. Claude M. Fuess, the

headmaster and a renowned historian and tough disciplinarian, summoned the entire body of eight hundred students into George Washington Hall, the school auditorium. Bush recalls the normal joking, kidding, and sloppy posture until Dr. Fuess called them to order and then said something like this: "Your country is at war. We have just played 'The Star Spangled Banner.' From now on when 'The Star Spangled Banner' is played, you will stand at attention, hands at your sides, and you will show respect."

From that point on, the schoolboys, especially the senior classmen, put aside their previous thoughts for the future and became preoccupied with the shadow of war, because most of the graduates would be of draft age.

George took Barbara to the senior prom, which was held in the school gymnasium festooned with paper streamers and balloons; for refreshments they served the mandatory fruit punch. Barbara was surprised to discover that her boyfriend was actually a BMOC (big man on campus). He seemed to know everyone, and it was clear to her that everyone knew him. Although not an academically distinguished student, George was involved in a remarkable list of activities. "Poppy" Bush was captain of the baseball and soccer teams, playing manager of the basketball team, president of the senior class, treasurer of the student council, deputy housemaster, and a member or officer of a dozen other boards, societies, and teams.

"George was terrifically competitive," a classmate recalls, "but his leadership qualities were as responsible for his athletic success as his strength and skill, if not more so." Another classmate, Walter J. P. Curley, remembers, "George was a star."

That summer, Secretary of War Henry Stimson delivered the commencement address to Bush's graduating class. The secretary, an alumnus of Andover himself, told the young graduates that the war would be a long one and that even though America needed fighting men, they would serve their country better by getting more education before going into uniform.

George listened to the secretary with mixed emotions. He had prepared for and been accepted by Yale, and he knew that most of his classmates would be going on to college. But as yet he had no specific career ambitions. At Andover he had become fascinated by airplanes and the navy: he had even considered trying for the Naval Academy. But now there was a war to fight. He lived in awe of his father but wanted to achieve something in his own name. As he was to put it much later: "I wanted to get out from under that powerful shadow."

With his brother Pres, who was then finishing his sophomore year at Yale, he talked over his plan to enlist. Pres had tried to enlist in the navy but had been classified 4-F because of his blind eye and leg infirmity. "I was proud of

George when he said he was going to enlist," Pres recalled recently.

When George told his parents he wanted to enlist, they were supportive. "It seemed so right," he says. "So many kids my age were going in." Barbara was also understanding. "I knew that George felt he really had to do it. I was proud of him, and when you're that young, you don't really consider death as a possibility."

After the graduation ceremony, in a crowded hallway outside Cochran Chapel, Prescott Bush, Sr., turned to his son, who was almost his height, and asked, "Did the secretary say anything to cause you to change your mind?"

"No, sir," George replied. "I'm going in."

Father and son shook hands.

George's birthday was June 12—he was 361 days older than Barbara—and on the day he turned eighteen he went to Boston and was sworn into the navy as a seaman second class by Walter Levering, Lt. USNR. "I was a scared, nervous kid," George recalls.

It was a week after the battle of Midway, the first decisive naval battle in history in which the participating ships never came in sight of one another, the entire battle being fought by opposing aircraft. The essential role of air power had been confirmed; the navy needed more pilots, and quickly. To get them, the navy changed the rules. Two years of college were no longer required to become a pilot, and the aviator training course in which George was enrolled had been trimmed to ten highly intensive months. George was ordered to go on active duty as an aviation cadet August 6, 1942.

On the night before he was scheduled to leave, George and Barbara had their last date together. He had saved some money from Christmas gifts and his allowance and bought her an inexpensive watch, which she pinned on her dress with a gold bow set with two rubies. She later lost the watch on a trip to New York City, and to this day remembers her despair: "I cried."

On a hot day in the first week of August, George, accompanied by his father, went to Penn Station in New York, where he was to board a troop train from Chapel Hill, North Carolina, with hundreds of other recruits. Prescott put an arm around his son and hugged him. "It was the first time I had ever seen my dad cry," George recalls.

Most of the young men on the train that night were from the New England states, from little towns and places George had never heard of like Yokun Seat, Watatic, and Contoocook. For many of them, it was the first time away from home and the first time in a Pullman. They sat alone or in small groups staring out the train window, making brave jokes, or writing letters to their loved ones at home. Many, like George, were shy with one another and subdued by thoughts of the danger that lay ahead.

George knew no one on that crowded train; to the best of his knowledge, he was the first of his graduating class at Andover to enlist, although there had been much talk at school of others intending to do so.

The first thing George did on arriving in Chapel Hill was to find a telephone and call Barbara, whom he considered his fiancée although they were not to become secretly engaged for almost a year.

Chapter Three

To meet the greatly increased demand for new pilots, the Bureau of Aviation decided that a completely new approach to flight training was required. Not only did student aviators need to know how to fly, but they had to be made combat-ready before being sent to an operational squadron.

A directive from the navy, issued shortly before Bush enlisted, detailed the thrust of the new V-5 cadet training program designed to train navy and Marine Corps fighter and bomber pilots at a starting rate of thirty thousand men a year. Each candidate was to undergo an extremely rigorous "toughening up," one more strenuous than any ever before attempted in America on an organized scale. The intention was to "condition pilot candidates for any danger or hardship they might have to face in, or as the result of, actual air battle." The program was deliberately aimed at making the so-called seahawks the "strongest, most daring and most determined type of airmen in the world." It was described as "a distinct challenge to patriotic young American men who are proud of their ability to take it. This training will be hard, but the time for pulling punches in words or actions is passed. The men who take this training will have proved that they can both take it and hand it out. That's the kind of fighting pilots the Navy wants and the country needs . . ."

Naval aviation had become the decisive factor in the Pacific war, and flying from an aircraft carrier was the type of demanding challenge that appealed to young Bush.

The preflight school at the Naval Air Station where Bush was assigned for training was on the outskirts of Chapel Hill, a lovely university town at the edge of the Piedmont. It was there that Bush was assigned to Sixth Battalion, Company K, Second Platoon. He lived at 317 Lewis Hall with three roommates: Blaine Hall, Deane Phinney, and Bill Robinson.

Among the group at Chapel Hill was Ted Williams, the famous home run hitter who, in 1941, had hit .406 for the Boston Red Sox, something no one had done in the major leagues for eleven years. All the cadets knew who "The Splendid Splinter" was; they had read the sports pages and followed the batting averages, and he was the first celebrity most of them had ever seen up close. Some even wanted his autograph. Williams was obliging but made it plain from the start that he was there to fight a war, not to talk about baseball. He was serious and quiet and, like the others, determined to succeed as a navy flier. The other cadets soon accepted him as one of the group. Bush, who also admired him, wrote home that Williams was in his class, and he felt a little more important because of him, even though they were not to become friends until long after the war.

George was given a regulation short-back-and-sides haircut and aviation cadet uniforms: khaki for working days, whites and blues for dress. His civilian clothes were sent home.

As one of the youngest inductees in the group, George was apprehensive: "I guess I was thinking, Will I be accepted?" Although he did not know anyone, he was open to making friends. To George, "the main thing was the people, in a variety I had never known before. Different people from different parts of the country, from all walks of life." Having made up his mind that he was going to give it his best, he had little trouble fitting in and adapted quickly to life in a crowded dormitory. He had always shared a room with his brother Pres and had had a roommate at Andover. "Having been at boarding school," Bush now says, "I was probably more attuned to life in a dorm than some kids who had never been away from home." There were common showers and common toilets, and a common mess hall, where everyone ate together at long tables.

For the first few days at Chapel Hill all new arrivals were occupied eight hours a day with tests. Every morning they were marched to a barracks, where they sat at long tables writing answers to hundreds of questions, from logic and math to psychology. After a short lunch break they went back to the tests until dinnertime. Bush sometimes cursed himself for not having paid more attention in math classes at school, but there were other times when he breezed through the questions.

Except for time out for meals and study, Bush and the others in his class were busy sixteen hours a day from Monday through Friday, starting at 0545 with a breakfast of pancakes, eggs, cereal, and coffee. The day ended with vespers from 1900 to 1915. At 1930 the cadets finally had free time to write letters, take care of their uniforms, polish equipment, and socialize. The bugles sounded tattoo (summoning them to their rooms) at 2125 and taps (lights out) at 2130.

His days followed a monotonous pattern alternating between classroom and physical activities. George found some of the classes—so different from his studies at Andover— interesting: "I enjoyed the navigation courses and did pretty well in that critical subject." The classroom instruction was followed by hours of close-order drill on the parade ground and nine sports considered the most effective in developing agility and strength as well as competitive spirit: the cadets competed against themselves as well as against one another. These were football, soccer, basketball, boxing, swimming, track, wrestling, gymnastics, and tumbling; to these was added hand-to-hand combat. Cadets were scored on every sport. Bush's records indicate he earned a "superior" in basketball and soccer, an "average" in swimming, boxing, wrestling, and football.

Because of his height, the bane of George's existence was the obstacle course, designed to test a cadet's physical stamina, agility, and courage. The course included a long rope to climb, a log over a ditch that had to be inched across, and then a high wall to be scaled. The only way to get over the wall was to run straight at it and then at the last moment extend a leg, which would act something like a pole enabling him to vault high enough to grab the top and throw himself over headfirst, turning in midair to land on his feet.

Bush had always been a good athlete, and his physical-training record at the time shows it. The aviation cadet physical entry standards were 5 chinups (Bush did 6), 15 pushups (Bush did 18), a 16-inch jump reach (Bush did 23), and completion of a speed-and-agility test over a short track course with turns, climbs, and hurdles within 35 seconds (Bush did the course in 31.6 seconds). The standard fitness was 60 points. His score was 77.

Meanwhile Barbara wrote to say she was coming to visit him en route to Ashley Hall in Charleston. Earlier George had asked Pauline Pierce for a picture of Barbara, and she'd sent an old one of Barbara with her cairn terrier dog, Sandy. Barbara still remembers that visit. "George asked me to tell people that I was eighteen although I was really seventeen, because he thought he'd be teased about being young himself and having a young friend."

George, looking handsome in his immaculate, newly issued whites, was waiting for Barbara at the railroad station. He gave her a hearty hug and then, discreetly holding her hand, proudly showed her around the campus and introduced her to his friends. "We walked around the campus, and I believe that I got on the train and continued on to Charleston," says Barbara, adding, "No one asked me how old I was."

George completed his preflight training at Chapel Hill in the Sixth Battalion. Upgraded to aviation cadet status, he was ordered to continue his flight training with Class 11A-42 at Wold-Chamberlain Naval Airfield in Minneapolis, Minnesota. He would be learning to fly in one of the most northerly states, a region famous for its bitter cold and deep snow.

When he took his first physical-fitness test at Wold on November 5, 1942, he was a quarter-inch over six feet in height and weighed 161 pounds, but he was still growing.

At Wold, Bush was instructed in subjects considered necessary for pilots—military history, physics, and aerology. He learned about Bernoulli's principle, which explains (indirectly) that an airplane can fly because the wing is shaped to produce more air pressure on its lower surface than its upper surface, thus providing lift; the flow of air over the wing literally holds the plane in the air. The angle at which the wing meets the wind is known as the angle of attack. The instructor demonstrated this by reminding the cadets that if they stuck their hand out the window of a moving car and angled the palm upward, the wind forced their hand higher; if they angled the palm downward, the wind forced the hand lower.

Bush was taught how to quickly recognize the fighter planes, battleships, cruisers, and carriers being used by the various combatant countries. He had signal flag practice, lectures on saluting, and the rules of prisoner-of-war resistance. He learned to tap ten words a minute using Morse Code and viewed the mandatory films on venereal disease.

He learned about the structure of the aerial torpedo, the technique of torpedo attack, and the elements of antisubmarine warfare. He was also taught the basics of discipline: to "brace the bulkhead," to jump to attention when the instructor entered the classroom. He learned to preface answers to questions from the instructor with a shouted "Sir!" and to sit rigidly at attention at mealtimes and eat only when given permission to do so by the ranking cadet.

In this first stage of training he spent hours plotting and triangulating courses. Step by step, with lectures, theory, and physical fitness, he was being prepared to pilot an airplane, but as yet he had not been near one. It was weeks before he was ready to take his first flight in an NP-1 Spartan, a rugged-fabric biplane with fixed landing gear. The Spartan had an open two-seater cockpit, with the instructor sitting in front and the student in back. It was a slow plane but responsive and forgiving, an ideal aircraft in which to learn to fly. His instructor was Ens. James Charles Crume, Jr.

Like most cadets going up for their first flight, Bush was nervous, worried about the impression he would make on the instructor, and tense. "'Excited' is the best word to describe the way I felt," he said recently. "All the training led up to this moment, and I was looking forward to learning how to fly." The first entry in his flight log and his first actual flight were dated November 10, 1942. Crume recalls the day as being bitter cold, down to zero with light snow. He and Bush were both wearing navy cold-weather flying gear: cumbersome sheepskin-lined leather flying suits and heavy boots.

With Crume at the controls they were in the air for more than an hour. Crume's report noted that the flight was for "instruction only . . . student shown area. Demonstration of climbing, glides, turns. Student shows normal reaction and appears interested."

Bush discovered that, as a left-hander, he had special problems because most of a stick aircraft's controls—propeller, throttle, fuel mixture—are on the left side of the cockpit and manipulated with the left hand, while the right hand controls the joy stick, which determines the airplane's movements in flight. He had to train himself to use his right hand for all of the delicate nuances of flying.

During that first week Crume showed him how to take off and land and demonstrated basic turns and climbs. Once George could perform those simple flying movements, Crume went on to the next step—stalls and spins. The first time Crume stalled and spun and the plane plunged toward earth George was frightened, but Crume pulled it out of the stall safely. "Bush was an outstanding student," Crume recalls.

Although a natural athlete, Bush was not a natural pilot. He had to learn to control the plane and his own fears and apprehensions and work hard to do what some of the cadets in his class did with ease. He was often frustrated—there were times when it seemed he could do nothing right in the air—but he was persistent and determined. Those traits more than made up for whatever natural talent he may have lacked, and he continued to get above-average marks in his reports. In a letter to his mother dated November 21, 1942, George wrote: "I sure am lucky for Ensign Crume hasn't *sworn* at me yet—something few others can say. He is a tall, thin, very young fellow and very quiet."

After ten hours of instruction George was ready to take his first solo flight in a Stearman N2S-3 trainer, an open-cockpit biplane painted yellow and known throughout the navy as "The Yellow Peril," although the flying cadets sometimes called it "The Washing Machine" because of the large numbers of cadets who washed out of training because of their inability to handle it properly. Nevertheless, it was probably one of the safest and strongest airplanes ever built. In its open cockpit students and instructors constantly wore their Gosport helmets (used for intercommunication) and chamois masks essential to guard against the bitter Minnesota cold. Even so, some suffered frostbitten faces. But Bush loved the open cockpit—he relished the sound of air rushing through the struts and the wind streaming past and around him, reminding him of the rush of air and sense of speed he'd had in fast boats in Maine.

On the morning of November 21, Lt. J. A.

Boyle, another instructor, checked Bush's first solo flight and noted: "Satisfactory check. Taxied a little fast. Landings were average to above with exception of one almost ground looped [Bush lost directional control of the aircraft]. Safe for solo." Bush was given a mark of 3.08, which was average. Recalling that first solo flight some forty-eight years later, Bush said, "It is hard for nonpilots to understand the joy of a first solo flight. All of us who soloed thought we were twenty feet tall."

George was then ready for the next stage of training, which meant that, weather permitting, he would be flying almost every day. By then he had fallen in love with flying in an open plane, which gave him a pure sensation of flight: all his senses were alive and in harmony with his body. The airplane soon became an extension of his own being—flying was becoming as natural to him as driving a car. He began to relish the sounds and smells as well as the feeling of joyous freedom from being earthbound, an experience unique to flying. Suspended in the sky, he saw the earth below as an exciting, multidimensional tableau. Most important, he even began to relax occasionally at the controls instead of fiercely concentrating on them and the instrument panel. As Crume warned him, "If you concentrate on one thing only, you'll soon lose awareness of the others, and that's when you'll get in trouble."

For six weeks Bush flew almost every day,

logging more than forty-three hours, many of them solo. And with an instructor by his side he began to learn the pilot's basic acrobatic vocabulary, including loops, split S, left and right snap rolls, Immelman turns, falling leaf, inverted spins, and wingovers.

After each stage of training there were check flights with an instructor to determine whether the cadet was ready for the next stage. There was no way to prepare for a check flight: he was either "up to snuff" or not.

Crume, who was his instructor much of the time, wrote on December 27: "Stage 'B' work reviewed . . . Student shows average to above reaction to stunts [acrobatic maneuvers] and instruction." George was judged ready to commence his Stage C training.

On February 1 George made his first nighttime flight with an instructor. The following evening he completed his first solo night flight. It was a moonless night—not even the stars were visible—and ground fog covered the field. Without the horizon for reference, he had difficulty retaining his spatial orientation. In the past he'd always had an instructor in the air or on the ground to coach him by radio, but now he was flying by instruments, and it was a lonely feeling. The runway had lights only along the sides. Approaching it was like entering the mouth of a coal mine. But he made a perfect landing. As he removed his flying helmet and walked off the field, and his instructor gave a subtle affirmative nod, he breathed an aspirant sigh of relief.

"I was thrilled," Bush still recalls. "Night flying was darn good fun. After my first solo, all my nervousness left."

To this day, however, Bush remembers a very dark night when he came in too low and the landing gear scraped the tops of some trees. "I was gripped with fear, but thirty seconds later, after making a successful landing, I was overcome with gratitude. A few feet lower and that would have been the end."

On February 6 his instructor noted: "All work average except stunts are a trifle weak." George later admitted to his friends that he did not really like acrobatics.

Three days later George took a check flight with an instructor, was again graded "average," and was judged to have completed his primary flight training. By this time he had made sixty-one flights as a student. His total flight time when he left Minnesota was 82.5 hours, of which 24.7 hours were solo. Having successfully passed every check flight, he was ready for the next stage of training.

He headed next for Gulf sunshine and Corpus Christi, Texas, for further advanced training. The changes in weather meant pleasant changes in flying conditions. "Until I got there," he has said, "I don't think I'd ever landed except on snow and ice."

On February 18 George joined Class 2C-43C

at Corpus Christi, where, if he had the right stuff, he would eventually earn his wings. From that point on, his days were devoted to reviewing everything he had learned. His "Fitness Report for Student Officers and Cadets," dated from March 1 to 21 and signed by Ens. Edward C. Fritz, shows above-average marks in every department, including intelligence, judgment, moral courage, loyalty, and endurance. His highest scores were for military bearing and industry. The report concluded with this note: "Aviation Cadet Bush is an upstanding lad with great self-confidence. It appears, however, that he may be somewhat eccentric." Asked recently what may have prompted that remark from his instructor, Bush laughed and jokingly replied, "I think Mr. Fritz meant erratic and not eccentric, but you would have to ask him."

Mr. Fritz, a lawyer before going into the navy, recalls George at the time as "outstanding and mature for his age," and he likes to believe that he was one of the first to see something special about the young cadet. "My definition of 'eccentric,'" he claims, "was taken from Webster's International Dictionary and means, 'divergence from the usual.' Events since we flew together have certainly proven me right."

Ensign Fritz next taught George how to fly the Vultee Vibrator, a dependable but underpowered, noisy, low-wing training airplane with a fixed landing gear. The Vultee was aptly named: it vibrated when airborne. Fritz's task was to guide George through the stages of the training program and to prepare him for the periodic check flights with an instructor. George had to learn to get the plane in the air fast and master the technique of making a three-point landing (wheels and tail touching the ground simultaneously).

On March 5, 8, and 11, Fritz checked George out in the Vibrator. After the first flight he noted: "Student serious and learns well. Has difficulty in maintaining altitude. Tends to make all turns in a tight skid. Took off several times with right wing low. Got onto flaps and prop pitch. Judged his first emergency [a spin or stall suddenly induced by Fritz] well . . . Instructed in stall and spin recovery." Of the March 8 flight Fritz wrote: "Has three main faults: (1) leveling off too high; (2) overshooting; (3) traffic pattern downwind of touch and go landing with the fieldward wing dipped down, therefore in a skid." By his third flight George had corrected his faults, and Fritz's comments reads: "Approaches were all on the head but did not have the knack of setting three wheels on the ground at the same time. Bounced on his takeoffs. Safe for solo."

Fritz occasionally commented on George's check flights, pointing out errors George might have made or giving him a pat on the back if warranted. But George would have to wait until later that day or the following morning when, pulses racing, he would join the other cadets in front of the scheduling board at the ready room and look for an arrow in front of his name. An up arrow meant he had passed his check flight; a down arrow meant failure. The cadets with too many down arrows were washed out of the course and reassigned. Their luckier friends commiserated with the washouts.

Bush then learned to fly by instruments in the Link Trainer, a simulated aircraft cockpit devised by Edwin Link with all the controls and instruments of an airplane. It was designed to do a good job of simulating anything that a plane could do, including taking off and crashing. Errors were recorded by the instructors, who sat outside the trainer at a long table with charts. It was they who determined whether the trainee passed or failed.

George spent more than thirteen hours in "the box" during the last week of March and passed the course with an above-average rating. The last note in his final check sheet reads: "Student did good work this period. Orientation good. Let down was fair. Bracketing [flying around simulated pylons] good."

Overall, Lt. Comdr. J. R. Dickey, skipper of Bush's training group, rated George as "fitted for commission" and judged him "fair" as instructor material.

On March 31, 1943, one of George's instructors, M. M. Honke, noted in his fitness report that "Cadet Bush is pleasant and ambitious. He does his work willingly and well. He is good officer material."

During the month of April, George spent more hours in the air with another instructor learning to do advanced aerobatics in the SNJ–North America's AT-6 Texan—a plane later to become familiar to decades of moviegoers because film producers discovered it could be used to simulate Japanese Zero fighter planes. He soon became more confident of his ability to fly a plane rather than just drive it. When he wasn't flying, he was at ground school learning, among other things, celestial navigation, strategy and tactics, practical navigation, and airplane identification, a subject at which he excelled.

Meanwhile he was continually being pushed to his physical limit to toughen him up. With his sports squad, called the Wildcats, he ran in the sand, did pushups by the score, boxed, wrestled, practiced hand-to-hand combat, and continued with tumbling. His "Physical Training Record Card" rated him above average. His overall fitness score rose from 77 points when he was inducted into the navy to 103.

The training—the most difficult and comprehensive the U.S. Navy could formulate—had lasted eight months. The simple fact that Bush had successfully completed it proved to his instructor and to the navy that he had what was needed to be a pilot. It proved the same thing to Bush himself, and perhaps something more. During the eight months of training his skills as an aviator had steadily improved, and he had gained confidence in himself and his ability to fly an airplane. Since enlisting, he had grown mentally and physically—he had lost one pound and was almost two inches taller. He had passed the first hurdle, the one purposely devised to identify only the very best, and he now sensed himself ready in all ways for the next.

Aviation Cadet Bush received his wings of gold (really, gold plate over silver) and gold ensign's bars June 9, 1943, at Corpus Christi. Payton "Pat" Harwell, one of his classmates, recalls it as a "simple ceremony": Capt. G. T. Owen, commander of the Corpus Christi Naval Air Station, said only, "You have completed the prescribed course for naval aviators. Congratulations and good luck."

Hats were flung in the air, and the graduates shook hands all around. For George, the ceremony was a time of "emotional and total excitement. I had an ensign's stripe and an admiral's confidence. I was a navy pilot." It was also a sad time for him because a few of his friends had washed out and some had been killed in accidents.

Although Barbara and his family were not at the ceremony, his parents sent him "lovely wings—now lost—real nice gold ones." They also gave him a set of gold cufflinks with navy wings, which he still treasures.

Ens. George Herbert Walker Bush was eighteen years, eleven months, and twenty-seven days old: if not the youngest commissioned pilot in the naval air service, he was certainly a front runner for that distinction.

Chapter Four

For the next eleven months Bush crisscrossed the country from air base to air base, honing his skills and preparing to play his part in the war that was still raging all over the world. He was only vaguely aware of what was going on in the country, other than what he learned from hurried glimpses of newspapers or snatches of news on the radio.

"Use it up, wear it out, make it do, or do without" was the slogan of the day for all Americans. There were shortages of almost every staple item, and rationing was put into effect. Ration stamps became a way of life and were issued for butter, sugar, coffee, and meat as well as tires, cigarettes, and almost all canned and frozen goods.

America's love affair with the automobile was curtailed when, in February 1942, the last new automobile to be produced until 1945 rolled off the Ford assembly line as auto plants turned to producing tanks, Jeeps, aircraft, and other material, thus giving rise to the growth of used-car lots.

All U.S. motorists were assigned A-, B-, or C-stickers, with holders of the A-sticker allowed four gallons of gas a week, later reduced to three. Travel was discouraged with slogans such as "Is This Trip Necessary?"—and a thirty-five mph speed limit was established on highways to reduce gasoline consumption.

Austerity was the name of the game, and most Americans played it well. Men's trousers went cuffless to save cloth, and an old toothpaste tube had to be turned in when buying a new one. There were tin can collections, wastepaper collections, and aluminum drives. "Victory gardens" were cultivated in backyards and communal plots as vegetables became scarce, especially in California, where two-thirds of the vegetable crop had been grown by Japanese-Americans, who were considered potential saboteurs and interned around the nation in camps encircled by barbed wire and watchtowers. In May 1942 the Women's Auxiliary Army Corps (WAAC) was established by an act of Congress, and women began to flood the enlistment offices. A few months later WAVES (Women Accepted for Voluntary Emergency Service) was authorized by Congress, and women were officially welcomed into the U.S. Navy.

Meanwhile, on the war front, German submarines were taking a heavy toll on Allied shipping; the combined RAF and U.S. Eighth Air Force were dropping thousands of tons of bombs monthly on targets deep within Europe; the Russian armies were pushing the German invaders out of their country; the Allies were preparing for the upcoming invasion of Sicily; and in the Pacific there was a major air battle near Guadalcanal. The Americans, continuing their island-hopping strategy, had retaken several of the islands of the Solomon group and were steadily heading toward the Japanese homeland.

From each training base George wrote letters almost daily to Barbara, telling her that he was all right, that he loved her, and that he looked forward impatiently to the day when "all this will be over and we can be together." Asked recently if she had saved any of George's letters, Barbara said, "Sadly, no," nor had she copies of any of her letters written to him that expressed basically the same sentiments.

The gold wings and bars George Bush now wore on his new green uniform validated him as a naval aviator. But he still had a lot more to learn about flying before he would be judged capable of taking off from an aircraft carrier and then landing on it at night. If he failed that test, he would undoubtedly join the other washouts assigned to fly target planes for night fighter training, and his dreams of being in a combat squadron would end. If successful in his training, however, he would be ready for the ultimate test of his skill and mettle—combat.

The pressure on the young pilots was relentless. They were in competition not only with themselves but with every other would-be combat flier. But, as George said in his letters home to his parents, he was happy. He loved flying and was in the air almost every day. He had made friends, and he was part of a team. The most important thing to him was that for the first time in his young life he was totally on his own.

At night before going to bed he sat in his quarters with his roommates, each of them polishing their shiny new gold bars with steel wool to make them look salt-pocked so it would not be obvious they were newly commissioned officers.

In mid-June 1943 he was assigned to Fort Lauderdale, Florida, an established navy flying base, where he would learn to fly torpedo bombers in a class of ten pilots. The senior instructor and torpedo training officer was Lt. (jg) Thomas B. "Tex" Ellison, who had flown an Avenger the previous year in the very first navy raids on the Marshall and Gilbert islands. Ellison does not have a clear recollection of young George Bush, but he says, "All the students were qualified pilots. Our job was to give them advanced training and tactics."

It was at Lauderdale, with the steaming

summer air sending shimmering waves of heat across the two runways, that Bush saw close up for the first time the plane he would ultimately fly in combat.

Called the Avenger, the TBF, which means "Torpedo Bomber built by Grumman" (later built by General Motors and designated TBM), was a huge plane—the biggest single-engine carrier-based plane in the navy. George's first impression was awe at its sheer size: it dwarfed almost every other plane he had seen. Tall as he was, he had to extend himself to full height to pull himself onto the wing and then into the cockpit, which loomed more than eighteen feet off the ground.

On the ground the Avenger, its huge belly bulging with a ton of bombs, looked like some aberrant barnyard fowl. For that reason it was known throughout the navy as the Pregnant Turkey.

Bush's flight log for June 18, 1943, records that after a week of becoming familiar with the bewildering array of levers, switches, and dials in the cockpit, and the flight characteristics of the huge plane, he made his first solo flight for "familiarization." He made eight more solo flights that month: following an instructor in the air, then flying with the instructor on his wing, and then flying wing on the instructor.

Bush soon came to love the Avenger. Despite its awkward appearance on the ground, the plane moved effortlessly in the air. It responded to even the lightest touch on its controls and had few faults: it flew ponderously but steadily, and it was more consistent on a landing approach than most of the smaller and faster fighter planes. The Avenger was stable, sturdy, adaptable, and slow until it nosed over into a dive, and then, because of its design, it accelerated with remarkable speed.

During the month of July he logged twenty more flights in the big plane, practicing field carrier landings. A section of the runway was marked out the same size as a carrier deck, and an LSO (landing signal officer) using flags guided him in to a landing. Emphasis on practice was the proper approach to a landing. He had to arrive over the edge of the field just above stalling speed at the right altitude, speed, and attitude (position of the aircraft) and follow the LSO's flag directions.

That summer, while Bush was learning to handle the plane he would fly into the war and his future, another American navy man, already deep in the Pacific war zone, was experiencing his own dramatic destiny. Early on the morning of August 2 a young officer commanding an eighty-foot-long torpedo boat on patrol in the Solomon Islands heard his turret gunner shout, "Ship at two o'clock!" and turned to see the surrounding darkness cut by the sharp prow of an oncoming Japanese destroyer. In a little more than thirty seconds the Japanese ship had sliced the small American craft in two. On a sea spread with burning gasoline the officer and his surviving crewmen clung to the flaming wreckage.

The officer was Lt. (jg) John F. Kennedy, another New Englander from a privileged family: his wealthy father, Joseph Kennedy, was a former U.S. ambassador to the Court of St. James (England); his preparatory school was Choate; like his father, he had gone to Harvard. Like the Bushes, the Kennedys summered on the New England coast. Both George and John had grown up in large, close-knit families, and both were raised to serve their country. Although they lived in proximity to each other during the summer, their families had never met.

Kennedy survived his ordeal in the water and led ten of his men to safety on a nearby island, from which they were eventually rescued. His experience in the Pacific had proved the value of his upbringing; George Bush's test was yet to come.

Bush continued practicing field carrier landings. Now he was no longer dependent upon his skills alone. The LSO was responsible for directing him in to a landing and for signaling when to cut his engine so that later, when landing on a carrier, he would catch one of a series of wires on the deck, which would drag him to a halt.

On August 24 Bush found out that it was one thing to practice landings on a field and another to actually land on a pitching and rolling deck. On that date, flying an Avenger, he qualified in carrier landings aboard the USS *Sable*, a converted paddle wheel excursion ship. He made six carrier landings and deck run takeoffs in little more than two hours. He now recalls the experience as "exciting, like when I soloed. One can practice carrier landings on land forever without knowing the thrill of actually landing on a moving ship at sea. There's something about the isolation, the ocean, the tiny carrier below that gets the adrenaline flowing."

After qualifying in carrier landings, he was given a week's leave. In one of his letters to Barbara, George had invited her, with his family's blessings, to join the annual Bush summer holiday in Kennebunkport before he went on to advanced training.

George and Barbara spent seventeen days together in Maine sunning on the beach, playing tennis, socializing with his family, and sailing. George's eleven-year-old brother Jonathan tagged along with them whenever possible. "I was crazy about Barbara," Jonathan said recently. "She and George were fun to be with because they laughed a lot—that is, she laughed because George was always kidding her. George invariably wanted to go sailing, but once we got on the boat he would just stretch out and go on kidding Barbara while I did the actual sailing and Barbara rubbed George's back."

Whenever they found time to be alone together, George and Barbara made plans for the future they planned to spend together after the war ended. "It was a great vacation at our beloved home there," he recalled recently. Barbara added, "I met all of his family—aunts, uncles, cousins—and I lived in very tight quarters with his immediate family. We swam, rode bikes, played tennis, picnicked, walked in the moonlight—and fell in love!"

George had never considered the possibility that he might die in combat. He knew that pilots were killed, were even considered expendable by the navy. But, like most nineteen-year-olds, he couldn't imagine that at some time in the future he might be one of those to be brought down by antiaircraft in a burning plane. He had too much faith in his training and ability. He would survive and try to keep thoughts of death from entering his mind.

He had already been accepted by Yale, and the GI Bill (a government program designed to help veterans with their college expenses) would give him financial help, making him independent of his family. He had faith in his ability to earn a living and support a family after graduation, and he knew that Barbara Pierce was *the* girl he wanted to marry.

That summer George and Barbara became secretly engaged, but without a ring. "Secret to the extent that the German and Japanese high commands weren't aware of it," Bush wrote in his autobiography, *Looking Forward.*

Their decision was simple and natural and didn't involve the traditional ritual: George didn't ask Marvin Pierce for permission to wed his daughter, nor did he suddenly pop the question to Barbara on one knee in accord with the tradition of old movies. To both George and Barbara, there really was no question at all. "Did he ask me if he could run for president?" Barbara says. "The answer is no, but he didn't 'ask' me to marry him, either."

To everyone who knew George and Barbara, it was obvious that they were very much in love. No one had to be told. When Barbara finally announced to her family that she was engaged, she again found herself offering news to the already well-informed. As Barbara recalled, "It was sort of 'How could you be so silly? We've known it all along.' Anybody who looked at us knew we were in love, which you don't think is true when you're young; you think you have a secret, but the secret shows.

"I thought they might put up a fuss about my getting engaged, but luckily my family had just gone through that with my sister, who, just before the war, after graduating from Smith, got engaged to and married a Yale senior, and they weren't up to going through that all over again.

"Also, there was a war going on. One has to remember that when you got engaged at that time you weren't sure you would ever see that person again when they went overseas. I know my mother and father really liked George, but I don't think they believed we would get married. I believe they were thinking they would take it one step at a time.

"George's parents probably felt the same way. He had yet to go overseas, and I think that although they had good reason to object because of his youth, they probably thought that anything that made him happy was fine. I know I wouldn't want my child going overseas without somebody other than his parents loving him. I suspect that may be what quieted his parents' objections."

Barbara was right. Dorothy Bush did indeed think they were "too young," but at the same time she and Prescott agreed that George and Barbara were "sensible and well suited to each other."

The formal announcement of the engagement appeared in the society pages of the *New York Times* on Sunday, December 12, 1943, another winter Sunday in a world at war. The newspaper's headlines reported that U.S. bombers had delivered a shattering blow to Emden, one of Germany's most important ports; the Russians were gaining in battles along the Dnieper front; five German U-boats had been sunk and three others crippled following a two-day battle in the Atlantic; the British Eighth Army had thrust a bridgehead across an important river in Italy . . . and on and on, with news of battles, both victories and setbacks, from around the world. Near the wedding announcement was an article reporting that some of the country's generals attributed much of the growing success of the Allied drives to the efforts of American women working behind the lines. That same Sunday the city of New York, already suffering a coal shortage, was being hit by a seventy-two mph gale, and the date also marked the sixty-first birthday of Mayor La Guardia. A small article noted that newly authorized honorable-discharge lapel buttons to be issued to all men and women who had served honorably in the U.S. Army were ready for distribution: at least some Americans were finally coming home from the war.

After his leave George reported to the Naval Air Base at Norfolk, Virginia, where he joined a new squadron then being commissioned. It was there that he met some of the men who, to this day, are among his best friends. But at first he shared little in common with them other than height.

Bush, Jack O. Guy, and Lou Grab were the three tallest pilots in the squadron. Every time a group photo was taken they were placed together in the center. At first they just exchanged pleasantries and traded information about where they had trained. In time they started to look forward to meeting and soon began to spend off-duty hours together.

Guy, a country boy from Claxton, Georgia, had been a bank teller in Atlanta when he enlisted. His father died when he was thirteen, and his mother ran the community house at Henry Ford's plantation, Richmond Hill, in southern Georgia. He got his first taste of flying when he was in his early teens and a barnstorming pilot asked him and some friends to clear a field for landing. As a reward, they were given a short plane ride over the town. From then on young Jack dreamed about being a flier himself. He earned his wings at Barin Field in Foley, Alabama, known throughout the navy as "Bloody Barin" because it accounted for more aviation-related accidents than any other training facility.

Guy recalls that when Bush once mentioned that he'd gone to Andover, he replied, "Well, I went to Claxton." Guy didn't know that Andover was an elite school.

Lou Grab was from Sacramento, California, where he lived in a tiny two-bedroom house behind his father's Chevron gas station. The navy was his escape from a domineering father (his mother had died when he was six weeks old) and an uncertain future. He was eighteen months George's senior, and they had been in the same class at Corpus Christi, where he also got his wings.

Stan Butchart had been raised in Spokane,

Washington, his childhood bedroom filled with model planes, and his dream was to be an aviator. He was in junior college taking the civilian pilot training course when he learned the navy had dropped its college requirement, and he immediately enlisted. Although the boot ensign (latest in rank) of the group, he was already an accomplished pilot and excelled in acrobatic flying.

"George was a lot of fun, a live wire," recalls Guy. "Everybody wanted to cotton up to him, and I don't know anybody who didn't like him for any reason."

Although the youngest member of the group, George was already showing traits of leadership. "We were all about the same age, but we looked up to George automatically," says Guy. "There just didn't seem to be any question about our confidence in his leadership ability."

At the end of September the new squadron was assigned to the Naval Air Station at Chincoteague, Virginia, a peninsula with Chesapeake Bay on one side and the Atlantic on the other, for the final phases of its training. Chincoteague, a provincial town where the women still wore sunbonnets, was well known for its oysters and even more famous as the home of a small breed of ponies.

His training there followed the prescribed syllabus, with principal emphasis on glide bombing and torpedo tactics plus extensive night flying involving radar tactics, formation work, and night navigation hops.

Bush's roommates at Chincoteague were Jack Guy, Doug West, and Francis "Tom" Waters. West, who had a baby face and pug nose and was one of the shortest cadets in the group, had a raucous sense of humor that kept them all loose. Waters was a ruddy-complected trombone player from Savannah, Georgia. The four men lived in a single room in the BOQ (bachelor officers' quarters) with a desk and two bunk beds and a locker between for storage of uniforms and personal articles. Most of their conversation before taps was about flying—that day's and the schedule for the following day. The navy published a monthly magazine, *Nav News*, that contained accounts, sometimes with photographs, of the month's accidents in naval aircraft. Most of the reported accidents were caused by pilot error, and the four young pilots discussed over and over the probable causes, trying to learn how to avoid such accidents themselves.

Sometimes they talked about current events, ranging from what was going on in the war—a battle was then being fought in the Pacific for possession of the island of Guam, and draft deferments had been slashed—to gossip, including the problems of Charlie Chaplin, who had been indicted for violating the Mann Act in transporting an underage female across state lines for the purpose of having sex with her.

On evenings when they had leave, the four usually piled into a Jeep or carry-all and drove to Salisbury, Maryland, to see a movie. It was on one of those excursions that Butchart met Miriam Young, a slim and pretty brunette who worked in Blizzard's Jewelry Store, and who would later become his bride. From then on Butchart took off every night after flight training to go courting, leaving his roommates to fend for themselves. "We'd go out partyin' and raise hell," remembers Guy. "But not George. He had Barbara. Pick up gals? Not George." (Bush's brother Jonathan once joked about why George was so dedicated to Barbara. "She was wild about him. And for George, if anyone wants to be wild about him, it's fine with him.")

Most of Bush's days were spent practicing glide bombing. The Avengers were loaded with water-filled bombs. The usual bombing target was a circle of whitewashed concentric rings laid out on a flat field a few miles south of the base. They were scored on how close they came to the bull's-eye. Day after day they flew back to that field, carefully keeping score and comparing hits.

The young pilots also practiced field carrier landings in preparation for landing on an aircraft carrier. This practice consisted of flying two hundred feet above the ground with the flaps and wheels down in landing position. The goal was to hit a spot on the field that had been painted the approximate length of the landing area on a carrier. A landing signal officer stood at the left on the marked area, signaling to the pilot with brightly colored flags and giving him instructions on setting up his plane for a proper approach. If the pilot was in an optimum position for landing, the LSO would signal for him to cut his engine.

One day the landing gear on George's Avenger collapsed and he crash-landed, totaling the eighty-five-thousand-dollar plane. "I'm not sure what actually happened, but I was more embarrassed than fearful," Bush says. "I kept worrying that it was a bad landing and not a fatally flawed landing gear."

For their practice runs the Avengers were frequently loaded with hundred-pound water-filled bombs. The student pilots would use an oyster house standing on stilts in Chesapeake Bay as their target. Butchart recalls, "We would make around a dozen passes, going in on coordinated attacks, as we might do to a carrier, and we would drop a water bomb so we could get an idea if it fell short of the target. One of our group skipped a water bomb, which went through the oyster house. Unfortunately, someone was in the house at the time and registered a complaint. The government later had to pay for it." The oyster house was eventually declared off-limits.

In Lou Grab's view, the people living in the vicinity of Chincoteague deserved some sort of medal because the young pilots did a lot of "flat-hatting" (flying as low to the surface as possible). "The fishermen would be out on the bay trying to earn a living, and we would go down and try to scare the hell out of them."

Roland "Dick" Houle, one of George's squadronmates, returned to base one day after flat-hatting with a huge hole in the landing edge of his wing. He was flying so close to the water that an unfortunate sea gull had no chance of getting out of the way.

Across the bay from Chincoteague, in Crisfield, Maryland, there was a piece of land and beach that stuck out by the end of the runway on Chesapeake Bay. As the young pilots soon discovered, it was a popular place for local girls to sunbathe in the nude. On their final approach to the field the pilots would come in low off the ocean and try to get a close look at the girls before plopping down on the runway. It soon became a game that even the girls enjoyed. Sometimes the pilots would even buzz the beach or beach houses.

One day Bush was flat-hatting over the fairgrounds in Crisfield where a traveling circus was setting up tents. The noise of his plane frightened some animals and an elephant promptly took off, in turn frightening some of the town's residents. One woman complained to the mayor. The mayor complained to the base commander. George was severely reprimanded. Years later Bush would recall, "I was grounded for causing an elephant stampede."

Always searching out nicknames for one another, the men promptly tagged George "Ellie the Elephant," a nickname that was to stick. George good-humoredly played along and was soon able to give a fair imitation of an elephant raising its trunk and bellowing.

All the pilots were assigned additional duties. Bush was chosen to be the squadron photographic officer and was sent to a navy photographic school for a week of training in the use of torpedo cameras, which were mounted under the wing of each plane. He also learned to use equipment that analyzed the photos taken by the cameras. He soon became expert at taking aerial photographs, and on his return he showed his buddies pictures he had taken of the James River Bridge.

While the pilots were being trained for their jobs in the squadron, the enlisted men who were to be assigned to them were being trained as well. Lee Nadeau, who would become George's gunner, had wanted to be a pilot when he enlisted in the navy—his room at home was filled with model planes he had built over the years—but because he had left high school at the end of his sophomore year to get a job, he didn't have the credits to get into Naval Air. However, he scored so high on the navy's aptitude tests that he was given the choice of any navy school he wished. He chose aviation ordnance because it at least involved working on airplanes. Like Bush—indeed, like all the

other thousands of young men being trained—
Nadeau was sent from base to base. His primary training was at an aviation ordnance school, where he was taught the use of all the navy's weapons, from machine guns to aerial mines and torpedoes. Although he was being trained to handle aircraft armament, loading and handling the weapons, he knew he would be serving on the ground, which disappointed him.

During his last days at the school he and the other students were convened to listen to an officer speak. The officer told them that the navy was in desperate need of air crewmen. He was, of course, asking for volunteers: as with service in the submarine corps, all aspects of service in the air were strictly voluntary. The idea that he could serve aboard an airplane was all Nadeau had to hear. When the officer asked if any of the men were interested, Nadeau's hand shot up. He was then sent to an aerial gunnery school in Hollywood, Florida. After six weeks of training he was sent to Chincoteague as an AOM 3/c (aviation ordnance man third class).*

Nadeau recalls the first time he met Bush. He'd gone into a hangar to look at the plane to which he'd been assigned and examine its ordnance. "The pilot was already in the cock-

---

* See table of navy rating codes in Dedication of this book.

pit when I boarded the plane. I was at my station in the turret, checking the gun out, when I heard a voice over the intercom saying, 'Welcome aboard.' It was a voice I was to hear many times over the next year in all kinds of situations."

Bush's radioman–tail gunner was John Delaney ARM 3/c, a feisty, happy-go-lucky Irishman from Rhode Island. Del was three years older than Nadeau, who was three months older than Bush. He, too, was at his position in the plane that day. Thus Bush and the two enlisted men who would be his constant companions for the next year in the skies over the Pacific Ocean were first joined in that hangar.

Bush now had men flying with him who relied on him to keep them alive and out of harm's way. Although they would be with him as passengers almost every time he flew, he never had the same bond with them that he had with the squadron pilots who were his friends. The crew was his responsibility. On the ground they separated at once, off to their segregated quarters, because navy regulations forbid fraternization between enlisted men and officers. Nevertheless, Nadeau came to like Bush as a person very much. "He was the kind of kid I would have been prone to associate with at home," Nadeau recalls. "I didn't know for a long time that he came from a well-to-do family. All I knew about him at the beginning was that he was a good pilot, and that was what was most important. The few times we did talk, it was about the aircraft or what we were doing. Ours was strictly a workaday business relationship."

On a weekend leave from Chincoteague, George went to New York with Doug West, Milt Moore, and Jack Guy. "It never occurred to me until then that George came from a privileged background, although it was apparent that he had a better education, a little more going for him," says Guy. "He invited us to go with him to his grandfather's or uncle's apartment in Manhattan. It was about the grandest place I had ever seen."

Moore, whose father owned a laundry, was also impressed. "I realized then that George was something more than I thought, but the members of his family that he introduced us to were real down-to-earth people."

A squadron consisting of nine TBFs and thirteen pilots was formed and soon assigned for more training in Norfolk, Virginia. By this time most of the young ensigns considered themselves hot pilots and thought they knew everything about torpedo bombers. That notion was soon dispelled when they met Lt. Comdr. Don Melvin, who was to be their squadron leader.

A tall, imposing man, Melvin was distant, cool, and dedicated to the job of training his men. Bush recalls Melvin as a "seasoned pro, steady and serious, and a disciplinarian. He didn't say a hell of a lot, but when he did give advice it was sound. He was probably as good a leader as we could have had. He was experienced enough so that we had respect for him, but he was never one of the boys."

Jack Guy still remembers how Melvin put his tyro pilots through the wringer. "On one of our first days in the air with him he had us play follow-the-leader. 'You stay right behind me,' he told us. I didn't think a plane could do what he did—but it did. We did wingovers and then dropped in forty-five-degree dives from twelve thousand feet, pulling out at one thousand feet and finally leveling off at one hundred feet. It was scary but great fun. Melvin wanted to find out who among us was going to fly and who was going to back off. Four men transferred out of the squadron in the first few weeks and had to be replaced."

Dick Playstead, a fourteenth-generation American and one of the few other New Englanders in the squadron, recalls that the operations manual for the Avenger detailed all the things that could be done but should *not* be done in the giant plane. "The book said you were not supposed to fly upside down. One day when we were flying, I said to Melvin, 'I think we were upside down.' 'We were?' Melvin said, pretending to be surprised. 'Well, how about that?'"

It was Melvin's responsibility to teach his

men how to really fly their huge planes, how to set their tabs in such a way that they could take off in a constant gradual climb, and how to fly in proper formation night or day. They soon got so good at maintaining formation that they became the envy of the other trainees. He also taught them discipline. His young charges were always clean-shaven and neatly dressed.

Melvin's follow-the-leader lessons were anything but a game: in the skies of the Pacific his men would have to follow him from a carrier to a target that must be bombed with coordinated precision. The approach to the target would be made with the planes flying in an echelon, a V-shaped formation of planes stretched out behind the leader. In sight of the target, the formation would descend from twelve or fifteen thousand feet in a steady, accelerating glide. At the precise moment, the leader would signal, pull up sharply, roll, and then suddenly drop toward the target, with each plane following, nearly rolling over to follow the leader, so that each pilot would pull the nose of his plane onto the target from an inverted position. One by one behind the lead plane, the pilots would drop their bombs on the target and then pull up to regroup.

A torpedo bombing attack is usually a coordinated group effort with the fighters arriving at the target area first and strafing the enemy in preparation for the immediate arrival of the torpedo bombers. The concentration of power was designed to reduce the effectiveness of the enemy defenses, thus making it possible for the torpedo planes to begin their attack in the safest and most effective way possible.

The pilots in the torpedo squadron usually flew at each other's wingtips. They took turns at flying wing—the wing man's job was to emulate every move of the plane he was assigned to protect. The practice runs soon became a form of teamwork, and Bush relished being part of a team.

After a few weeks of grueling training under Melvin's watchful and critical eyes, the new squadron, now named VT-51, was assigned to the naval air station at Hyannis, Massachusetts. It was raining steadily there, and the field was little more than a dirt runway, the control tower a Quonset hut. Lee Nadeau recalls the entire squadron sloshing around in the muck and mud.

The pilots with their crews aboard practiced gunnery. One member of the flight towed a long canvas sleeve at the end of a long cable. The rest of the squadron followed him to a predetermined altitude and then attacked the sleeve as though it were an enemy plane. Nadeau and Bush scored high in the practice runs: the years spent skeet shooting at Duncannon, his grandfather's plantation in South Carolina, had sharpened Bush's eye for moving targets.

The main purpose of the practice, however,

was to learn how to drop torpedoes. In those days the attitude of the plane was critical in guaranteeing the success of the torpedo run. The squadron continued with torpedo practice in Narragansett Bay, using an abandoned lightship for a target.

On Thanksgiving Day, after the squadron had feasted on a turkey dinner with all the fixings, the skipper announced that they had orders to move to another base, where they would complete their training. Within hours they were in the air for the thirty-five-minute flight to the naval air station at Charlestown, Rhode Island. Here they sharpened their shooting skills on fixed and free (moving) targets, escort problems, and fighter direction work in conjunction with the twenty-five F-6 Hellcats and their pilots that would complete AG-51 (air group).

When the weather was bad, the air group pilots practiced field carrier landings combined with field catapult shots. The landing gear of the Avenger was attached to wires leading to the hydraulic catapult. At a signal the catapult hurled the Avenger off the carrier deck. Then there was a moment when the plane cleared the edge of the deck and started to drop before the pilot could gain altitude. Bush recalls his first "cat shot" as being "exciting but pretty much routine. As the plane dropped, I wondered if the power would be enough. The first shot went smoothly although there would be many times in the future when too little 'cat' power or too little wind across the deck made for some hairy experiences."

While the pilots were in the air, their crewmen worked out on the bomb sight trainer and were given lectures on the use of radar and minimum-altitude bombing using radar.

Dorothy, George's mother, came to visit him at the base. Bush's friend Legare "Gar" Hole, the squadron executive officer, was on duty that day. "A stylishly dressed woman came to the visitors' quarters and asked to see George Bush. I was surprised. She was the only mother I ever knew who had come to the base."

Dorothy spent the entire day with the squadron and even attended briefings. Then she had lunch with the men, and after the day's flight she went to the debriefings. "She was just as sweet as she could be," recalls Stan Butchart.

While at Charlestown, Nadeau qualified as a gunner. One day after a flight Bush, with a big grin on his face, gave him a small black box. Nadeau opened it. Inside was a pair of silver wings, a gift from Bush.

On December 15, 1943, the air group was invited to Philadelphia to attend the commissioning ceremonies of the USS *San Jacinto* (CVL30), the new carrier to which they were to be assigned. It was a day of excitement for everybody but especially for George. He knew he would soon be going to war, so he had a private telephone conversation with his mother. He had invited Barbara and his mother to the commissioning ceremony if they could get space: transportation was rationed, and military personnel had priority on trains, but they managed.

It was to be the first time that Barbara and Dorothy Bush were really to be alone together, and Barbara recalls that she was apprehensive. "I was scared to death of George's mother anyway, not because she was scary but because she was so perfect, and has remained so for forty-five years. I adore her today, as does everybody who knows her, but then I was just a kid.

"All the way down on the train Mother Bush asked me what kind of engagement ring I would like. I'm dumb but not that dumb, so I said, 'I don't care.' 'Does it have to be a diamond?' she asked me. Again I said, 'I don't care,' not knowing that she had a star sapphire ring in her purse that had belonged to George's aunt Nancy Walker. Just before the commissioning ceremony started, George took the ring out of his pocket and gave it to me. I was thrilled. I don't know to this day whether it's real, and I don't care. It's my engagement ring, and it hasn't been off my finger since the day George gave it to me."

The *San Jacinto* was a war-born hybrid. When her keel was laid, she was to have been the cruiser *Newark*, but American experiences at Pearl Harbor and Midway had determined that more aircraft carriers were needed, so, while still on the ways, she was redesigned to become the light carrier *Reprisal*. After the sinking of the USS *Houston* the citizens of that city patriotically doubled their bond drive to replace the missing cruiser. The extra money was contributed for another ship, which the Houstonians chose to name *San Jacinto* in honor of the battle that took place there on April 21, 1836, when General Sam Houston's small army of Texans, outnumbered almost two to one, defeated the Mexican dictator Santa Ana and preserved the independence of the Texas republic.

The *San Jacinto* was rushed to completion. Her fitting-out time was cut in half and her commissioning advanced six weeks. She was ugly but functional when she slid down the ways under the command of Captain Harold "Beauty" Martin and was christened before a deputation of the Sons of Texas. The *San Jac,* as she was called, flew the Lone Star flag from her masthead below the Stars and Stripes.

She had a sleek cruiser hull but a high center of gravity with a bulky hangar deck and a narrow wooden flight deck that ran almost her full length. Instead of the armor plate that protected most carriers, she had only the thin steel skin of a merchantman. She carried 500,000 gallons of fuel oil and 100,000 gallons of aviation gasoline. A direct hit to any of her vital areas would have turned her into a flaming inferno. She was built to be expendable, having cost less to build than a conventional carrier.

But none of this was important. What did count was that she could steam at thirty-four knots and operate thirty-four planes—twenty-five fighters and nine torpedo bombers. At 14,399 tons, she was one of the fastest light aircraft carriers in the navy. Although the *San Jac* carried a lot of armament for a ship her size, the fighters and torpedo planes were her chief weapons in battle. But the pilots had to be especially skilled: she had a very short deck for landing space.

AG-51, including the men and torpedo pilots of VT-51 along with the fighter pilots of VF-51, reported aboard the *San Jac* on February 6, 1944, as "plank owners," meaning part of the ship's original complement. The carrier embarked the following day on a two-week shakedown cruise to the Gulf of Paria, Trinidad, B.W.I. The time on board was well spent; pilots and their crews conducted practice air searches. Gar Hole had to make a forced landing in the water because he had insufficient power on takeoff.

Bush's other close friend, Jack Guy, also had to make a splashdown (water landing) when the engine of his Avenger failed on the downwind leg of his approach to the ship. His radioman, Jerrold Ward ARM 3/c, suffered a broken leg and face lacerations. (Ward was to spend fourteen months in the Philadelphia Naval Hospital and was replaced by Harold Fuchs S1/c.) Another ensign-pilot was killed while making an approach for a landing on the carrier.

A captain's inspection was held in port at Trinidad, at which time personnel and materiel were inspected. On the return trip, about two days out of Norfolk, the ship struck extremely rough weather. Most of the ship's company and the pilots were new to sea duty: at mess call only 8 of her 150 officers showed up. One of Bush's roommates, Francis "Tom" Waters, had a red face, but the seas were so bad that his face literally turned green. Bush weathered the storm well, however, thanks to his childhood experience with boats.

After the shakedown cruise the *San Jac* returned to the Philadelphia Navy Yard for repairs and more supplies, and Bush and his squadronmates were given a short leave, after which they reported to Norfolk, where they spent several days in final training activities. VT-51 set something of a record by qualifying, two landings each, aboard the USS *Charger* at dusk, which made it somewhat easier although Bush recalls being "tensed up. The *Charger* looked awful darn small." But the landings were made without damage to any aircraft.

Gar Hole, who was leading four Avengers, saw only one ship with lights on in the bay and, thinking it was the *San Jac*, circled it—only to find that it was the Cape Charles Ferry.

On March 25, 1944, the *San Jac* left a cold and snowy Philadelphia and headed for San Diego, where the air group's planes were to be hoisted aboard. The ship traveled south around Florida down the Yucatan Channel to Panama, stopping at Panama City, which is midway through the canal locks.

Butchart recalls the stopover in Panama City. "The first drink I remember us having together is there. We went someplace, and all of us in the squadron had a planter's punch in a hotel. The fighter pilots in our squadron always seemed like the wild bunch to us because few of us torpedo pilots boozed it up or even smoked. Except for that one time, I don't remember any of us even going into a bar."

That was not the case with most of the other crewmen; Gar Hole recalls that he never saw so many drunks in his life. "When the men came back to ship, most of them were completely sauced. Many were out of uniform and they were carrying dolls they had won at amusement arcades—and kissing girls they had met."

While the crew was on shore leave, the ship took on fifteen hundred army troops and all their equipment. By the time she set sail again, her original complement had been doubled. Most of the army men slept with their vehicles on the hangar deck.

The *San Jac* stopped at San Diego before

heading out for Pearl Harbor. It was while the carrier was en route that Bush met Frank Paoletti AMM2/c, who was to be his plane captain (responsible for all of his airplane's maintenance) for the next eleven months. Paoletti, who was ten years older than Bush, came from Lodi, California, where he worked in a mill making slats for pencils.

Paoletti recalls that on the way to Pearl Harbor he was told he had been assigned as an "Airedale"—one pilot/one dog taking care of one plane—to torpedo plane 2X. "I was aboard ship talking to a couple of buddies when I saw this tall, skinny ensign coming along the flight deck toward us. I had just remarked on how much he looked like a young Charles Lindbergh when he came up and said, 'I'm Ensign George Bush, and I'm assigned to plane 2X. Do any of you know who is supposed to be my plane captain?' I said, 'Aye, sir, I am.' We shook hands and started talking about the plane."

Paoletti, who was as tall as Bush but weighed less—at 140 pounds, he was 5 pounds under the minimum weight, but the doctor had fudged his weight upon enlistment—saw Bush from them on almost daily. He was responsible for keeping the plane shipshape and buckling Bush into his harness before each flight. "I never realized anything about Mr. Bush's background, that he came from a well-to-do family, until after he left the ship. We were never buddies, but in my book he was a top-class guy, a real nice Joe."

The *San Jac* arrived at Pearl Harbor on April 20, 1944. Bush felt like a tourist as they steamed into port, where he saw the ships that had been sunk on December 7, their superstructures still thrust up out of the water, with their trapped dead below. The *San Jac* docked behind the *Essex* in Pearl Harbor. Nearby the *Utah* was still lying on her side, where she had settled after the Japanese attack. The *Arizona*, sunk at the same time, was also dramatically visible. To Bush, the skeletons of the big battleships were both grim reminders of the war that had begun there and portents of the possible fate of his own ship.

The squadron was land-based at the naval air station at Kaneohe, Oahu, T.H. There they practiced more gunnery and glide-bombing runs on moving targets. When attacking a maneuvering ship at sea, Avenger tactics called for dropping a "stick" of four bombs (their entire bomb load) using an intervalometer, which controlled the spacing of the bombs. The intervalometer was mounted in Delaney's station, and it was his job to set the Avenger's air speed and the desired bomb spacing. The target was usually attacked in a thirty- to forty-five-degree glide from at least fifteen hundred feet, dropping to an altitude of five hundred feet or lower. Bush released the bombs as he leveled off, and the intervalometer spaced the bombs sixty to seventy-five feet apart, practically guaranteeing one or more hits on the target from a stick. Bush and his crew scored high on all their runs.

On May 2, 1944, the squadron was officially deemed ready for action. The *San Jac* was assigned to be part of the growing might of Adm. Marc A. Mitscher's Task Force 58/38, the fast-carrier striking force of the Pacific Fleet.

After almost a year of arduous and intensive training Bush and the other pilots of AG-51 expected that they would soon be in the air fighting against the Japanese enemy. It was to be sooner than they anticipated.

Chapter Five

Pearl Harbor: American naval missions against the Empire of the Rising Sun began where the war had begun, at the scene of a tragic defeat. The pilots and crew of the *San Jac* were eager to avenge that defeat, but they were also understandably nervous about encountering the enemy. The Japanese seemed invincible: they had destroyed the fleet at Pearl Harbor, defeated one of America's greatest generals—Douglas MacArthur—in the Philippines, overrun American bases throughout the Pacific, blasted the best warships of the British navy, and handily captured fortresses, such as Singapore, that were believed impregnable. Japanese planes—in particular the feared Zero— were widely held to be superior to those flown by the Allies. In a very short time the Japanese had turned their island nation into an enormous empire.

Looking back now, with a hindsight made

clear by ultimate victory, it could be said that the tide turned in the long Pacific war on May 3, 1942, two years to the day before the *San Jac* pulled out of Pearl Harbor. On that date the battle of the Coral Sea began, and shortly thereafter was won: just a month later the Allies defeated the Japanese at the battle of Midway.

Despite those victories the war in the Pacific was far from over, and Bush and his comrades knew they were going out to meet a powerful and skillful enemy. They had been well trained and had weapons equal to those of the Japanese, but their fighting spirit—and their courage—were as yet untried. That moment was about to come.

The *San Jac* eased out of the dawn mist and headed west from Pearl Harbor on May 3, 1944, along with two large carriers and support vessels. Five days later, without encountering any sign of the enemy, the small fleet reached Majuro, a beautiful coral atoll with a sapphire-blue lagoon surrounded by palm trees in the eastern Marshall Islands. There the *San Jac* reported for duty as part of Task Force Fifty-eight. They were to join in Operation Forager, code name for the invasion of the Marianas, which was scheduled to begin within a month.

On May 15 Bush's carrier, with a small task group consisting of the *Essex*, the *Wasp*, five cruisers, and twelve destroyers, set off on its first combat mission: strikes against Marcus

Island, a Japanese island with a naval base, and Wake Island, the American island attacked along with Pearl Harbor on December 7, 1941.

By May 18, when the group neared Marcus Island, the *San Jac*, accompanied by four destroyers, had been ordered to search the area north of the island for enemy ships. No Japanese vessels were found. This diversionary mission brought the *San Jac* and the accompanying ships to within six hundred miles of the Japanese mainland, at that time the deepest penetration of Japanese-dominated waters by American surface craft.

On May 21 the *San Jac* rejoined the main task force. Two days later the carrier's planes took off to attack ground installations and the harbor on Wake Island—the first combat mission for Bush and his squadron. "We were all tense because it was our first bombing mission over an active target, and we didn't know what to expect," Nadeau recalls. "I don't think there was any time we were in the air when the adrenaline wasn't flowing, but much as we dreaded that first flight, we knew we had to do it. Luckily, George seemed confident, which relaxed Del and me somewhat. I think the worst part was sitting and waiting to take off. Once we were airborne, we were so busy taking care of business that it was just another flight until we pulled up out of our dive and I could see black shellbursts below us. I was fascinated by them until I realized that the Japanese were shooting at us."

Although Bush appeared calm to his crewmen, he recalls that he was really tense and nervous. "The first sight of the antiaircraft bursts made a lasting impression on me." Yet he adds, "I have never forgotten the beauty of the area from the sky."

But the sky that day was also hostile. Jim Wykes, Bush's friend and roommate aboard the *San Jac*, disappeared that day while on an antisubmarine patrol. When a plane goes down at sea, it usually goes to the bottom without a trace unless it breaks up on impact, in which case floating debris sometimes gives away its location. Search patrols were sent out, but all proved fruitless: the Avenger, with Wykes and his two crewmen, Robert Whalen and Charles Haggard, had disappeared in the ocean (their bodies were never found). They were listed not as combat casualties but as missing in action. The technical difference in terminology was unimportant to the men who had known them. That night Bush lay in his upper bunk and cried for his friend. "No one saw me—that wouldn't do," he recalls.

The *San Jac* returned to Majuro on May 31 and celebrated a "happy hour," an event all hands had been anticipating for weeks. The officers and enlisted men put on an evening of entertainment that included boxing contests and music by the Flat Toppers (aircraft carriers are called "flattops") orchestra led by Tom Waters, who played a mean trombone. Jack Guy was the bass-fiddle player. Despite the heat and humidity, the entire crew enjoyed the show and was surprised by the array of talent aboard. They wildly applauded the remarkable variety of singing and acting acts. The evening's door prize was less astonishing: the inevitable war bond.

Entertainment on the ship was one thing; what the airmen and sailors wanted was shore leave. Much of the time aboard was spent in training exercises and resupplying the ship in preparation for action, but the men were finally granted a few hours' leave—half were allowed ashore on June 2, the other half on June 3.

The small atoll didn't have a great deal to offer in the way of diversions, so a beer party was given for the crew and officers, all of whom soon discovered that it was unusual to be leaning against a tree with a can of beer in hand and not have a lizard crawl up a leg or down the back. "The foliage was so dense a bloodhound would have been needed to retrieve a volleyball," the company historian reported.

A baseball game was organized between the men of the *San Jac* and the *Bunker Hill*. One of the AG-51 fighter pilots had been an All-American halfback, while another had played with the Red Sox. Bush was on first base, and Dick Playstead was an outfielder. "There was a dispute over a call, and the *Bunker Hill* guys said they were going to beat us up," recalls Playstead. "Suddenly the guys in our ship's company rallied around us. It was the first time that the crew of the *San Jac* ever showed complete support for their air group, and it was a good feeling. The argument was finally mediated."

Asked whether George was a good first baseman, Playstead said, "He more than held his own."

The men were dependent for war news on the AG-51 newspaper, the *San Jac Sun*, which reported that on June 4, while they were still at Majuro, Rome was entered by elements of the United States Fifth Army. On June 6, 1944, the day Allied troops stormed ashore at Normandy in France in the D-Day invasion, the *San Jac*, along with the *Lexington*, the *Enterprise*, the *Princeton*, and the other ships making up Task Force Fifty-eight, weighed anchor and slowly steamed out of the lagoon entrance. It was to take almost five hours for the entourage—consisting of seven fleet and light cruisers, seven fast battleships, three heavy and seven light cruisers, plus sixty destroyers—to clear the lagoon. The 902 airplanes carried on the flattops made them an imposing force. Their destination was the Mariana Islands, where the invasion of Saipan was to commence.

The action began on June 11, a beautiful, clear day. The fifteen carriers launched a strike of more than 230 planes against Saipan and nearby Aslito airfield. During this mission fighter planes of the *San Jac* shot down their first enemy aircraft: a Betty (attack bomber) and an Emily (flying boat).

AG-51 had drawn its first blood. It was to pay the next day when the fighter planes and Avengers flew over Aslito again and encountered fierce antiaircraft fire. "They were firing at us like mad," recalls Stanley Butchart. Ens. R. D. McIlwaine's Hellcat was hit and crashed in the area of the Aslito airfield. McIlwaine was the first member of AG-51 shot down in combat and also the first American pilot to lose his life on Saipan in the Marianas campaign.

The following day the task force lost twenty-three planes in combat, including sixteen pilots and eight crewmen. But they had badly hurt the Japanese air units in the Marianas. During the next few days of preinvasion air strikes the squadron encountered less defensive fire from the Japanese antiaircraft gunners who had quickly learned that as soon as they fired, the cruisers and battleships in position around the island would home in on their installations with their heavy guns. The lack of antiaircraft fire made the fliers believe they had knocked out the guns. They found they could fly over the island almost unopposed. According to Butchart, "We were carrying hundred-pounders, twelve of them. Usually, if there was a lot of ack-ack, you'd just try to get on target and release your bombs and then get out. But during those few days we just formed into a big long line and went around and made twelve different runs because there was no opposition, so we could just pick targets and do what we wanted."

At mess that night one of the pilots read aloud an item from the ship's newspaper to the effect that Rosie the Riveter and a partner were credited with assembling the entire wing of a torpedo bomber in one shift, ramming in a record 3,345 rivets. There was a lot of kidding about the effects such speed might have on the finished product.

Bush, who flew constantly during the days before the invasion was scheduled, had cause to remember the joking when, on June 13, he flew three strikes in three planes. Each plane developed a problem. The first lasted only three hours, the second didn't even stay aloft that long, and in each instance he had to make an emergency landing aboard the ship. The third flight lasted only half an hour because the hydraulic line was leaking so badly that the entire rear of the fuselage was loaded with fluid, forcing him to make another emergency landing back on board the *San Jac*.

The following day, June 14, he was in the air again over the island, dodging flak and strafing and bombing targets for more than five hours. On that day he made a good hit on one of the island's coastal guns.

The planned invasion of Saipan began on June 15, and the Japanese antiaircraft gunners came to furious life. While VT-51 planes took part in strikes against the island in support of the troop landings, the *San Jac* itself saw action for the first time—precisely six months to the day after its commissioning ceremonies. Near sundown a large group of enemy aircraft attacked the ship. A combat air patrol that was up when the attack began managed to shoot down seven enemy planes and damage two others, but eight planes made their way to within one hundred yards of the ship before being shot down by antiaircraft fire and crashing into the sea. One of the enemy planes burst into flames and skimmed over the stern of the *San Jac*, coming so close that the gun crew could see the pilot's face. A second Japanese bomber exploded in the sea one hundred yards in front of the carrier. And then the ship heeled over sharply to evade the first of the bubbling torpedoes that were bracketing her length.

The task group commander radioed to ask if the ship was hit. "Not yet," replied Captain Martin.

From the deck of the *San Jac* the fliers and their crewmen watched the progress of the battle. To this day the sight before Bush remains one of the most spectacular he has ever seen. As the historian of the *San Jacinto* reported, "It was like a gigantic Fourth of July display with the myriad patterns of arcing bright-red tracers, the mushrooming puffs of black flak, and the flaming orange-yellow brilliance of the exploding bombs all set against a backdrop of gray battleships and the beautiful colors of the sunset."

When the Marines stormed ashore on the morning of the fifteenth, they found that the enemy was still entrenched and dangerous: many targets had not been damaged by the bombardment and aerial strikes. The fighting was savage, frequently hand-to-hand, and Marine losses were heavy.

Later that afternoon Stan Butchart landed the two-thousandth plane aboard the carrier. After every thousand landings a celebration was held in the officers' wardroom, and a cake, specially made for the occasion, was served. Everybody counted strikes (missions against the enemy)—"We used to argue like a bunch of kids as to whose turn it was to go on the next strike," recalls Butchart—but carrier landings were of equal importance to the pilots, and each was dutifully recorded in logbooks.

At dusk some Hellcats from the *San Jac* flying at twenty-two thousand feet encountered six enemy planes, destroying five and damaging the sixth.

On June 16 Bush and others from his squadron took part in attacks on the nearby island of Guam, scheduled for invasion in July. Bush flew through heavy antiaircraft fire to bomb or strafe Japanese troops and towns. VT-51 pilot Dick Houle, a friend of Bush's and perhaps the most daring and carefree pilot in the fighter squadron, disappeared on one of the sorties. Either his Avenger had made a water landing near a reef and sunk or it was shot down, and once again Bush mourned for a lost comrade.

Two pilots in the fighter squadron were hit by antiaircraft fire and made landings on the ocean. Lt. B. F. Griffin was immediately picked up by a submarine on lifeguard duty. The other pilot was hit by flak over Guam and forced to splash down. He was seen getting into his life raft, but darkness prevented rescue efforts, and he was listed as missing in action.

Meanwhile Bush's plane continued to have hydraulic problems. On takeoff from the carrier the wheels would fold up into the wings perfectly, but when he returned to the carrier and tried to land, he invariably had difficulty getting the wheels down. On many such occasions he was forced to put the plane into a steep dive and then snap it out and up, hoping that this popping maneuver would lock the wheels into place. The carrier's mechanics were unable to straighten out the plane's problems.

Operations in support of the landings on Saipan continued until June 17, when the task force steamed westward, hoping to locate and engage the main body of the Japanese fleet, which was reported moving nearby in Philippine waters. On the morning of June 19, before the task force aircraft had located the enemy fleet, the Japanese struck with a force of 542 planes. Six Zeros managed to get past the swirl of defending American aircraft and attack the ships. Accurate antiaircraft fire from the *San Jac* brought down one.

While the *San Jac*'s fighter planes scrambled to engage the horde of incoming aircraft, Bush and other torpedo bomber pilots were ordered to take off to keep their precious planes from being bombed on the deck. Nadeau recalls that Bush taxied their Avenger to the catapult, where they were tied down. "We needed to be catapulted, instead of making a deck takeoff, because of our heavy load of ordnance. Once we were tied down for the cat shot, a wave of Japanese planes attacked the *San Jac*. We couldn't take off, however, because the ship wasn't into the wind."

As the *San Jac* guns traded rounds with the enemy planes, Bush, Nadeau, and Delaney sat in their Avenger with the engine running, praying they wouldn't get hit.

Poised on the catapult ready for takeoff, Bush attuned his senses to the sound of his engine. He listened intently to make certain it was running properly, so that when he revved up he would have full throttle (power). Something seemed wrong to him, and he looked down at his instruments and discovered that he had little oil pressure. Bush signaled the launch officer to abort the launch, but it was

George's maternal grandfather
(and namesake), George Herbert Walker.

George Bush's birthplace in Milton, Massachusetts.

A young Barbara Pierce.

The Bush brothers in 1937. From left: George, Jonathan, and Prescott, Jr.

The Bush family bungalow in Kennebunkport, Maine, 1937.

George Bush with his high school baseball coach, George L. ("Flop") Follansbee, Sr.

The graduating class of Phillips Academy, 1942. George is in the second row, fourth from left.

George and Barbara "courting."

Barbara Pierce at Smith College.

The location of Chichi Jima and the Bonin Islands is marked with an arrow.

George Bush and his roommates at pre-flight school at the Naval Air Station in Chapel Hill, North Carolina, 1942. From left: Blaine Hall, George Bush, Bill Robinson, and Deane Phinney.

George's class at the Fort Lauderdale Naval Air Station in July 1943. Top row, from left: Bill Donovan, Ralph Cole, Mort Landsberg, George Bush, and Louis Grab. Bottom row: Mike Goldsmith, Leslie Mokry, Bill Shawcross, Tom Campion, and instructor Tex Ellison.

A frozen-faced George Bush in Minnesota.

The members of Squadron VT-51.

George Bush with flight crew members Leo W. Nadeau (center),
and John L. Delaney (left).

The USS *San Jacinto* (CVL 30).

The Avenger torpedo bomber.

George in the cockpit of *Barbara III*, 1944.

Recording flight information in the cockpit.

George Bush's rescue at sea, September 2, 1944.

The USS *Finback*, the submarine that plucked George Bush from the sea.

On the deck of the *Finback*, George is pictured with the other rescued airmen (front row) and officers (standing).

52

Miss Barbara Pierce And Ensign Bush, Navy Flyer, to Wed

Marvin Pierces' Daughter, Smith College Student, Is Engaged to Officer

Mr. and Mrs. Marvin Pierce, of Rye, N. Y., announce the engagement of their daughter, Miss Barbara Pierce, to Ensign George Herbert Walker Bush, pilot in the Naval Air Service, son of Mr. and Mrs. Prescott S. Bush, of Greenwich, Conn.

Miss Pierce is a graduate of Ashley Hall, Charleston, S. C., and is attending Smith College. She is the granddaughter of Mr. and Mrs. Scott Pierce, of Dayton, Ohio, and of Mrs. James E. Robinson, of Columbus, Ohio, and the late Judge Robinson.

Ensign Bush was graduated from Phillips Academy, Andover, Mass., and received his wings at Corpus Christi, Tex., last June. He is a grandson of Mr. and Mrs. George Herbert Walker, of New York, a[...] Bush, of [...]

An Ensign's Fiancée

Kaiden Karanjian
Miss Barbara Pierce

Mr. and Mrs. Marvin Pierce
request the honour of your presence
at the marriage of their daughter
Barbara
to
George Herbert Walker Bush
Lieutenant, junior grade, United States Naval Reserve
Saturday, the sixth of January
at four o'clock
The Presbyterian Church
and afterwards at the reception
The Apawamis Club
Rye, New York

R.S.V.P.

To accommodate both families the wedding date was changed—after the invitations were printed.

After the ceremony, Lt. and Mrs. George Bush.

George and Barbara Bush with bridesmaids on the receiving line.

George, his brother, Prescott, Jr., and Prescott's wife, Beth.

The Bush family. From left: Jonathan, Nancy, George and Barbara, Prescott and Dorothy, Prescott, Jr. and Beth, and Bucky.

Settling into married life.

too late: the deck had to be cleared. As the bomb-laden Avenger was catapulted into the air, the engine sputtered.

Bush flew for a while and then realized the plane was in real trouble. He flew back along the starboard side of the ship, the established method to signal his need to make an emergency landing. But the deck officer, busy launching planes, waved him off.

Within minutes Bush came on the intercom and asked Nadeau if he had seen something go by his turret.

"Yes," said Nadeau. "I saw a big black cloud of smoke on the starboard side."

"We just lost all our oil," Bush said. "We're going to have to ditch. Prepare for a water landing."

Bush could not use his radio to signal his situation, because the squadron was under radio silence, so he made another fly-by on the starboard side of the carrier from stern to bow, signaling that he was going to put the plane down in the water.

Any sea landing is hazardous because the pilot has to hit the crest of a wave into the wind: if he doesn't hit just right, the plane can cartwheel. This time his landing was even more perilous because the Avenger was carrying four five-hundred-pound depth charges. There wasn't time enough to jettison them, so Bush flew ahead of the fleet. During his childhood in Maine and later on in flight training he had learned to gauge wind velocity and the height of the waves. He estimated the winds to be about fifteen knots, with a light chop on the sea, so he trimmed the nose of the plane as high as possible without risking a stall. Although he had never done it before, he made a textbook landing—tailfirst—and set the huge plane down on the water.

Lee Nadeau recalls, "I was scared as hell riding on two thousand pounds of TNT, but Bush made a beautiful landing. We skidded along until the nose dropped. Then it was like hitting a stone wall. The water cascaded over the entire aircraft. I pulled the escape handle on my hatch, unhooked my seat belt, and started to climb out . . . and damn near broke my neck because I had forgotten to unplug my earphones.

"When I finally made it out, Bush was standing on the starboard wing inflating the life raft. I turned to look for Del, but his exit had been jammed and he was stuck trying to get out through the turret—he had on his Mae West and parachute harness. He'd apparently hit his head on the radio and was bleeding, and his eyes looked glazed. I grabbed his harness and yanked him out. Then we stepped over the canopy down onto the other wing and walked down to the raft. After he came aboard the lifeboat, Del and I started singing, 'Sailing, sailing, over the bounding main.' Mr. Bush turned around and said, 'You guys had better shut up, or they're going to think we're having too good a time out here.'"

Bush rowed as hard as he could to get them away from the rapidly sinking plane. Moments after it had dropped below the surface, the safety devices gave way to deep undersea pressure and the depth charges exploded, shaking the water. The concussion rocked the raft and nearly dumped the three men into the water.

They had no radio and could not use their signaling mirror, for fear the Japanese would spot and strafe them. "We hoped the first thing we saw would be an American ship and not a Japanese," recalled Nadeau. Luckily, they were spotted by the destroyer *C. K. Bronson*, which dropped a cargo net over the side, enabling them to climb aboard.

Meanwhile one of the most dramatic—and one-sided—battles of World War II was raging in the sky over the American fleet. During the day of June 19 the Japanese carriers launched four waves of planes at the American ships. The Japanese tactics and planes were those that had brought them victory after victory during the first years of the war; but those years were over. Many of the best Japanese pilots were dead and had been replaced by hastily trained newcomers. Now the American pilots, such as Bush and his squadron members, were tough and experienced, equal to or better than their Japanese adversaries.

Enormous in scope, the battle involved hundreds of swarming planes engaged in combat from above twenty thousand feet down to sea level. From the very beginning the American pilots proved their skill. As each wave of Japanese planes approached, it was met and furiously blasted from the sky, many American pilots downing as many as four enemy planes, often one right after the other in a space of minutes. The few Japanese planes to make it through the protective wall of fighters fell prey to the fleet's antiaircraft gunners. When not firing, the men manning these weapons stared up at the sky, awed by the spectacle of swirling aircraft, the fireballs of Japanese planes streaking toward the sea.

By nightfall the battle was over; the skies had been swept of Japanese planes. In only a few hours the Japanese lost 294 planes, and only twenty-two American fighters had been downed. Twenty pilots and seven crewmen had been killed, and four officers and twenty-seven sailors had lost their lives aboard ships. There were losses, but it was a victory and a fabulous day for the American fliers.

History records the day's fighting as the battle of the Philippine Sea, but it has another name. Listening to his men excitedly recount their exploits, an officer aboard the carrier *Lexington* heard one pilot exclaim, "Why, hell. It was just like an old-time turkey shoot down home!" And so the battle has popularly become known as the Marianas Turkey Shoot.

One of the American planes lost during the battle belonged to VF-51: Ens. T. E. Hollowell did not return from the fighting. Marines taking part in the invasion later found his body and plane near the airfield on Guam.

Meanwhile Bush and his crew had yet to return to their carrier. Finally, in what Bush recalls as a "hairy experience," they were hauled aboard another carrier via breeches buoy and ropeline. They were then hoisted aboard the *San Jac* by breeches buoy and assigned a brand-new Avenger. All that remained to personalize it was to paint *Barbara II* under the cockpit. Nadeau obliged.

On June 20 the task force moved west, trying to close with the fleeing Japanese ships. That morning Bush's squadron went on a search of the area, finally spotting the enemy 250 miles to the west, at the extreme range of their fuel supply. Additionally, the distance was so great that it was clear the Japanese fleet would escape if not attacked immediately. A long-range strike was ordered launched in late afternoon. Already short on fuel, the planes arrived over the Japanese fleet at sunset, when the sun had become a bright-red circle.

VT-51 participated in the attack, which soon developed into a wild melee over the Japanese ships. The American pilots knew they had barely a half hour of daylight left in which to fight, time enough only to make one pass and then head back to their carriers. With no time for coordinated action, they dove on the Japanese ships in individual attacks.

Avengers piloted by Jack Guy and Don Melvin flew through clouds of bursting flak and spotted a carrier. The two pilots nosed over and began their bombing run. Guy dropped his four bombs from 5,000 feet and scored two hits. But when Melvin began to pull out of his dive, he discovered his bombs had not released. He pushed over again and found himself in position to attack a destroyer. Manually releasing his bombs from 2,500 feet, he saw one hit the ship's bow wave. However, their work was not done. Melvin and Guy had a return flight of 350 miles in the dark. Melvin's accurate navigation brought them directly to the *San Jac*. Both pilots realized, however, that they were dangerously short of fuel. Guy landed on the carrier with only four gallons of gas left in his tanks. Melvin's plane was almost on empty, so he decided not to take a chance and instead made a water landing alongside the carrier. Melvin and Guy were the first members of the squadron to actually hit the Japanese fleet, and for their feat they were each awarded the Navy Cross.

Because of the extremely long range, the other planes on the mission did not return to the carriers until after nightfall, and they, too, were all dangerously low on fuel. Normally, each flattop had individually colored, foot-square glow lights for identification, but these were visible only from directly above, and the deck outline lights could only be seen from astern. To avoid enemy attack, the carrier decks had been blacked out. Few of the pilots were able to see their carriers, much less land on them. The carrier crews could hear the planes circling overhead, the engines coughing and sputtering as they ran out of fuel. There was also the occasional loud splash as a desperate pilot made a blind landing on the dark water. Finally, Admiral Mitscher decided to take the risk and ordered the ships to turn on their lights. Searchlights lit up the sky, the carriers turned their flight deck lights up bright and used special lamps to illuminate their decks, ships lit their running lights, destroyers fired off star shells. One pilot said the resulting kaleidoscope of illumination looked like "a Hollywood premiere, Chinese New Year's, and the Fourth of July all rolled into one."

Gar Hole, who was standing on deck with the LSO when the lights came up, recalls that he had a perfect view of the action. "Planes were coming in from all directions. A TBF from another carrier whose engine had quit came in with gear down to make a landing. He landed dead-stick on his wheels and bounced up, but he had caught the cable and pulled it about twenty-five feet until it came to the end. When he came down to the deck, the plane broke in half. But none of the crew were hurt. The deck crew shoved the plane over the side."

Planes landed on any carrier they could find; ten planes from other carriers made emergency landings on the *San Jac*. In the end almost 90 percent of the fliers had been saved.

During this period a strange aircraft made two excellent approaches at the landing deck of the *San Jac* but was waved off by the LSO each time because the plane's landing hook was not down. "The plane sounded funny," says Gar Hole. "After the second waveoff, the pilot flew the length of the flight deck about fifty feet above the deck into the glare of the searchlight, where the red 'meatball' [slang for the Japanese national insignia] markings on his plane were visible."

The radio operator on the *San Jac* reported to the commander of the task group: "I believe there is a Jap plane over *San Jac*," and moments later: "The plane with bright red light over formation appears to be a Zeke dead ahead of me now."

Four minutes later the operator added: "That plane passed low over us and his red circles were quite discernible on his lower wing." The plane was probably a Judy (Japanese dive bomber), but the pilot made no attempt to strafe or bomb the *San Jac*. And the gunners on the *San Jac* made no attempt to shoot him down, because there were too many other planes in the sky. Instead, the Japanese pilot flew down the port side and turned westward, where he was tracked by radar for fifty miles before disappearing.

Another pilot came in to land on the deck, but his tail hook failed to catch one of the seven arrestor cables that would have brought the plane to a halt. The plane crashed into a gun mount a few feet from Bush. The pilot's leg, severed in the crash, suddenly appeared in front of Bush, who recalls it as "quivering and separated from the body. The poor guy got cut in half. We young fellows were standing there stunned when this big chief petty officer came along, yelling to the crew, 'All right, clean this mess up,' and everybody snapped back."

There was one humorous sidelight to the night's activities. Among the ten aircraft that did not belong to the *San Jac* but landed on her either mistakenly or for lack of fuel was one piloted by Ens. John F. Caffey, who had been waved off from a landing on his own carrier. With his Dauntless sputtering and almost out of gas, Caffey told his gunner, Leo D. Estrada, AOM 2/c, to prepare for a water landing. Estrada put on his chute. When the plane touched down and stopped, he leaped out and found himself on the deck face to face with a *San Jac* sailor. Equal to the occasion, Estrada told the seaman, "This water landing isn't as bad as I thought it'd be."

Caffey, still in the cockpit of the Dauntless, was ordered to fold his wings. He tried to explain that his plane's wings couldn't fold. "God damn it, fold them anyway," was the retort.

Bush's flight log for June 1944 shows that he was in the air for more than thirty-two hours, at least half of that time in successful strikes against the enemy encamped on Saipan, where the Marines and the army were still trying to gain a foothold.

While on one of those flights he felt strong stomach cramps. There was no way to relieve himself, so he squirmed out of his flight suit and relieved himself into a handkerchief, inadvertently mooning Milt Moore, who was flying wing. Bush then threw the handkerchief out of the canopy. From then on Moore referred to George in his logbook as "Skin Bush."

On July 3 the VT-51 fighter pilot who had been shot down near Guam on June 16 and was listed as missing in action was returned to the ship, having been recovered by a seaplane. He had gotten clear of his sinking plane, though badly lacerated about the face and hands, and managed to get into his raft. He spent seventeen days paddling about offshore in the daytime and pushing into an isolated stretch of beach on Guam at night to grub for roots, gather shellfish, and drink springwater. Japanese planes flew over him constantly but never spotted him. Although emaciated and blackened by constant exposure to the sun, he was determined to remain with his squadron rather than be sent to Pearl Harbor for hospitalization. His wish was granted.

No one, however, had taken into account the stress the young pilot had suffered. On his next mission, after making contact with enemy planes, he returned to the *San Jac*. Dick Playstead, who was set to land after him, saw everyone on deck scattering and wondered what was happening. The pilot had forgotten to put his six wing guns on safe before landing, and when he set down on the deck, all the guns started firing, killing two men and wounding twenty-four: Captain Martin received a bullet in the hand. The next day the crew assembled at quarters and stood at rigid attention as Chaplain Deitrich Cordes officiated at solemn memorial services. The *San Jac*'s flag and those of the accompanying ships were at half-mast. A Marine honor guard fired the traditional volleys as the flag-draped shroud was consigned to the deep. The mournful notes of taps echoed in the stillness of his shipmates' grief. It was the first time Bush had witnessed a burial at sea, and although he had known the men only slightly, he again shed tears for his squadronmates. The hapless pilot, near the point of breakdown after the accident, was sent back to the States.

Bush had won his crew's respect as a steady-nerved flier. "No matter how long the mission or how heavy the action, he was always calm and did what was needed," Nadeau recalls. "On return to the carrier, he always managed to land without a problem. We took very few waveoffs, and those were because of equipment on deck or something."

Like the other men in his squadron, and like thousands of other fliers in the Pacific, Bush had finally met the fearsome enemy and engaged in combat, had proved himself a capable pilot, and had taken part in one of a continuing string of American victories against the Japanese. Much was still to be done: victory was still a far-off hope, and for each man on each ship, the same was true of survival.

Chapter Six

When VT-51 was not in action, life aboard the carrier followed a set routine. The squadron's pilots, young and very much aware that they might die at any time, did their best to enliven the days in an attempt to keep away frightening thoughts. At officers' mess they joked a lot about the big carriers like the *Essex* and how easy it was for its torpedo pilots to land on its massive deck, in contrast to the short stretch they faced on the smaller *San Jac.* Some of their comments about the larger carriers were biting. In their view, the torpedo pilots aboard the bigger carriers got all the medals, while they were just the "toolies" who followed them. The Germans gave their best pilots an Iron Cross, and the joke among the pilots of VT-51 was that their efforts would probably earn them only "the Bent Nail."

The torpedo plane pilots spent hours in their shorts sunbathing on the bow below the flight deck—the deck itself had to be left free at all times. They often stood at the rail watching and betting on the flying fish or played volleyball games on the hangar deck. George was one of the best at volleyball and, thanks to his height, expert at spiking the ball. "He certainly wasn't the man to be in front of when there was a volleyball game taking place on top of the hangar elevator," recalls Gar Hole.

Bush was only twenty years old. "No one realized he was that young," says Hole. "We thought that all these young officers had to be college graduates. We couldn't believe that he had been the youngest commissioned pilot in the navy. But he proved to be an accomplished pilot. He never shirked a job and was definitely the leader of the squadron men. His natural interest in people made him liked all around."

When the weather was bad, the pilots hung out in the ready room, partly because there wasn't anywhere else to go and partly because it was air-conditioned and a good place to sleep. The ready room was the flight crew's home away from home. It served as office, classroom, movie theater, and living room. The walls were covered with bulletin boards, charts, maps, posters, and briefing guides.

When they weren't flying, the next best thing was talking about flying. They discussed techniques and torpedo bombing tactics and swapped accounts of missions they'd been in, going over each one endlessly and playing it out with hand gestures and sound effects. Stories about wrong decisions or wrong responses that had led to a pilot's death were of absorbing interest, each pilot imagining himself in the same situation as the dead pilot. This was easy to do, for they all wore the same uniforms, flew the same planes, and daily faced the same possibilities.

There was always a card game of some sort in progress, usually acey-deucey with low stakes. Acey-deucey was the naval pilots' game, something like backgammon and often played for money. The men spent hours in "the green country" (officers' quarters and mess) playing cards, socializing, and watching occasional movies such as *Casablanca* with Humphrey Bogart and *Holiday Inn* with Bing Crosby. Music was frequently piped in, the favorites being sentimental ballads such as "I'm Making Believe," "You're Nobody Till Somebody Loves You," and "When the Lights Go On Again."

Every day Bush wrote letters to Barbara, his parents, and his brother Pres, who was in Brazil for Pan American helping build air bases for strikes against Nazi submarines.

The destroyers were the mailmen of the fleet. They zipped around between the carriers, delivering mail by breeches buoy between ships. These deliveries were made about once a week, and mail call was a big event in the lives of all the men, both officers and enlisted. Pushing and shoving, they'd gather around the yeoman with the mail sack and eagerly reach out when their names were called. When the letters and packages had been distributed, the men quickly separated, each going off alone to reenter the world he had left behind. When the letters had been read and reread, the emotions absorbed, the men would gather in groups to exchange news, pass letters or photos around— new photos soon became worn from handling— and share with closest friends their private thoughts and reactions to words from home. "Mail was everything, our contact with home and our loved ones," Bush remembers. "If I got five letters it was the biggest deal in the world."

Bush would seek out a quiet place where he could read and reread letters from his family and Barbara, who by then was a freshman at Smith, the women's college in Northampton, Massachusetts, where she lived at Tyler House on Green Street.

Her letters were full of school gossip, reports on the scores of the intramural soccer and lacrosse teams on which she played, the movies she had seen on Saturday nights (usually much newer than the ones he had seen), and repeats of conversations she'd had with her father— who often called the college wanting to know why his daughter was not doing so well, and then spent a good deal of time on the phone with her, telling her to do better. But Barbara's heart was not in college. Her thoughts and prayers were always with George. As one of her roommates remembers, she began each day singing, "'Oh, what a beautiful mornin', Oh, what a beautiful day, I got a beautiful feelin',* George Walker Bush is okay." The musical *Oklahoma!* had recently opened on Broadway and was a big hit, as was the song from it that she paraphrased. She ended each letter to George with reiterations of how much she missed him. Occasionally she enclosed photographs.

Unlike his friends, Bush rarely confided his innermost thoughts to the other men, but he eagerly shared in their news, congratulating them on the good and consoling them on the bad. The major topic for everyone aboard the carrier, of course, was girlfriends. Most of the pilots were too young to have children, but nearly every one had a wife or a girlfriend and wanted his pals to agree she was the best, wanted them to look at her picture—but not smudge it—and compliment her beauty. The men were all familiar with the names of their friends' sweethearts, and the course of many romances was tracked publicly. There was the occasional "Dear John" letter, and these hit hard not just the recipient but all his friends: like the stories of mistaken moves in dogfights,

---

*From "Oh, What a Beautiful Mornin'" by Richard Rodgers and Oscar Hammerstein II, 1943.

it was a danger they all faced and worried about. They would commiserate with the unfortunate friend, convince him the girl in question had never been right for him anyway, distract him with other stories, or just pat him on the back and leave him alone with his thoughts.

Many of the pilots were contemplating marriage when they returned home, and there was a lot of kidding about that. Lou Grab recalls Bush singing a song to him with the melody of the famous song from the movie *Casablanca*. The words went: "You must remember this, Lou. A kiss is just a kiss, Lou. A sigh is but a sigh, Con."

"We were always kidding around, the kind of jokes ball players play," says Grab. "Everybody had a nickname. George's was Georgeherbertwalkerbush, all run together and said very fast, just as Jack O. Guy's was Jackoguy said the same way. George called my girlfriend Hot Connie."

The kidding included practical jokes. Jack Guy was the squadron safety officer, and it was his job to check on the parachute riggings, which were later inspected by another officer. On the day it was George's turn to do the inspection, Guy arranged with the parachute rigger to stuff pieces of cloth into the parachute packs so they would be clearly visible.

When Bush saw the ragged edges of the

cloth, he stiffened. "What's this?" he asked Guy.

Guy picked up a pair of scissors and trimmed the pieces. "Does that look better?" he asked.

"You're crazy," said the astounded Bush.

"When we all broke up laughing, George knew he'd been had," recounts Guy.

Their delight at spoofing George was made all the more sweet because he was usually the one who stirred things up. Dick Playstead recalls that when things were quiet, some of the squadron would go into George's quarters, where he could be counted on to start something. "He'd get a conversation going, take a position opposite to 'most everyone else, and then after riling us all up he'd disappear, returning in a few minutes to add more fuel to the conversational fire."

When they weren't flying strikes (combat missions), most of the squadron participated in what Jack Guy describes as RAPs (red-assed patrols), boring searches for enemy submarines, sometimes for as long as four or five hours at a time flying from five hundred to one thousand feet above the water.

Despite the tedium, there was always a stimulating tension in the air because the ship was constantly under the threat of attack from land or sea, and violent death was always imminent.

Bush's flight log for the month of July 1944 indicates he was in the air more than forty-six hours and participated in thirteen strikes against the enemy. VT-51 was in constant action, making strikes on Pagan and Guam, culminating in the Marine landing on Guam on July 17. The *San Jacinto* resumed strike operations on July 18, focusing on Guam and Rota. On July 20, Jack Guy made the three-thousandth landing aboard and was rewarded with the traditional cake.

On July 25 a group of *San Jacinto* fighters on an antishipping strike spotted an enemy destroyer thirty miles northeast of Babelthuap escorted by a lone "Jake." While Ens. L. A. Bird pursued and shot down the Jake, the other three fighters made strafing runs on the destroyer. The Japanese ship, apparently loaded with munitions, blew apart with a terrific mushrooming explosion that sent smoke and debris billowing upward three thousand feet. One of the Hellcats, piloted by Ens. Nat J. "Blackie" Adams, was still firing when the destroyer exploded. The force of the explosion was so great that flying debris severely damaged Adams's plane, and he was barely able to reach the task group, where he made a water landing. He was then picked up by a destroyer. Adams was awarded a Distinguished Flying Cross for the action.

Photographs of Palau and surrounding islands taken by *San Jac* planes (including Bush's, rigged with special cameras) received high praise from authorities in Pearl Harbor and were used as guides in subsequent landing operations.

On July 27 the Avenger piloted by "Whiskey Dick" Houle, one of Bush's friends, was shot down over Malakal Harbor. Nadeau recalls, "We didn't see him get hit, but we saw one chute going down. There were no other planes around, so we stayed in the vicinity and strafed some Japanese boats that were going out to get him while the shore batteries opened up on us. The island was shaped somewhat like a horseshoe, and we hoped that the wind would push the chute clear of a last hump so it would land on the far side of the island, where he would have a chance to be picked up. But he didn't make it. We kept circling overhead until I told Bush I had a malfunction with my gun and couldn't clear it. Bush came back on the intercom and said he was out of ammo. 'We can't do any good here, so we're going to have to leave.'"

Bush was disconsolate that he had failed to find any trace of Houle, but he had done what he could and dared not risk his plane and crew any longer. It was with a heavy heart that he gave up the search and flew back to the *San Jac.*

Two days later Bush wrote a letter to his parents. In it he said: "Last week has been one of sadness and sorrow. We lost another one of our pilots. Four of us went out and three of us had to return without him. I can't give you any more details but it's sad. There is still a chance that he will be rescued and that's what we're all hoping . . ."

Barbara was constantly on his mind, and he told his parents that he had written a letter to the Pierces asking them how they felt about a wedding when he got back. "I have been thinking about it so much . . . I don't like to think how it will be if they say no . . . I am counting on it so much . . . If they approve, I shall apply for instructor duty as soon as I return to the States. I don't know what my chances are for that duty. Not too good I am inclined to believe, but I could apply anyway. If I don't get it I shall rate a few months in the States anyway either training other VT squadrons or shifting units . . ."

The task group retired to Saipan for supplies on July 31. There plans were made for the traditional ceremony to be conducted when the ship crossed the equator. All the polliwogs (crew members who had not yet crossed the equator) were separated from the shellbacks (those who had). The shellbacks gave up shaving until after the initiation. The polliwogs, including Bush, had to wear their whites to dinner and the movies.

From Saipan the task group proceeded to the Bonins for a two-day attack on Iwo Jima and Chichi Jima on August 4 and 5. Many ships were sunk in the harbor at Chichi Jima, and the town was heavily bombed.

Early in August the *San Jac* was struck by a typhoon while most of the crew were at chow in their mess room. The ship pitched to port and then swung right over to starboard, sending plates, folding tables, chairs, and the men tumbling across the room. Suddenly there was a thunderous rumble from the ready room. One of the men looked through the open bulkhead door and discovered that the chairs had come loose from their brackets and were crashing from one side of the ship to the other. Carrying ropes, Nadeau and two other enlisted men entered the room by hanging from the overhead pipes and going hand over hand. Even with the wildly rocking floor, they managed to corral all the chairs to one side.

Shortly after the typhoon the ship retired to Eniwetok to replenish supplies and provisions and repair damage. Hundreds of other items of deferred maintenance occupied the time of all hands, night and day, in preparation for their next sorties. In spite of this the crew was allowed to go ashore on the bomb-pocked and shell-cratered atoll for their first series of formal recreation parties since departure from Pearl Harbor three months earlier. Movies were shown nightly. Basketballs and volleyballs were issued, and the men were sent to the beach. Volleyball matches were held every day, with Bush much in demand by each side. Boxing competitions were arranged with men from other ships. George also spent hours collecting shells in the atoll waters to give to Barbara as souvenirs.

The Marianas campaign was behind them,

and on August 18 all the ensigns in VT-51 were promoted to Lieutenant (jg). That month the Fifth Fleet was reorganized as the Third Fleet under Admiral Halsey's command.

The *San Jac* got under way on August 28, destination Palau and the Bonin Islands, including Chichi Jima. Three days of air strikes were planned, beginning on August 31, and supporting cruisers and destroyers moved in to shell the islands.

VT-51's primary target for the September 1 air strikes was a radio tower on Chichi Jima. The tower was not destroyed, and as Bush and the rest of his squadron headed back to the *San Jac*, they knew they would have to return. Once again they would have to dive down through flak toward the tower on the slope of Yoake Peak.

Meanwhile, on Chichi Jima, the complex of buildings around the radio tower was in flames, and thick smoke was rising from the area of the harbor. When the last plane had flown out of range, the antiaircraft guns stopped firing. The relative silence that followed was broken by occasional explosions and shouting voices. It was time again to dig out those trapped beneath collapsed shelters, to count the dead and wounded. Once more Chichi Jima had been struck by American planes, and once again the damage had to be repaired as quickly as possible: the Americans would be back.

The island, a volcanic creation in the middle of a clear, blue sea, had once had a stark beauty. Discovered by Spanish explorers in 1543, it and the rest of the Bonins had been claimed by Japan only in 1875. Until recently the population had been composed of Japanese, Koreans, and Formosans, most of them involved in harvesting sugar cane or cocoa or making ornamental jewelry from the surrounding coral. A peaceful place, one of the world's backwaters, it basked in its subtropical climate, only occasionally battered by Pacific typhoons.

The Japanese realized the island's strategic importance: with proper armament it could help protect the mainland from sea attack, so they laid claim to it in 1875. Thirty-nine years later the Japanese decided to fortify Chichi Jima. Heavy-artillery pieces were dug into its slopes, and in 1917 a naval radio station and a weather station were set up. The resident Koreans and Formosans were forced into labor gangs. Following Pearl Harbor the garrison had numbered only fourteen hundred, but by 1944 the threatening advance of American forces had led to a strengthening of the island's defenses: a naval base and antiaircraft batteries were installed. Like Iwo Jima, 150 miles to the south, Chichi Jima was being prepared for attack. The soldiers stationed on the islands were not impressed by the area's raw beauty. Water was scarce, and the rocky, treeless terrain made their lives difficult. As one officer wrote, there was "no sparrow and no swallow."

The senior officer on Chichi Jima was Vice-Adm. Kunizo Mori, but actually he was the administrative subordinate to the island's army commander, Lt. Gen. Yosio Tachibana. The army had been given control of any prisoners that might be taken on the island. The officer directly responsible for such prisoners was Maj. Sueo Matoba, a cold-eyed, bull-necked officer, who at five feet ten inches was big for a Japanese; his men referred to him as "the giant."

On June 15, 1944, American planes struck Chichi Jima for the first time. The Japanese defenders were taken by surprise: the attacking planes appeared out of a gale. The air attacks continued through the next months. The island defenders brought down planes and often managed to capture the pilots—who were listed in the American record books as MIA.

The fate of Allied airmen captured by the Japanese was often grim; reports of grisly deaths—prisoners beheaded or used for bayonet practice—reached Allied intelligence, and the fliers were warned. Squadrons in the Pacific were shown a picture, purportedly taken by a Japanese soldier on Chichi Jima, that showed a Japanese officer lifting a samurai sword about to behead a bound and blindfolded Australian aviator. The photograph was later reproduced in *Life* magazine, and Bush recalls having seen it and thinking that if a pilot survived a crash in the water it would be far better to drown than be captured by the Japanese.

No one then knew, however, that on Chichi Jima, thanks to the depravity of Major Matoba, American prisoners were being mistreated in a way that defies belief. Several of the Korean laborers reported after the war that many of the captured pilots had been executed and then cut into pieces—and eaten. Major Matoba, they said, had ordered his doctor to cut out the liver of an American aviator, which was then fed to the enlisted prisoners, and had even tricked the naval officers into eating flesh from the thigh of the body: it was served in place of goat meat at the admiral's mess. When they learned what they had eaten, many of the officers vomited, but the major often boasted of his little joke. His men hated him, but they continued to carry out his orders.

Following the September 1 attack, Matoba and his men began to repair their installations and waited for more American planes to enter the sky over the island. They would not have long to wait.

Chapter Seven

September 2, 1944.

At sunrise George Bush was in the *San Jac*'s ready room being briefed for that day's air strike on Chichi Jima. Bush and three other pilots from VT-51, with air support from accompanying Hellcats, were to try again for the transmitter in conjunction with an attack on Futami Harbor by fifteen other torpedo planes from their sister ship, the heavy carrier *Enterprise*.

Immediately after the scheduled strike—code name "Baker"—Task Force Fifty-eight was to head south to join Task Force Thirty-eight under the command of Adm. William "Bull" Halsey. The transmitter had to be put out of commission before the scheduled U.S. Marine assault on the island of Peleliu.

When the briefing was over, Lt. (jg) William Gardner "Ted" White, the squadron ordnance officer, approached Bush. A handsome six-footer with black hair and brown eyes, White was six years older than Bush and a graduate of Yale, where he had been head of the Political Union and a member of Skull and Bones. White's father had been a Yale classmate of George's father, but he and George had met for the first time on board the *San Jac*. White, who was not a pilot, wanted to check out the Avenger's weapons systems, which he was responsible for maintaining. For weeks he had been asking Bush to take him on a mission in place of his regular gunner, Lee Nadeau.

"What are you hitting today, George?" White asked.

"The radio station on Chichi Jima."

"We're moving out later today, and this may be the last time I can go with you," White said. "How about it?"

"It could be a rough trip," Bush warned.

White persisted. Bush thought for a moment and acquiesced. Naval intelligence reported that Chichi Jima's airstrip had been knocked out on the previous day's mission. Since fighter opposition was not anticipated, Bush believed he would not need an experienced rear-seat gunner and could afford to take along a rookie. "It's okay with me, if Commander Melvin approves," Bush said finally.

Melvin agreed. Nadeau briefed White in the procedures used for abandoning the aircraft.

White was strapped into the turret behind Bush. Bush checked out the Avenger and taxied into position on the flight deck while Del tested the radio gear. At 0715 four Avengers from the *San Jac* with four Hellcat fighter planes for protection took off and joined a dozen Hellcat fighters off the *Enterprise*. Each of the Avengers carried four five-hundred-pound bombs.

It was a hazy morning with light fog. Visibility was poor, and Bush knew it would be a particularly bad day to be shot down, since anyone on the surface of the ocean would be difficult to spot.

By 0815 the formation was over the island, flying in a diamond formation with Milt Moore as "Tail-End Charlie." Don Melvin led the first pair of bombers in through a barrage of intense antiaircraft fire from the Japanese shore batteries. Melvin and Doug West, his wing man, dropped all eight of their bombs on the radio station and the buildings nearby. By this time the Japanese had the attacking Avengers in range and in their sights. Bush was piloting the third plane over the target, with Moore flying on his wing. He nosed over into a thirty-degree glide, heading straight for the radio tower. Determined to finally destroy the tower, he used no evasive tactics and held the plane directly on target. His vision ahead was occasionally canceled by bursts of black smoke from the Japanese antiaircraft guns. The plane was descending through thickening clouds of flak pierced by the flaming arc of tracers.

There was a sudden flash of light followed by an explosion. "The plane was lifted forward, and we were enveloped in flames," Bush recalls. "I saw the flames running along the wings where the fuel tanks were and where the wings fold. I thought, This is really bad! It's hard to remember the details, but I looked at the instruments and couldn't see them for the smoke."

Don Melvin, circling above the action while waiting for his pilots to drop their bombs and get out, thought the Japanese shell had hit an oil line on Bush's Avenger. "You could have seen that smoke for a hundred miles."

Nat J. "Blackie" Adams, pilot of one of the four Hellcats off the *San Jac*, was flying at about ten thousand feet when he saw a torpedo bomber smoking but still continuing its bomb run. "I knew it was one of our TBMs, and later learned it was Bush."

Dense smoke poured out of the TBM's engine, and flames swept back along the wings. Bush nevertheless continued his bomb run. Finally over the target, his view from the canopy all but blinded by the thick smoke, he released his bombs. All four bombs made direct hits on the radio tower, which disappeared in swirling flames and flying debris. He lifted the plane from its dive and then turned back out toward the water.

By then the wings were covered in flames and smoke, and the engine was blazing. He considered making a water landing but realized it would not be possible. Bailing out was absolutely the last choice, but he had no other option. He got on the radio and notified squadron leader Melvin of his decision. Melvin radioed back, "Received your message. Got you in sight. Will follow."

Milt Moore, flying directly behind Bush, saw the Avenger going down smoking. "I pulled up to him; then he lost power and I went sailing by him."

As soon as he was back over water, Bush shouted on the intercom for White and Delaney to "hit the silk!" The intercoms on the Avengers allowed all the planes in the formation to copy transmissions from one another. Dick Gorman, Moore's radioman-gunner, remembers hearing someone on the intercom shout, "Hit the silk!" and asking Moore, "Is that you, Red?"

"No," Moore replied. "It's Bush, he's hit!"

Other squadron members heard Bush repeating the command to bail out, over and over, on the radio.

There was no response from either of Bush's crewmen and no way he could see them; a shield of armor plate between him and Lt. White blocked his view behind. He was certain that White and Delaney had bailed out the moment they got the order.

Bush turned back over the water, leveled his plane, disconnected his headset, released his safety belt and harness, and then pushed himself out of the seat and canopy. The wind tore at his body and blurred his vision. He knew he was about two thousand feet above water, which meant he had time to dive headfirst onto the wing so that the wind could pull him away from the plane and the tail section. But he had never done it before, nor had any other pilot he knew. When he plunged over the side, he banged his head on the tail and jerked the parachute ripcord too soon. The slipstream (air driven backward) had caught his body, all 161 pounds of it, and thrown him toward the tail of the plane. His head grazed the starboard elevator, and his chute snagged on the tail and ripped.

Because of the torn panels in the parachute he plummeted through the air far too fast. All at once the tedious hours of emergency training paid off. Rule Number One in bailing out at sea: don't get tangled in the parachute after hitting the water—the weight could sink you or the chute could wrap around you, making it impossible to move. Although stunned by the blow to his head, Bush had sufficient presence of mind to start unbuckling his seat straps on the way down. The parachute drifted away from him, and he plunged the last twenty feet straight into the water. He saw his parachute blowing off toward Chichi Jima, but his Avenger was nowhere in sight. Kicking with his legs to stay afloat, he yanked the toggles on his flight vest. It inflated properly, but he was not yet out of trouble. He was being nearly pulled under by the weight of his water-soaked flight suit. Gasping, he removed his shoes and struggled to the surface. Blood streamed down from the cut on his head as he began to tread water, searching for the life raft that had been his seat cushion. A Hellcat swooped and drew his attention toward the raft bobbing about fifty feet away. He swam for it, hoping it hadn't been damaged by the fall and would inflate. It did. Bush hauled himself aboard and discovered that the emergency container attached to the raft had been smashed. The realization that he was without fresh water brought him near despair. The raft's paddles had also been lost during the splashdown.

Don Melvin radioed the raft's position to the submarine *Finback*, which was cruising on lifeguard duty some ten miles away. Doug West had seen the Avenger go down and one man parachute into the sea. He skimmed over the raft. From one hundred feet above he could recognize Bush and see that he was bleeding. West circled again, and one of his crewmen dropped an emergency medical kit, which landed some fifty feet away. Bush hand-paddled to it and splashed Mercurochrome over the cut.

He then checked out his regulation .38 caliber pistol, which was wrapped in a navy-issue condomlike case to keep it dry in case of a splashdown. The pistol was in working order— for all the good it would do him. He would gladly have traded it for one small paddle. Meanwhile the tide was slowly pulling him in toward Chichi Jima.

There was no sign of another yellow raft on the horizon, but visibility was limited. All he could see was a hazy blue sky and choppy green water. He could only hope that White and Delaney were already safe in the water, and he reflected on the sad irony of White's choosing to come along on this mission. But there was no time for such thoughts. He had to hand-paddle vigorously just to stay put and maintain his position in the event a lifeguard submarine was in the vicinity. His head ached. His arm was burning from the sting of a Portuguese man-of-war. To further complicate matters, he had swallowed some seawater during his splash into the ocean and occasionally had to stop paddling to vomit over the side.

Still, he was alive. He reached deep inside himself to stay calm and assess his predicament. He was alone without water in an enemy-controlled area. He knew that if help did not come soon, he would either be picked up by the Japanese or die within a couple of days of thirst and exposure. He prayed that Don Melvin or Doug West had radioed his position to a friendly ship in the area, or that his message to Melvin had been relayed by the squadron leader to the submarine that was supposed to be on lifeguard duty.

He heard the drone of an airplane coming in

low, looked up, and recognized Doug West's plane. His heart fell when he saw West waggle his wings in farewell and head off.

For an hour and a half Bush paddled with his cupped hands, trying in vain to keep his raft from drifting. His head throbbed from the sun burning down on it. He was nauseated and exhausted. Stories he had heard of what happened to airmen captured by the Japanese flashed through his mind, and he began to panic. Fear that he might never see his family or Barbara again gave him the strength to continue struggling.

Melvin reported the details of Bush's misadventure over the skies of Chichi Jima in the squadron log:

> The attack . . . employed normal glide bombing tactics in an attack from South to North encountering in the area intense, heavy and medium A/A fire of accurate variety from areas surrounding the target.
>
> Lt. Cmdr. Melvin and Lt. j.g. West put all of their bombs on the radio station building and towers to destroy the tower and destroy or badly damage the buildings. Debris in large quantity was seen to arise from these hits.
>
> Lt. j.g. Bush was piloting the third plane over the target. Bush's plane was hit in the engine shortly after the final pushover at

8,000 feet. In spite of this hit, which caused his engine to smoke and catch on fire, Lt. j.g. Bush continued in his dive, releasing his bombs on the radio station to score damaging hits. Ensign Moore in the fourth plane likewise dropped his bombs on the latter installations.

After releasing his bombs, Lt. j.g. Bush turned sharply to the east to clear the island of Chichi Jima, smoke and flames enveloping his engine and spreading aft as he did so, and his plane losing altitude. He advised the C.O. by radio that it was necessary to bail out. At a point approximately nine miles bearing 045′T (degrees) from Minami Jima, Bush and one other person were seen to bail out from about 3,000 feet. Bush's chute opened and he landed safely in the water, inflated his raft and paddled farther away from Chi-Chi Jima. The chute of the other person [either Lt. j.g. White or J. L. Delaney, ARM 2/c] who bailed out did not open. Bush has not yet been returned to the squadron . . . so this information is incomplete.

While Lt. j.g. White and J. L. Delaney are reported missing in action, it is believed that both were killed as a result of the above described action.

It should be noted that VT-51 has established a standard doctrine whenever wind and other conditions permit to make bombing runs on targets near water so as to retire over the water. This puts the pilot and crew in position for water rescue in the event of forced landing such as that described herein . . .

The *San Jac News*, the carrier's newspaper, reported on September 2, 1944:

Our torpedo planes flew four flights over Chichi Jima. They had over the targets twelve planes, each carrying four 500-pound bombs. They hit and destroyed one radio station with eight hits. The second radio station was also hit. The VTs also hit an ammunition dump storage area and a large explosion occurred with heavy flames. The anti-aircraft fire was very heavy and intense.

Lt. (j.g.) Bush, while in a dive bombing attack over the target, was hit. The plane caught fire. Mr. Bush and one of the crewmen bailed out somewhere near the target. Mr. Bush's chute opened. . . . Unfortunately, the chute of the crewman failed to open. The crewmen in Mr. Bush's plane were Lt. W. G. White and J. L. Delaney.

For years it was impossible to document George Bush's experience over Chichi Jima from the Japanese side. But one record of the antiaircraft battalion responsible for shooting him down was located in secret government archives in Tokyo. The official document translated below corroborates all the known facts about George Bush's crash and the death of his two crewmen.

Summary of Combat Results of
Allied [Japanese] Forces.
The 1st Anti-Aircraft (Asahiyama)
DATE 9/2 1944
WEATHER Fair
TIME (Zulu time)

04:45	Prepared for air raid.
05:46	Fired upon enemy aircraft passing over Ani-jima on their way to Taki-ura Bay.
05:55	Fired upon enemy aircraft passing over Ani-jima on their way to attack the transmission station at Mt. Yoake.
06:08	Confirmed downing of one enemy bomber in the sea at 240″ 20′.
08:07	Formation of sixteen enemy aircraft circled Ani-jima.
08:09	Fired upon them as they attacked in the direction of Mt. Asahi.
08:25	Confirmed downing of one enemy in the sea at 80″ 10′. Two men descended in parachutes and disappeared into the sea.
08:57	One submarine surfaced at 250″ 20′ proceeding north.
10:11	(submarine) at 130″ 25′ was confirmed proceeding north.

The submarine the Japanese defenders had spotted was the USS *Finback*. Although the Japanese could see the submarine from their lookout stations, George Bush, on the surface of the sea, was completely unaware of its existence.

Chapter Eight

Most of the men and officers on board the USS *Finback* were unhappy about doing lifeguard duty. Many of these bearded veterans—all of them volunteers for their hazardous service— were on their tenth war patrol. They were eager to make another strike against the Japanese Empire and felt it ridiculous to risk a five-million-dollar submarine and eighty-two men on the off-chance they might pluck a downed flier or two from the ocean. The men were proud of their ship: at 311 feet by 33 feet, the *Finback* was one of the biggest submarines in the navy, and its two sixteen-hundred-horsepower diesel engines made it one of the fastest. It was a powerful weapon made for use against the enemy, not a babysitter. Their commander, Robert R. Williams, Jr., understood their feelings but also knew the importance of their role: any downed fliers would find themselves in enemy-held waters and far from any other aid. The knowledge that an American submarine was in the area and watching out for them gave the carrier pilots a big boost in morale.

Williams's orders were to provide lifeguard services for scheduled Task Force Thirty-eight carrier strikes from September 1 through September 4 in the vicinity of the Bonin Islands. So, on September 2, 1944, he was maintaining a position on the surface ten miles northeast of Minami Jimi. Two navy Hellcats from the *Enterprise* flew overhead to provide protection for the sub, which was vulnerable to air attack while on the surface.

At 0933 the sub's radio came to life: Don Melvin reported that Bush was down around the southern end of Chichi Jima. He reported he had seen another chute streaming. Williams gave orders to the engine room to proceed at full speed to the location. The big American flag draped across the stern of the sub to identify it to friendly aircraft fluttered and flapped as the *Finback* raced through the calm sea toward the downed flier. It was a race, and the Americans were not the only participants. The Japanese defenders of Chichi Jima had seen the smoking plane go down, and they too wanted the pilot.

Doug West was still circling above Bush when he saw Japanese craft leave the wharf. He circled the plane around toward the island and went into a dive to strafe the boat and drive the Japanese back. He could see the bullets from his .50 caliber machine gun cut across the water and hit the boat. And then he saw the men jump overboard: West had done all he could and had just enough fuel left to reach the *San Jac*. As he passed over Bush for one last time he waggled his wings in farewell.

Bush heard the drone of the plane as it left, and then he heard only the water sloshing against the gunwales. He leaned over the side and paddled again, but even as he did so he could tell it was a losing battle against the wind and current. No matter how hard he struggled, the ocean was going to take him to the island he had just bombed, right into the hands of the enemy. He felt tired and knew he was alone: the sky above him was bright-blue and clear—no planes anywhere in sight. He prayed and thought, This is it—it's all over.

The sky was clear: the weather that day was in fact excellent, the sea relatively calm with two-foot swells and no whitecaps. Visibility was about ten miles, but Bush's small craft alternately appeared and disappeared as it rose and fell on the rolling water. Three miles away Japanese observers on the island occasionally caught sight of the yellow mark in the water. Twelve or fifteen miles away lookouts on the *Finback*, hanging on the periscope shears while anxiously scanning the ocean through binoculars, finally spotted the craft, too, and excitedly relayed word to the skipper.

Ens. Bill Edwards was among those on the *Finback*'s conning tower. Edwards was delighted by the sighting of the flier, not just because of the pleasure in rescuing a comrade from the drink but also because, like most officers on board the submarine, Edwards had more than one job—he was also the photographic officer. He had a Kodak spring-wound 8 mm movie camera, which he used to record the sub's activities.

Shortly after noon the day before, he had photographed the rescue of Ens. Thomas Keene and his two crewmen, James Stovall and John Doherty. While attempting to return to their carrier, the USS *Enterprise*, their Avenger had been hit by antiaircraft fire and had lost power near the southern tip of Iwo Jima. Keene ditched his plane in the sea. The Avenger quickly sank, but the crewmen, unharmed, had gotten into their raft and begun paddling furiously with the small, blue regulation-issue paddles. They were still paddling away when the *Finback* pulled up alongside them.

From up on the conning tower Edwards had hailed down to them in proper navy fashion, "Boat ahoy! What's your destination?"

Although breathless from their effort with

the little paddles, the fliers had shouted back up to him, "Saipan!" That had given Edwards a good laugh, although he thought at the time that from the way they were rowing they might even have made it the 750 miles to Saipan. Those fliers had no intention of falling into enemy hands.

Now it appeared Edwards would have another opportunity to photograph a rescue on a calm and clear day. A true navy man, he also looked forward to the opportunity of joking with a few new pilots. He had no way of knowing that the film he was about to shoot would, forty-four years later, be shown on national television and be instrumental in helping the downed flier become elected president of the United States. Perhaps he would have been even more surprised to know that he, too, would someday be a pilot and that in November 1950, during another war, he would have the experience of being shot down.

A tall, solidly built man who had been a football player at Louisiana State University, Edwards had forearms like Popeye's and the beard submariners were proud to grow. He wound the spring tight on his camera, jostled for position among the men on the conning tower, and mounted his film camera to a bracket on the periscope. He was ready.

Bush recalls that he had been struggling in the water for almost three hours when the subma-

rine appeared. At first it seemed like an apparition. He saw it grow, first a small, dark speck
glimpsed—or was he seeing things?—between
one swell and another, then a larger spot,
finally a massive form coming right toward
him. "At first I thought maybe I was delirious,
and when I concluded it was a submarine all
right, I feared that it might be Japanese. It just
seemed too lucky and too farfetched that it
would be an American submarine."

The first thing Bush saw as the sub drew
closer was a huge metal logo mounted alongside the conning tower. It was of a flying
torpedo, with a red head and a bridle in its
mouth, being ridden cowboy-style by a dog
wearing a pirate's hat and holstered pistols.
And when he saw American sailors running
back and forth across the deck, he knew that he
was going to make it—that for some reason
he was going to live through this thing. For the
first time since he had been shot down, the
young pilot was able to breathe easy.

At 1156 four enlisted men from the *Finback*,
including Chief Petty Officer Ralph Adams,
suited up as part of a "man-overboard party."
Adams, the best swimmer of the group, was the
first to reach the yellow life raft that was
bobbing only a few feet from the *Finback*'s bow
planes, which had been rigged to give the men
a platform. The four men helped snug the raft
against the side of the sub.

Don Kohler, torpedoman 2d class from Wapakoneta, Ohio, grabbed Bush's left hand at the wrist with his right hand while gunner's mate Bill Connolly grabbed Bush's other hand. Together they pulled Bush up onto the bow planes.

"Welcome aboard, sir," Kohler said to the cold, shivering, and wet young pilot, who was still wearing his flying helmet and yellow Mae West life jacket.

"Happy to be aboard," said Bush.

"Let's get below," said Kohler. "The skipper wants to get the hell out of here."

As Bush walked shakily toward the conning tower, Edwards got a picture of him looking up toward the camera.

The official report of Bush's rescue is given in the log of the *Finback* for September 2, 1944. It reads: "1156. Picked up Lt. (j.g.) George H. W. Bush, File No. 173464, USNR, pilot of plane T-3 of VT-51, U.S.S. San Jacinto, who stated that he failed to see his crew's parachutes and believed that they had jumped when plane was still over Chichi Jima, or they had gone down with the plane. Commenced search of area on chance they had jumped over water."

Bush was taken directly to the bridge, where he was greeted by the skipper while sailors on deck sank his raft with gunfire; Keene's raft had been taken aboard, the sub had neither need nor room for another, and they did not want the raft to fall into Japanese hands. In that moment on the bridge, as another group of planes flew overhead, Edwards asked Bush what carrier he was off. On learning it was the *San Jac*, he asked if Bush knew a friend of his, a certain Leo Bird, who was also off the *San Jac* and with whom Edwards had played football at LSU. In response Bush pointed up at the planes droning over the sub and said, "I know him, and he's probably in that plane right there."

Commander Williams then sent Bush below to put on some dry clothes. The hatches slammed shut, the horns sounded, and the skipper gave the orders to take her down.

At the top of the ladder leading to the cramped control room, one of the sub's officers noticed the still-holstered standard .38 caliber Smith & Wesson police-type pistol Bush was carrying. "You won't be needing this on board a sub," the officer said and relieved Bush of his sidearm. Navy officers other than pilots were issued Colt .45s, and the .38 was a treasured weapon. Bush later reported his sidearm lost at sea.

The first person Bush met in the ward room was Lt. (jg) William "Hugo" Parkman, the communications officer, who at five feet eleven weighed only 125 pounds. In his Alabama drawl Parkman told Bush he was glad they had been able to pinpoint his location so quickly, and gave the shivering pilot a cup of coffee. "He was cool as can be, and wet," Parkman recalls.

"I don't think he ever realized the danger he was in out there."

While a medical corpsman treated the bleeding cut he had sustained over one eye, Bush met the pilot, gunner, and radioman from the USS *Franklin*, rescued the previous day. Keene, who had also been flying an Avenger, told Bush how he had lost power from a hit, most probably in the hydraulic lines. Bush said that he'd had to abandon his plane because it was on fire. Keene warned Bush that they faced a month's war patrol off Japan. The *Finback*'s tour as a lifeguard vessel was ended. The sub was loaded with torpedoes and could not return simply to deliver navy pilots to their carriers.

It was about then that Bush felt calm enough to take in his surroundings. He was a pilot, used to having the open sky above him: above him here was a steel wall. He knew life aboard ship—he was a carrier pilot—but this was something else. This was like being inside a machine. He could hear the machine and feel it throbbing. Here inside the submarine there was no horizon, no distant views, no direction offering escape from danger. At least during his first few days aboard the sub his own physical size endangered him: he was forever bumping his head.

Bush was told to strip and take a warm shower in the officers' compartment opposite the ward room while dry clothes were being organized for him. "The uniforms the pilots were wearing disappeared immediately," said Jack Peat, who was in the ward room. "Everybody wanted to get hold of them because they were prized souvenirs."

Peat, a lanky, twenty-two-year-old six-footer, was one of four Naval Academy graduates on board the *Finback*. The other three were Jim Griswold, Lawrence Heyworth, and Williams, the skipper.

Forty minutes after Bush was picked up, one of the Hellcat pilots spotted a rubber boat being shelled about one and a half miles from the beach west of Haha Jima. The pilot said he would fly cover for the *Finback*. The crew was again elated. "Spirits of all hands went to about 300 feet," Commander Williams reported in his log of the day.

Bush hurried to the control room. Although it seemed unlikely that either of his crewmen had gone into the water so far from the downed plane, he prayed for the man's safety and sweated out the wait.

As the *Finback* raced to the location, a lookout spotted Japanese planes overhead. Commander Williams gave the order to clear the deck and prepare to dive. Within thirty seconds the *Finback* was fifty-five feet below the surface— maximum periscope depth. Through the periscope a spot in the water was seen one mile west-southwest of Meganen Iwa.

What happened next was one of the more

unusual occurrences of the war. With only its periscope breaking the surface of the water, the *Finback* headed for the location of the life raft. Williams was hoping the airman would spot the periscope and grab hold of it. The sub reached the raft and passed it; the flier just watched it go by. He did not grab hold. With their submarine now in dangerously shallow water and the flier failing to understand their movements, the *Finback*'s crewmen were getting more than a little worked up. They couldn't leave the flier and had to hope he would understand the next time by. Another pass at him required turning the big sub around, a difficult and trying operation that took half an hour.

Commander Williams's log of the day tells the rest of the story:

1620. Pilot hooked on [the periscope] and we headed out away from the beach. Tried to make two-thirds speed, but the pilot had one arm around the periscope and the other around the life raft with a bailing bucket bringing up the rear. Stopped to see if he would get in the boat. This took about 10 minutes, during which a discussion developed below concerning the precedence of simultaneous orders to blow, pump, and flood [keeping the submarine in trim at slow speeds was difficult and involved a complicated series of commands]. Finally got away towing pilot in his boat. Two-thirds speed filled the boat, and there he was in the water again. Finally came up to 38 feet to keep him out of the water until at range of 5 miles from beach, planed up and opened the hatch. [The airman had held on to the periscope and then slid down it as the sub surfaced.]

Got on 4 engines and cleared area to westward. Pilot was Ensign James W. Beckman, File No. 301442, USNR, VF-20, U.S.S. *Enterprise* who stated that it was known [or so Beckman heard on the radio] that only one man had parachuted from Bush's plane. This decided us to discontinue any further search of that area, particularly as our air cover had left.

What Williams's concise log does not reveal is that the Japanese on the islands of Ani Jima and Tatumi Shima had Beckman in range and were constantly firing small arms and machine guns at him. Jack Peat recalls that "it sounded like rain on the water." When the *Finback* surfaced some five miles from land, the Japanese shore batteries began lobbing shells at the larger target offered by the submarine. But the rescue was accomplished without any losses or damage.

Edwards greeted Beckman in the ward room and lifted the Smith & Wesson pistol out of his holster. "You aren't going to have much use for that thing anymore, are you?" he asked. "No, sir," said Beckman, and Edwards had his prize.

Beckman's uniform went the way of Bush's. Later Beckman gave Hugo Parkman his compass as a souvenir.

By nightfall the *Finback* was heading north with Bush and the rest of her guests. There were not bunks enough for the five members of the air crews, so the visitors had to "hotbunk" with other crew members: as one man left a bunk, another took it, still warm from the last body.

Just after midnight, sixty miles northwest of Chichi Jima, the *Finback*'s radar picked up an enemy plane, a Japanese Nell bomber, heading toward them. Commander Williams gave the order to dive.

Bush lay in Hugo Parkman's narrow bunk in the clammy torpedo compartment and silently prayed for the safety of his two crewmen. The engines throbbed, the bulkheads trembled, and the air smelled of diesel fuel. He tried in vain to sleep. When sleep finally came, he had a nightmare—one that would recur for weeks. In it he was shot down again, and he woke up in fear that his plane was blazing around him.

The following morning, as they were preparing to leave the Chichi Jima area, Commander Williams invited Bush to look through the periscope. "It was weird," Bush recalls. "There we were, sitting off an enemy-held island and watching the battle still going on from below—a totally different view from what I was accustomed to seeing from above. I even saw a plane come in and go up on its nose."

That afternoon Bush wrote a letter to his parents, giving them all the details of his being shot down and his rescue. He also told them that Ted White was missing, and "you know his family. Please don't write to them until you get word from me or until the family has been officially notified. There is a possibility that he parachuted into the sea but I am afraid it is quite remote. We received a message saying that only one chute opened . . . " His parents received the letter, postmarked October 2—exactly one month after he had been shot down—with a big, red six-cent airmail stamp on it. He didn't write a letter to Barbara, because he didn't want her to worry. He knew how long it would take for his letter to reach his parents, and at some point when he was returned to his ship or shore he would send them a telegram saying he was safe.

Later that week Bush learned that the one parachute that had emerged from his plane had streamed out (failed to open). It was officially confirmed that either White or Delaney had gone into the sea with the Avenger.

George Bush had already suffered a warrior's rites of passage by the time he was rescued by the *Finback*. But there was to be more testing of his mettle. As a member of VT-51, he had thrived on the feeling of freedom that came with flying an airplane. He was part of a team, yet on his own. But while living with the officers and crew of the *Finback*, he learned about a different kind of teamwork, as well as a different kind of danger.

There were some terrifying moments in store for the twenty-year-old pilot. Like most submarines, the *Finback* ran on the surface during the day as much as possible, to avoid draining the ship's batteries and to cover a larger search area. But when a lookout or the radar spotted an enemy plane headed its way, the sub's Klaxon would sound, the bridge would be cleared, and within minutes the submarine would dive.

While Bush was aboard, the *Finback* was depth-charged twice by Japanese ships. The rescued pilots sat in the ward room along with one crewman. "We just had to sit in there and be still," Bush recalls. "That experience was far scarier than an airplane bombing run. At least in the plane you controlled your destiny to some extent: you could see puffs of smoke coming at you, and you knew what the problem was. But there, under water, all you could do was hope like hell that the enemy wouldn't put an explosive on top of you. The real submariners weren't that worried about it; they'd been through it all before. But for me, there was a certain helplessness. Having no assigned duty made it even worse—waiting for one explosion and then the next. There were times when it felt as though the sub would shake apart. I felt trapped and scared, far more scared than I was being shot at in my plane."

After the first attack on the sub a chastened Bush told Lawrence Heyworth, the torpedo and gunnery officer, that he wasn't so sure whether he had been rescued or not. Being depth-charged was a frightening experience, and the longer it lasted the more he grew to respect the crew of the *Finback*.

"I thought I was scared at times flying into combat, but in a submarine you couldn't do anything but sit there," Bush says. "The submariners were saying that it must be scary to be shot at by antiaircraft fire, and I was thinking that it really wasn't as bad as what they were going through. The tension, adrenaline, and fear factor were probably about the same, though."

But there were some pluses along with the minuses. On Bush's first night aboard, the officers' mess served filet mignon for a main course, with strawberries and whipped cream for dessert. Bush was astounded. "Where did you get this chow?" he asked Edwards. "We've been eating nothing but Spam and beans on the carrier for the last few weeks." Edwards beamed. One of his duties was keeping the commissary supplied, and he performed that duty with particular skill.

Edwards's nickname was "Grogan" after the character Willy Grogan, who died at the key of his telegraph set in the 1943 movie *The Human Comedy*. Even today, in letters written to Edwards, Bush refers to him as Grogan.

Bush's sense of humor soon endeared him to

the *Finback* officers. Heyworth recalls that when the men were all together in the ward room, Bush told them how he had caused a herd of elephants to stampede at Chincoteague, earning himself the nickname of "Ellie the Elephant" on board the *San Jac*. "He crooked his hand by his ear and then slowly extended it and bellowed like an elephant. From then on, when things were dull, someone was sure to call out, 'Come on, Ellie, let's hear you roar.' He would, and the men would all break up with laughter."

Bush was also popular with the enlisted men, who, like everyone else on submarine duty, were volunteers. He respected them for that and often sat sipping coffee in their mess room. "We had no idea who he was or where he came from," recalls machinist's mate Richard Peat. "All we knew was he was good company and we were glad we picked him up."

Although Bush was the youngest of the pilots picked up by the *Finback*—they were ensigns, too—he was their senior in rank, so the others accepted him as leader.

Thomas Keene, the young pilot who had been plucked from the water just before Bush, soon became his best friend on the submarine. "We spent most of our time in the ward room, on watch, or decoding messages," recalls Keene. "And we watched movies whenever we could." The men aboard the *Finback* watched over and over the movies they had; and when they knew them by heart, they would run them backwards. Coming by new movies in the middle of the Pacific was no easy matter, but when circumstances permitted, two subs would rendezvous and sailors would lean across the bobbing prows in the ocean spray and exchange film cans. The men at sea did not always enjoy the same films as the people back home in the States: no one on a sub wanted to watch such wartime hits as *Back to Bataan*. What they wanted were Hollywood musicals with lots of girls, the more and the prettier the better.

"I gave George my copy of *The Robe*, which was a popular book at the time," Keene recalls. "He read it within a few days and told me how much he enjoyed it. Any copy of *Time* magazine, no matter how old, was read from cover to cover. And, of course, we played a lot of acey-deucey. George was mighty good at that."

Whenever the *Finback* was not on alert, popular music was piped through the sound system: records like Frank Sinatra's "I'll Never Smile Again," Dinah Shore's "I'll Walk Alone," and Vera Lynn's "The White Cliffs of Dover."

The men regularly tuned in to the music popular in America that Tokyo Rose (Mrs. Iva Ikuko D'Aquino) made a feature of her propaganda broadcasts. One night she announced, "Here's to the men of the submarine force. We have sunk sixteen of your submarines this month." She mentioned that the *Finback* was one of the submarines, and the men screamed with laughter.

On the evening of October 15 Tokyo Rose gloated, "All of Admiral Mitscher's carriers have been sunk tonight—*instantly!*" The men, who had heard such nonsense too often, jeered heartily at such a preposterous claim. Yet the Japanese public awoke the next day to the news that its "Wild Eagle" naval pilots had won a "Second Pearl Harbor" in the waters off Formosa. The emperor announced a public victory holiday, the first in over two years. The triumphs of American carriers and submarines delivering a catastrophic hammering to the Japanese had forced Japan to invent a face-saving victory.

Although most of the men had pinups in their lockers of sex symbols like Rita Hayworth, Betty Grable, and Marilyn Maxwell, there was very little talk of girls, recalls Edwards. But there was one girl who was foremost on nearly everyone's mind. After dinner every Saturday night, Heyworth, the communications officer and a slim, handsome six-footer who had graduated from the Naval Academy at the age of twenty-one in 1942, would go to the captain's safe and open it. With everyone paying attention, he would take out an eight-by-ten portrait of the Park Avenue debutante who had caught his hat when he threw it up in the air at his Naval Academy celebration. The hat had his card in it, and the debutante started to correspond with him. Heyworth would carefully remove and then pass around a cellophane bag with a lock of hair in it. Everybody was allowed only one deep sniff of heavily scented perfume. Then Heyworth would hold up a piece of her debut dress that she had cut off and sent to him. After the men had seen the picture and the hair and sniffed the envelope, everything would go back in the safe until the next Saturday night.

Edwards remembers that Bush oohed and aahed with the rest of the men. "But the only girl he ever mentioned was Barbara, who he said he had met at a school dance."

Six days after his rescue Bush wrote another letter to his parents, in which he described his feelings at the time. "I try to think about it as little as possible, yet I cannot get the thought of those two [Delaney and White] out of my mind. Oh, I'm O.K.—I want to fly again and I won't be scared of it, but I know I won't be able to shake the memory of this incident and I don't believe I want to completely."

He also wrote daily letters to Barbara, who was in his thoughts constantly.

Life aboard the *Finback* was unlike anything Bush had ever experienced or imagined. Although one of the largest submarines in the navy, the *Finback* was designed without one extra foot of unused space, and there was very little room to move around. The sub had so-called overheads, storage areas for gear and locations for valves and piping. With his six-foot-three frame, Bush had difficulty at first, but he soon learned how to negotiate the narrow passageways and, after a few days, was able to go dashing around, automatically ducking in the right places—most of the time. But even the most experienced of the crew often came into sudden and painful contact with a door or lever or tube, and the water-tight doors between compartments were so low and narrow that the shortest men aboard had to duck to get through them.

There were also very few of the amenities to which he had grown accustomed aboard his carrier. For example, all the water on board had to be processed by two evaporators in the engine room, so there was little water available for bathing. The sub did have showers—aside from the officers' shower located in a battery compartment opposite the ward room, there were a few in the crew's quarters—but fresh water was strictly rationed, even for the officers. Each officer was permitted one shower a week, during which he would quickly wet his body, then turn off the water and soap up, and then quickly rinse. This method used little of the precious water. Most of the submarine crew stopped shaving and grew beards to save water (some found that their beards also protected their facial skin from the constant salt spray and winds while standing watch). Bush, who was accustomed to shaving daily, had to make do with seawater and soap for lather when the *Finback* was on the surface.

Commander Williams spent as much time as possible on the surface to avoid draining the ship's batteries. But if there was any sign of the enemy he submerged because the submarine had very little firepower for defense. The *Finback* relied on concealment and its load of twenty-four torpedoes. "Bush and the other aviators really got into the submarine experience," recalls Lt. Comdr. Dean Spratlin, the *Finback*'s executive officer at the time. "Every time an enemy plane would force us down, they'd curse it just like we did."

The sub's diesel engines were used only when running on the surface; these engines pulled a vacuum in the boat exhausting the oxygen in the air so much that a match would not burn. The air, always heavy with diesel fumes, sometimes became so bad that there was very little conversation. When submerged, the *Finback* traveled at slow speeds—around four knots—because the batteries would last only forty-eight hours. The moment it got dark the *Finback* would surface and begin to charge the batteries with the diesel engines. Part of the engine power was siphoned off for that purpose: one or two engines would be used to charge the batteries, while one or two others were used for main propulsion.

When not standing watch, the members of the crew ate or slept or performed various duties. There was always work to be done in the engine rooms or with auxiliary equipment to keep the sub in shape and battle-ready.

Bush served as junior officer of the deck under Bill Edwards and stood bridge watches with him. "He was a hell of a good lookout," Edwards reports. "He was trained at aircraft identification, and he had real good eyes. One day when we were on watch, he suddenly yelled out, 'Aircraft! Zero two zero. Elevation ten. Betty bomber closing fast. Twin engine, crew of seven, four machine guns, and one cannon.'

"I gave orders to clear the bridge and dive and then told him, 'Ellie, I don't give a damn how many people are on that thing or how many engines or guns it has. I don't even care whether it's one of ours or one of theirs, because if an airplane is coming our way, we're getting out of here.'"

Jack Peat, who had wanted to be a flier but had failed the eye test and volunteered for submarines, also shared many hours on watch with Bush. Peat, from Webster Groves, Missouri, had immediate rapport with the New England blue blood. "He was an extremely curious person," Peat recalls. "He wanted to know everything about submarines and I wanted to know about flying, so we spent our time on watch exchanging information about each other's jobs."

Bush recalls that he would often argue over which navy duty was the most dangerous. "Many of the *Finback* officers said that they would never want to be a pilot, because you were too vulnerable as a pilot, and if you got hit, it was all over. Yet here I was, living proof that you could fall out of the sky and live to talk about it. I would tell them that this was going to be the last submarine duty I ever did."

It was those times when the *Finback* was on the surface at night and he was standing the midnight-to-0400 watch that Bush most enjoyed. "I'll never forget the beauty of the Pacific—the flying fish, the stark wonder of the sea, the waves breaking across the bow," Bush recalls. "It was absolutely dark in the middle of the Pacific; the nights were so clear and the stars so brilliant. It was wonderful and energizing, a time to talk to God.

"I had time to reflect, to go deep inside myself and search for answers. People talk about a kind of foxhole Christianity, where you're in trouble and think you're going to die, and so you want to make everything right with God and everybody else right there in the last minute.

"But this was just the opposite of that. I had already faced death, and God had spared me. I had this very deep and profound gratitude and a sense of wonder. Sometimes when there is a disaster, people will pray, 'Why me?' In an opposite way I had the same question: why had I been spared, and what did God have in store for me?

"One of the things I realized out there all alone was how much family meant to me. Having faced death and been given another chance to live, I could see just how important those values and principles were that my parents had instilled in me, and of course how much I loved Barbara, the girl I knew I would marry.

"As you grow older and try to retrace the steps that made you the person that you are, the signposts to look for are those special times of insight. I remember my days and nights aboard the *Finback* as one of those times— maybe the most important of them all."

Much as he fraternized with the other men, Bush rarely spoke about Barbara or his family. Hugo Parkman, who spent many long, cold nights alone on watch with Bush, recalls, "All he ever said about Barbara was that he had a girl at home waiting for him and he'd named his plane after her. He was a clean-cut young man, and I never heard him use any bad or foul language. Everything he said was high and honorable. It was only years later that I learned how prestigious his family was."

"He never once mentioned that his father was a prominent stockbroker," says Heyworth.

To help while away the boredom, Bush volunteered for the duty of censoring outgoing mail of sensitive information. "You were together and shared the other fellow's joys and sorrows," he recalls. "Human friendships came through. That's always been important to me, making and keeping friends, understanding people. It was all put in bright colors by that experience."

During the period the pilots were aboard, the *Finback* was attacked by a Japanese Nell

bomber and sank two ships. Since the pilots had
no duties in a combat situation, they were sent to
the ward room and given a set of sound-powered
headphones so that they could plug into the
battle circuits and keep abreast of the activities.
"The excitement factor was unbelievable," Bush
recalls. "Keene put on the phones and gave us a
running account of the battle." It required a total
of only eight torpedoes to sink the two ships.

Now, more than forty-five years later, Bush
looks back on his time aboard the *Finback* as a
maturing experience. "Things just took on a
better perspective," he says. "There was never
any doubt about our cause in the war. That was
all crystal-clear. But I had vivid recollections
about what my mother and dad meant to me,
and Barbara. I thought about the people
around me, the differences in our experiences,
our backgrounds. There wasn't a sudden revelation of what I wanted to do with the rest of
my life, but there was an awakening.

"There's no question that underlying all that
were my own religious beliefs. In my own view
there's got to be some kind of destiny and I was
being spared for something on earth."

Thirty days from the time Bush had been
picked up the *Finback* arrived at Midway for
refitting. The pilots were put ashore. Before
leaving, however, one of the *Finback* officers
cut Keene's life raft into pieces. Bush, Beckman, Keene, and his two enlisted men signed

one of the pieces. A larger piece was signed by all the *Finback* officers. The departing pilots promised to join up with the sub crew for one last party when they reached Pearl Harbor.

The pilots were given new helmets and uniforms and were flown to Pearl Harbor. The first thing Bush did on arriving at Pearl was to send a telegram to his parents letting them know he was safe. His younger brother Bucky recalls how every night his family prayed for George's safety. When they got the telegram from him, both parents burst into tears. "I remember asking them why they were crying if he was all right," he says. After pulling herself together, Dorothy Bush called Barbara to relay the good news.

"I thought George was missing in action because I hadn't heard from him in such a long time (it took a month for mail to arrive from the Pacific war zone), and I was sick with worry," Barbara recalls. "Then I learned in a letter from Doug West that he had been shot down. My worst fears were realized. And then, four days later, his parents called to say they had a telegram from him and he was all right. I cried for joy."

The pilots went to the mansion of businessman Alexander Holmes, which had been turned into a rest home for pilots in Honolulu. There they spent a brief R&R (rest and recreation) sunning on the beach, playing volleyball, and sight-seeing in Waikiki.

Bush was in the air again for a refresher flight on October 13, 1944. In his flight log of that day he noted: "Forced landing at Barber's Point." "I really think I imagined difficulty," he now says. "I hadn't flown in a long time, and the plane just didn't feel right. Maybe some minor glitch, but nothing serious. Some of the older TBFs made strange sounds. But I've often wondered if it wasn't just 'coming-back syndrome.'"

The *Finback* arrived at Pearl Harbor within a few days; its crew enjoyed a rest at the Royal Hawaiian Hotel. The pilots threw the party they had promised for their submarine friends at the Holmes mansion.

Bush had the option of rotating home after his experience, but he was determined to rejoin his ship and get back into combat. "We were supposed to stay in Hawaii for two weeks' R&R," said Keene, who had become good friends with Bush aboard the sub. "But Bush was concerned about what had happened to his crewmen. He wanted to get back to the *San Jacinto*, and Beckman and I wanted to return to our carriers. We were not getting much cooperation from the navy until George took the matter in hand and somehow got us seats on a DC-3 to Johnson Island and finally Guam. We spent a few days there trying to find our carriers and finally located them at Ulithi. We said good-bye at Guam and went back to our separate carriers."

Keene had borrowed twenty dollars from Beckman and sent him a letter with the money in it. It was returned. Beckman had been killed over Leyte Gulf on his first mission back in action.

Chapter Nine

Bush finally caught up with the *San Jac* at Ulithi, eight weeks after being shot down. He was welcomed aboard and made his way to the ward room. One of the first people he saw was Lee Nadeau, who had been replaced on the fatal flight by Ted White. Nadeau recalls that Bush was wearing newly issued khakis. "He looked peaked but was cheerful as ever. He seemed a little older maybe, maybe more mature. Everyone, including the enlisted men, gave him a big greeting. He was that popular with all of us. We shook hands but we never discussed the crash. I figured his hurt was just too great. It was just something that happened in war—bad luck or fate—and we all accepted it."

Nadeau has a theory about what happened aboard the Avenger when Bush told Delaney and White to bail out. "When we got over the target area, Del always snapped on his chest chute. The plan we had rehearsed countless times was for Del to unhook my chute from the bulkhead and hand it to me when I came down the hatch into his compartment. And then he would bail out first through the starboard-side entry door.

"I'm sure Del did as we rehearsed and stayed in the plane until he could hook up White, unless White had been killed by the gunfire that raked the plane. Del was wearing a chest chute, and they were notorious for not opening, particularly if they had been packed a long time, as his chute had. Chances are that Del was the first one out and White went down with the plane. Since both men were wearing khaki coveralls, it would have been impossible for Moore's gunner to know whether it was an officer or enlisted man whose chute failed to open."

Nadeau was not worried about flying again with Bush. "He was a mighty good pilot, and I always felt safe with him."

The navy also considered Bush a good pilot. He was awarded a Distinguished Flying Cross soon after rejoining the carrier. The citation accompanying the medal reads:

Opposed by intense antiaircraft fire, his plane was hit and set afire as he commenced his dive. In spite of smoke and flames from the fire in his plane, he continued in his dive and scored damaging bomb hits on the radio station before bailing out of his plane. His courage and complete disregard for his own safety, both in pressing home the attack in the face of intense and accurate antiaircraft fire and in continuing in his dive on the target after being hit and his plane on fire, were at all times in keeping with the highest traditions of the United States Navy.

Although Bush had spent only a month aboard the *Finback*, much had changed during that time, both in the war raging in the Pacific and in Bush himself. During those solitary nights on the *Finback* he had realized he was no longer a kid. He had seen pilot friends shot down on missions but never believed it could happen to him. It had, and he had survived. While aboard the *Finback*, he had lost three more friends in the squadron, including Tom Waters, one of his roommates at Chincoteague and the trombone-playing leader of the ship's orchestra. Waters had been shot down by antiaircraft fire over Peleliu on September 15. Again Bush shed his tears in private and wondered why he was fortunate to still be alive when so many other good men were dead.

He had a lot of news to catch up on. The war was nearing its final phase: from fierce battles for distant island strongholds the fighting had finally reached the Philippines.

After the September 2 strikes during which Bush had been shot down, the *San Jac* had proceeded south to the area of Yap and Ulithi, where her planes had wrought such devastation on the enemy positions that further strikes were considered unnecessary and called off. From there the ship had begun operations against Peleliu, Anguar, and Ngesebus. It was during one of these strikes that Waters had been downed. The carrier had then retired toward the Admiralty Islands, and on September 20, 1944, the *San Jac* had crossed the equator. Bush thus missed his initiation into the Neptunus Rex Society and the Order of the Deep. To this day he remains a polliwog. He did, however, receive a charter membership in the Sea Squatters Club, given to anyone who had to use a life raft made by the Kidde Company for survival. And he is a member of the Caterpillar Club because he used a parachute to save his life.

His friends also told him that he missed out on some unforgettable days aboard the carrier. On October 10 the *San Jac*'s planes had taken part in attacks on Okinawa. These attacks had caught the enemy by surprise, so the planes managed to destroy twenty-four enemy aircraft on the ground at Naha airfield, strafe and bomb the town of Yonabaru, and sink two cargo ships in Naha Harbor. Two days later the Japanese, having finally succeeded in locating the carrier, counterattacked. A VF-51 fighter had shot down three of the attacking aircraft, but a much heavier attack came the next day, October 13. During that day, although most of the incoming enemy planes had been shot down, some had penetrated the screen of defending ships and aircraft and had made coordinated attacks on the ships in the fleet. The *San Jac* had been attacked by dive-bombers and torpedo planes. Two torpedo planes in particular had singled out the *San Jac* and had aimed straight at it. Both were quickly shot down by the ship's antiaircraft gunners, but not before they had released their torpedoes. Some of the pilots who were on deck saw these "fish" launched and watched them head for the carrier, one for the bow and the other for the stern. Just as one torpedo approached the bow, the carrier rose on the crest of a wave and the torpedo passed underneath. The other fish passed beneath the stern. An hour later a Japanese Judy bomber headed directly for the carrier was shot down by the combined guns of the *San Jac* and a nearby destroyer.

All these events were made more dramatic by the fact that the *San Jac* had just changed skippers, Capt. Michael H. Kernodle assuming command from Captain Martin, who had received orders for other duties (he was later promoted to admiral and became commander of the whole Pacific operations). The new captain had taken over in the midst of these constant, aggressive attacks.

One week later, on October 20, Gen. Douglas MacArthur waded ashore on Leyte Island. With film cameras rolling, he announced, "People of the Philippines, I have returned." With him came the United States Sixth Army, troop and cargo transports, and the Seventh Fleet. The liberation of the Philippines had begun. On that day the *San Jac* was en route to Guam for resupplying and additional armament. The ship was immediately ordered to turn back and head for the Philippines, where the Japanese were landing heavy reinforcements in Manila. The carrier and its air complement were needed to help halt the enemy; VT-51 was assigned to operate against land targets and enemy shipping in Manila Bay.

The Japanese reacted to the invasion of the Philippines with a long-prepared massive fleet operation named *Sho-Go* ("victory"). The plan involved sending a carrier fleet to draw away the main American naval forces, while battleships and cruisers would attack the invasion transports and their comparatively vulnerable escort ships.

The ensuing battle, one of the long war's most furious, lasted three days. On the first day, the Japanese attacked and sank the American carrier *Princeton*—the first American carrier lost in two years. That same day American torpedo planes sank the Japanese superbattleship *Musashi*. The monster ship survived more than eighteen torpedo hits and ten direct bomb hits before finally capsizing and sinking.

During the next two days the American ships

protecting the invasion transports, although outnumbered and outgunned, successfully drove off the attacking Japanese. During the furious fighting in the Surigao Strait, American battleships—some of them raised from the mud at Pearl Harbor and refitted—defeated a superior force of Japanese battleships.

Very much aware they were losing the war, and desperate to turn the tide somehow, the Japanese fought to the death. It was during this battle that the special assault corps known as *kamikaze* ("divine wind") first appeared. The *kamikaze* creed was "one plane, one warship." These suicide pilots were young volunteers, mostly teenage schoolboys with only a few hours of flight training. The engine of the plane, loaded with explosives, was a solid rocket with fuel enough to last fifty seconds at a speed of 535 mph. The human bombs were carried within a few miles of the target by a mother plane, usually a Betty bomber, and then released. Whether or not the young pilot scored a hit, he gave up his life for the emperor.

On October 25 the *San Jac* formed part of the task force sent to intercept the Japanese carrier group off Luzon's Cape Engano. During the engagement the *San Jac*'s planes had destroyed a Japanese carrier, the *Zuiho*, with two bombs and three torpedo hits.

The battle of Leyte Gulf ended as a shattering defeat for the Japanese. Their material losses included four aircraft carriers, three battleships, nine cruisers, and ten destroyers. Already suffering a serious shortage of experienced pilots, the Japanese navy was forced increasingly to put hope in the successes of the new suicide attacks.

On October 29 Captain Kernodle assembled the entire ship's complement and gave them a lecture on the *kamikaze*, warning the ship's gunners that they had to do everything in their power to shoot the planes out of the sky upon spotting them. On the last day of the month two *kamikaze* planes made it through the heavy barrage of antiaircraft fire. One crashed along the port bow of the carrier. The other headed directly for the "island"—the ship's control center—but was knocked off course by the ship's gunners and crashed on the flight deck. Pieces of the plane and pilot splashed all over the flight deck with an explosion that was felt below decks in the ready room. Fortunately, there was little damage to the *San Jac*, and the crew was able to clear the decks and jettison ten damaged planes in order to make room for other carriers' planes to land.

Bush's friend Dick Playstead and his crew, radioman Wendell Tomes and turret gunner Joe Smith, were shot down in flames. Playstead gashed his head on the torpedo sight, and Smith helped pull him out of the plane. The trio somehow managed to get clear and into their life raft, which they flipped over and hid beneath: the bottom of the raft was painted blue to blend with the water. Don Melvin chased away a Japanese destroyer. The hapless airmen floated for almost fifteen hours until search planes spotted their flashlight and directed the destroyer *Caperton* to their rescue. The destroyer's skipper was wary, however, and demanded their name and air group. Playstead shouted the information back. The skipper was still cautious until one of his crew said, "He comes from Boston. No one else talks like that."

When Playstead returned to the *San Jac* some weeks later, he had grown a mustache to hide the scars on his upper lip received when his plane had crashed. Following the action at Leyte Gulf, the *San Jac* had returned to Ulithi in the Carolines for replenishment. It was there that Bush rejoined her. On November 5 the carrier left Ulithi, headed back to Leyte.

Packages arrived for Jack Delaney from his sister Mary Jane. Knowing what was probably in the package, Lee Nadeau opened them and passed out the cakes, cookies, and candies. He then wrote a letter to Mary Jane:

Dear Miss Delaney,

. . . I am writing to tell you that the packages have arrived here. I think you know about John. The packages were rather banged up, so I have taken it upon myself to pass their contents out among all of his friends here. I know I am speaking for the whole squadron when I say thanks. We only wish he were here to divide them with us, as he always did. I don't know if John ever mentioned me, but I was the gunner in the plane that he always flew in. By a queer trick of fate, I didn't go along that day. He was a swell buddy, and I'll always remember him. I have his flight log here, and the first opportunity I have I will send it on to you. Thanks for everything. I know you'll understand.

Sincerely,
[signed] Lee Nadeau

Bush was busy, too, writing letters to the families of the men who had died in his plane, because the navy considered them missing in action and had not yet officially notified the families. Ted White's sister, Barbara, had married Judson Bemis, a friend of his. She was in the hospital having a baby when she learned of her brother's death through a letter written by a pilot on the *San Jac* to a friend in Minneapolis. A few days later her parents received a letter from Bush telling them how their son had died. She recalls that the letter was "warm and compassionate."

Bush soon received a letter back from Mary Jane Delaney. It read:

Dear Lt. Bush,
I must apologize for not writing sooner. It isn't that I did not try—I just could not.

You mentioned in your letter that you would like to help me in some way. There is a way, and that is to stop thinking you are in any way responsible for your plane accident and what has happened to your men. I might have thought you were if my brother Jack had not always spoken of you as the best pilot in the squadron. I always had the greatest confidence and trust in my brother Jack's judgment. I still do as I have not given up hope.

I want to thank you for your beautiful letter and the kind things you said about Jack. It was a message of sadness, but you made it much easier to bear.

With every wish for your continued safety.

Very truly yours,

[signed] Mary Jane Delaney

Meanwhile George had written to Barbara saying that he was scheduled for rotation back to the States and wanted to get married as soon as possible. In her reply Barbara was enthusiastically agreeable.

George, who wrote often to his brother Jonathan, then fourteen, sent a special letter to him on November 9, 1944. In it he wrote: "Whip out your top hat and tails, cause I want you to be one of the featured ushers at my wedding— when it will be I do not know, but get hot on shining your shoes, cause the day is not far off. Also get pants that are plenty big, because we're going to fill you so full of champagne it'll be coming out of your ears . . . It's nice to be flying again after my so-called vacation. Lately the weather has been terribly rough—so rough that waves have even been breaking over the flight deck."

Even though he was scheduled for rotation back home, Bush flew eight more missions in the Luzon area, including four strikes. On November 13, VT-51 had orders to join in the attempt to disrupt enemy shipping in Manila Bay. Lee Nadeau was in his usual place in the aft turret. The radioman-gunner was Joe Reichert, who had been overseas on other carriers for more than thirteen months and had recently been assigned to the *San Jac*, where he had been radioman–turret gunner for Grab and Butchart. Reichert had grown up in Queens, New York, and had always been a radio buff. At lunchtime on December 7, 1941, he was listening to his father's shortwave radio tuned to the control tower at Hickam Field, Honolulu, and heard a firsthand report of the Japanese raid. By that Christmas, just after his seventeenth birthday, he had enlisted in the navy.

With Reichert and Nadeau as crew, Bush took off at dawn and circled above Manila Bay with other planes of all varieties, waiting to find a slot so that he could go down and seek out a target. Finally he saw an opening and dropped down to attack. "The flak was heavy as we started our run," Reichert recalls. "There were four heavily armed ships firing at us, but we dropped our four five-hundred-pound armor-piercing bombs and hit a couple of light cruisers tied side by side. As we pulled up and out over the jungle, Bush started circling around. He came on the intercom and said he was going to hang around a bit to see the extent of the damage. About then I noticed a truck convoy going through the jungle. Every once in a while I saw an opening in the foliage, so I started firing at them just for the heck of it. Bush came on the intercom and asked me what was going on. When I told him, he laughed. 'At three thousand feet you'll never hit them,' he said, 'but go ahead. Enjoy yourself.'"

When Bush pulled up, he found himself alone in the sky. Instead of re-forming and returning in a group to their carriers, as was the usual practice, the planes had all returned to their own carriers separately.

As he headed back to the *San Jac*, Bush realized that he was low on fuel: they had been in the air almost four hours. He notified the crew that they might have to ditch in the sea. An SB-2C dive-bomber from another carrier flew alongside. The pilot pointed to his instruments and then pointed down, signaling he was low on fuel.

The two planes flew in formation for about fifteen minutes; then the other pilot waggled his wings and started to descend, presumably to make a water landing. Bush radioed the plane's position and continued on, trimming the Avenger to get the most efficiency out of the limited amount of fuel.

Nadeau recalls that at about the time he was beginning to give up hope, he saw a section of carriers, including the *San Jac*, with planes circling above waiting for the signal to land. Some of the planes were being waved off because the sea was rough and the deck was bobbing up and down. Bush came in from the stern of the carrier, and Nadeau, who was listening on the radio, heard him ask for permission to land instantly. Permission was granted.

"We came right in on the fantail, and Bush sat it down on the first approach," says Nadeau. "They unhooked us, and we taxied up the deck and shut down." The landing—in the worst kind of sea, with other pilots being held back from the risk—was perfect. Bush hoisted himself out of the cockpit and climbed down off the wing to join Nadeau. "Well," Bush said, "we made it." Nadeau remembers that Bush looked relieved. He had always been a capable pilot; now he had demonstrated the value of experience—he had saved the lives of the men in his care.

The squadron logbook corroborates the effectiveness of the sortie with this entry: "Again on 13 November in Manila and Luzon Bay, Philippines, Lt. (j.g.) Bush and several other members of VT-51 were credited with scoring four torpedo hits and sinking a floating dry dock, two bomb hits on a medium AK and four torpedo hits on two Japanese AKs."

Bush and his crew were in the air the following day. His log for November 14 records: "Bombing strike on Japanese shipping—Manila Bay." The flak was heavy, exploding all around the American planes, some of which were shot down. "The Jap fleet was moving out, and we caught them just outside the harbor," recalls Reichert. "Our first bomb landed alongside a supply ship. As we were diving again, I saw a gaping hole in the wing. I got on the intercom and told Bush about it. He came back to me in a moment and said, 'You're right. We have a hole in the wing.' But he continued straight in on the run and scored a hit. He was just as cool and calm as he could be."

On Thanksgiving Day a mass memorial service was held aboard the carrier for those pilots and aircrewmen who had made the supreme sacrifice. The tribute included those missing in action as well as those known to have been killed. It was a sad time for everyone on board as Chaplain Cordes conducted the service attended by the entire crew. The colors were at half-mast.

The final entry in Bush's wartime log, dated November 29, under the column "Character of flight," reads: "A/S" (anti-submarine patrol). "Duration of flight" was 3.7 hours, and "Passengers" were Reichert and Nadeau. The flight in the "Luzon area" was uneventful.

Later that day the *San Jac* sortied under escort of two destroyers en route to Apra Harbor, Guam. VT-51 was long beyond its three-month tour of duty: it had been in action for eight months and was to be replaced by a new squadron. All the torpedo bomber pilots were to be sent back to the States for a thirty-day leave. The *San Jac* dropped anchor at Apra the following day.

The pilots and their aircrewmen were put aboard the USS *Bougainville* on the island of Guam, which had been only partially seized from the Japanese: there was still fighting in the hills when they departed.

AG-51, of which VT-51 was the torpedo bomber squadron, had established itself as one of the foremost air groups of the Pacific fleet. Its planes had shot down fifty-one enemy aircraft and had been largely responsible for sinking the carrier *Zuiho*. The *San Jac*'s planes had also sunk two destroyers, two cargo vessels, and three armed trawlers, plus numerous smaller craft. The air group destroyed and damaged many aircraft on the ground and laid waste enemy airfields and ground installations. The pilots and crewmen of AG-51 had won an aggregate of six Navy Crosses, one Silver Star, twenty-eight Distinguished Flying Crosses, forty-nine Air Medals, and two Purple Hearts.

Bush had not only earned the DFC but had also been awarded the Air Medal with Gold Star, the Asiatic Campaign Medal with three battle stars, and the Victory and American Campaign medals.

The battle-weary men of VT-51 arrived December 22 in San Diego, where they were quickly processed. That night Bush and Playstead went into the city for a hamburger (meat rationing had just ended) to celebrate their coming home. Not much had changed since they had left for the Pacific a year before, except that women in the streets were now wearing form-fitting slacks instead of trousers.

It was on that visit, Playstead recalls, that he heard more about Barbara than at any time on the carrier. "She was all George could talk about. He said that he was going to get married at once if she'd go for it, and he asked me if I would go to his wedding."

The following morning Bush and Playstead flew on a commercial plane to Pittsburgh and then transferred to a sleeper-train heading for Boston via New York. Barbara met George at the railroad station at Rye on Christmas Eve. "I gave her a big hug, and then we went on the same train for the ten-minute ride to Greenwich, where Mom and Dad met us," George recalls. "There were tears of joy all around. I remember a mother's love and a father's pride and a fiancée's love as well. The next day was

Christmas, and we went to church. There I thanked God I was home, and in the quiet of our church I thought about Jim Wykes, Dick Houle, Tom Waters, Ted White, John Delaney, and the others who would never come home for Christmas."

Barbara had dropped out of Smith in August 1944, at the beginning of her sophomore year, after only one year plus a summer session. "I wasn't very interested in college," she admits. "I was just interested in George." Barbara and George confirmed their engagement and decided to get married as soon as possible.

In 1945 a man under twenty-one had to have parental consent to marry, although a woman of eighteen did not: a fact that tickled Barbara. "If it had not been for the war, neither my family nor George's would have considered our marrying so young," she said. "The timing of our wedding was set by the war."

Theirs was a typical wartime romance set against the background of the times. Although George and Barbara had known each other for a little more than two years, they did not really know each other well and had actually spent very little time together—overall, probably less than two months—and much of that time they were chaperoned, either by family or friends. Most of their courtship had been conducted via brief telephone calls while George was training in the U.S., and then by mail while he was overseas. But they were in love and determined to get married, and that made all the difference to them and their parents, who, if they had objections, never voiced them.

Wedding invitations were printed and immediately sent out to family and friends. The invitation read:

Mr. and Mrs. Marvin Pierce
request the honour of your presence
at the marriage of their daughter
Barbara
to
George Herbert Walker Bush,
Lieutenant, junior grade, United States Naval
Reserve
Monday the eighth of January
at four o'clock
The Presbyterian Church
and afterwards at the reception
The Apawanis Club,
Rye, New York
R.S.V.P.

But first there was to be another wedding in the Bush family. Five days after arriving home, George was best man when his older brother, Prescott, married Elizabeth "Beth" Kauffman on New Year's Eve. George brought Barbara to the wedding.

Although invitations to George and Barbara's wedding had been printed, the date had to be changed to January 6 to accommodate everyone in both families. Bush was resplendent in his blue uniform with gold pilot's wings and campaign ribbons as he stood beside his glowing, nineteen-year-old bride, who was wearing Dorothy Walker Bush's veil and a long-sleeved white satin gown. The eight bridesmaids, including some of Barbara's friends from Smith, wore kelly-green satin dresses.

George's brother Pres interrupted his own honeymoon to be best man. The ushers included Jonathan, wearing a new tuxedo, and Milt Moore and Dick Playstead, both in full-dress uniforms. George's brother Bucky, then only seven years old, remembers how impressed he was because so many of the men were in uniform.

It was an elaborate affair, with more than 250 friends of the Bush and Pierce families gathered at the Apawanis Club reception, where, coincidentally, George and Barbara had first met. Milt Moore was impressed. He'd known, of course, that Bush's family was well-to-do, but the elegance of the festivities made him feel a bit awkward. Everybody was polite and very friendly to him, but, as he later told his wife, "after the wedding couple, college seemed to be the guests' favorite topic of conversation." No one in Moore's family had ever gone to college.

Marge Playstead, who accompanied her husband, Dick, recalls the wedding as one of the friendliest she had ever attended. "Each bridesmaid introduced the next in line to guests at the reception. George's parents treated Dick and me like long-lost relatives."

When Pauline Pierce insisted that the bride and groom dance together at least once at the wedding reception, George reluctantly escorted Barbara to the crowded dance floor. As the celebrants cleared space for them, he whispered in her ear, "I hope you're having a good time. Enjoy it. It's the last time I'll ever dance in public."

It was bitter cold in the East that January, so the newlyweds opted to spend their honeymoon week at The Cloister on Sea Island, Georgia, just a few steps from the Atlantic Ocean. With its soft breezes, pools and magnolia gardens, the resort had long been a traditional spot for newlyweds, especially from the South. The Bushes were honeymoon couple number 1,768.

Coincidentally, Stan Butchart married his Miriam the following day, and Lou Grab married "Hot Connie" two weeks later. Jack Guy and Bea were wed the following month.

After their leave ended, George, Doug West, Jack Guy, and Milt Moore reported back for active duty in Norfolk at the office of Admiral Martin, who had been promoted from captain of the *San Jac*. He suggested that the four pilots get some special training and then return to Norfolk as the nucleus of VT-153, a

Joe Hyams

navy torpedo bomber group being readied for the invasion of Japan. They were sent to Florida, then Michigan, then Maine, and then back to Virginia to be retrained for assignment to another carrier in preparation for what was hoped would be a final assault on Japan. Bush's former comrades aboard the *Finback* were also preparing for the coming invasion; the sub had been chosen to act as a radar picket to aid planes attacking the Japanese islands.

Barbara stayed with either her family or George's most of the time while he was moving from base to base. While at Grosse Ile, Michigan, Milt Moore, who was waiting for carrier landing requalification, wrote to Lou Grab and Stan Butchart enclosing a letter from George updating his squadronmates on what was going on in his life at the time.

The letter, dated March 14, 1945, tells a lot about young George Bush and how he interacted with his friends. It reads:

Hi Louie and Butch,

Your letter was exceedingly fine. Gracie [George's nickname for Milt, after Grace Moore, an opera and movie star of the Thirties] is a little hard to get along with and at present, has a hard nose. But if all goes well, I'll stick this in the letter he is writing. He has told you about our prospective new squadron, etc. There is little left for me.

I bought a car up here. A '41 Plymouth two-door sedan Grand Coupe. It is a grand car if only the paint weren't flaking off. We propose to drive to Maine or wherever our new outfit forms now that the war has gone its way.

We have flown a few times and have completed an instrument course, which gives us a pink card. Flat cut. This you take off if two guys are smoking cigars on duty runway. It is a far cry from the master instrument carrier which Melvin had.

Give my best to the loopy one [Carl Woie]. Tell him that I really appreciate his letter of a month or two ago. Tell Raqucpau [a replacement pilot who joined the squadron in the Pacific] I want to meet his wife and tell Ricky [Playstead] to give my best to Marge. Also, if Ricky or Rack need squaring off, work with them. You guys are too apt to get discouraged. You lose sight of the long range objective for which we are striving. Well, work with them.

It is a great feeling to have an improvement for which you are responsible. Even as I write, Gracie is beside me, as physical proof . . . of course he slips into dirty holes every so often. But for the most part my work has reaped its reward and so my final word is "keep up the fight." If Rack says cards count eight in casino and spades don't count for two owl poop, humor him along and then deck him. The kid will learn.

Heaven this summer if we are here that long. Your skipper must be a dogger if he has only one cross. Give my regards to Hot Connie and Hot Pamela [Miriam Butchart] and keep the old pictures coming.

George

Later that month George and Barbara drove in the Plymouth (for which he had paid $350) from across Canada to Lewiston, Maine, where he joined the new squadron.

He checked out in the F-4U, the hotshot gull-wing Corsair fighter, and began to wonder if the "low and slow" Avenger was good enough for him anymore.

President Franklin Delano Roosevelt died on April 12, 1945, at the "Little White House" in Warm Springs, Georgia, while sitting for a portrait. It was a day of mourning for most Americans and their allies. Bush couldn't remember when FDR had not been president. "Bar and I were in our tiny apartment in Auburn, Maine, when we heard the news together," he recalled recently. "We were both shocked. His politics had drawn my dad's fire, but the day FDR died we wept for our commander-in-chief. He was the symbol of our determination—good over evil."

Jack Guy recalls that when he heard news of

the president's death, "we all thought the world was coming to an end."

Vice-President Harry S. Truman was rushed to the White House, where he was sworn in as the thirty-third president of the United States. But FDR's death changed nothing. The war was still raging.

Bush left the Naval Auxiliary Airfield in Lewiston for Oceana Naval Air Station in Virginia Beach, Virginia, just as the war in Europe was drawing to a close. He remembers little about V-E Day, May 7, 1945, the day when the war in Europe finally ended, except "feeling relief that the killing in Europe was over. But my war was still very active, and I expected to go back to the Pacific."

Despite their awareness that VT-153, their new squadron, was definitely going to the Pacific—or more likely because of it—"the Four Musketeers," as Bush, Grab, Guy, and Moore referred to themselves, spent their off-duty time with their wives or girlfriends as pleasurably as possible. One night George and Barbara went with Jack and Bea Guy to a USO show in Norfolk, where Fred Waring and His Pennsylvanians were the entertainment. Guy remembers that after the show ended, George suggested they go backstage and "say hello to Mr. Waring." "I thought George had gone off the deep end, but it turned out that Fred Waring *was* a good friend of the family! You can imagine what kind of impression that made on this 'ole country boy.'"

The planned invasion of Japan was canceled. The expected losses were just too great. On August 6, just before Bush received orders to return to combat, the B-29 Superfortress bomber *Enola Gay* (named after its commander's mother) dropped a single atomic bomb on Hiroshima, destroying 80 percent of the buildings and killing or critically wounding at least eighty thousand people. President Truman called upon the Japanese government to surrender and thus avoid "a rain of ruin" from the air. The Japanese leaders did not respond, and on August 9 Nagasaki suffered the same fate: the entire city was vaporized. Asked recently what he knew about the atomic bomb at that time, President Bush replied, "I knew *nothing* at all about it, but I was horrified when I heard about the human suffering it had caused."

On August 14, 1945, Japan unconditionally surrendered. On August 15—V-J Day—George and Barbara were in their rented rooms in Virginia Beach, Virginia. Like almost all other Americans, they were by their radio when President Truman announced from the Oval Office: "I have received this afternoon a message from the Japanese Government in reply to the message forwarded to that government by the Secretary of State on August eleventh. I deem this reply a full acceptance of the Pots-

dam Declaration which specifies the uncondi-
tional surrender of Japan . . ."

The Bushes joined the throngs of navy families who streamed into the streets of Virginia
Beach, celebrating late into the night. Bush
recalls, "It was unbelievable joy, rejoicing with
our fellow pilots down the street, with this
tremendous outpouring of emotion. We were
free to live normal lives. The killing would be
stopped—nine or ten of the fourteen original
pilots of our squadron had been lost.

"I remember laughing, yelling—crying, too.
The impact of the announcement was unbeliev-
able. We jumped and yelled and cried like kids.
We *were* kids—seasoned by war, but *kids.*"

Jack and Bea Guy, along with Doug and
Jacquie West and another couple, had rented a
house on the beach that had become the squadron hangout. "None of us knew then what an
atom bomb was and what devastation it could
cause," recalls Jack Guy, echoing Bush. "We
just knew the war was finally over, and we
were going to have the celebration of our lives.
Midway into the party someone asked where
George and Barbara were, and we telephoned
them at their rooms. But no answer. About half
an hour later they showed up. I asked where
they had been. 'We went to church to say
thanks to God for His blessing,' said George. Of
all the people in the squadron, they were the
only ones who went to church. That kind of

maturity and character impressed me more about George than almost anything else."

On September 2, 1945, at 0930, representatives of the Japanese government and general staff formally surrendered to representatives of the Allied powers led by General Douglas MacArthur on the deck of the battleship *Missouri* in Tokyo Bay. It was, coincidentally, one year to the day, and almost of the hour, since Bush had been shot down.

On September 18, 1945, George Herbert Walker Bush was discharged from the navy on "points" compiled by his months in combat and the decorations he had been awarded. After logging 1,228 hours of flying time, 126 carrier landings, and 58 missions, his role in the Pacific campaign was over, and he had survived. He was married to the woman he loved, and a new life full of promise was about to begin.

Epilogue

There were 16 million Americans in uniform during World War II, and of these 400,000 were killed and a half-million others wounded. George Bush is quick to point out that he was no more or less a hero than any other combat serviceman. "In terms of objective analysis, the real heroes to me were the Marines going ashore at Iwo Jima," he said recently. "I wore clean laundry every night and ate well. For a few minutes my life was in danger, but when we covered the landings in Guam and Saipan and I saw those boats going ashore, I realized how lucky I was to be in an airplane above. I'd look at those grunts down there going in, and that was real courage."

But George Bush had done his job well, and he could take pride and satisfaction in that. He had been anxious to get out from under the shadow of his father, to be his own man, to fly with the eagles—and he had succeeded. He'd made real friends, had real adventures—and he had survived.

The closeness of his early family life, the spirit of competition, the joy in the outdoors, the high standards of personal conduct, and the religious faith—gifts from his parents, continuations of a certain tradition—were all intended to strengthen his character and make him a better, more valuable person. But they had also made him a superior officer and a popular and courageous leader. Thrown back on himself, forced to confront alone the very real danger of violent death, he had not been found lacking: within him, strong and ready, were beliefs and strengths equal to each situation. George Bush has said he found the three years he spent in the navy "sobering." He did not entertain doubts—although he often wondered why he had been "chosen" to survive—and instead found that the traditions handed down to him had only been forged stronger by the flames of that terrible war.

Nor were the lessons of the war lost on him. As with so many other young men of his generation, his years of military service were a special kind of schooling, studies beyond textbooks in the world's realities undertaken before going to college for further learning. Bush had matured into a man with a unique knowledge of himself and his world. The price of war had been made painfully clear to him, and was the price of unpreparedness. His service career put into perspective for him the human side of military conflict and, he claims, "taught me the realities of death."

During a recent interview he said, "When it came time for me to send our kids to Panama, and later to the Middle East, I thought back on my own experiences in combat and what it was like to be shot at. Those memories were constantly in my mind when we were discussing committing troops and estimating expected combat losses. I'm not saying that I had to have that experience in order to make a decision as commander-in-chief, but having been in combat rounded out my awareness of the human cost of war. That experience is not essential for a president, however. We have generations of kids who may one day become president, and I hope that they will never have to fight or be in a war."

Bush returned from the navy to marry the woman he loved. There had never been any doubts: for George Bush and Barbara Pierce the war was an unwanted but necessary period of separation. And although far apart, they had done everything possible to share even that experience. Together again, they went on with their life, never wavering in their shared love and trust.

As his father had done, Bush went on to Yale, where he studied economics and became captain of the baseball team. He completed Yale in two and a half years—thanks to a special, speeded-up program for veterans—and graduated Phi Beta Kappa in 1948. Like his father, George became a member of Skull and Bones, an honor given only to the best and brightest of the classmen. As the "last man tapped" at his induction into the secret society, he was, according to long-established ritual, the most highly regarded man in his class. It was no small honor: past Bonesmen include Averell Harriman, William Howard Taft, Henry Luce, and Henry Stimson. He did not, however, follow his studies at Yale with a career on Wall Street. Instead, shortly after graduation he headed west to Odessa, Texas. "There was an oil boom going on, and it seemed to me that it was the right place to be," he said. "I hadn't heard of Odessa in those days, but it proved to be a marvelous thing to have done."

The Bushes began a life much different from the one they had originally planned, a life far away from the New England of their childhood. It has not always been easy, and they have had to face—always together—crises and challenges. Barbara's mother died in a car crash in 1949; their second child, a daughter named Robin, died of leukemia in 1953, at three and a half years old; Prescott Bush, Sr., died in 1972. There were also business losses and setbacks in Bush's political career. But he never lost his faith in himself, nor did Barbara.

Never claiming more than his fair share, never seeking the limelight—but always steadfast, laboring ardently for his beliefs—Bush moved step by step up the political ladder. He began his public career in January 1967 as the first Republican elected to a Houston congressional seat and was reelected without opposition; in 1970 Richard Nixon nominated him chief U.S. delegate to the United Nations, and he held that post from 1971 to 1973; from 1973 to 1974 he was national chairman of the Republican Party. He was chief of the U.S. Liaison Office in the People's Republic of China from late 1974 through 1975. President Gerald Ford then asked him to take over the post of director of the Central Intelligence Agency. He was there from 1976 to 1977. In July 1980 be became Ronald Reagan's running-mate and in January 1981 was sworn in as vice-president. In 1988 he was elected president of the United States.

George Bush's story might have been otherwise, of course. Had the *Finback* not been where it was, the Japanese might well have captured him. What would have happened then can only be conjectured. Chichi Jima, the island VT-51 had pinpointed for the September 1 and 2 strikes, was the scene of war crimes that stagger the twentieth-century imagination.

The official United States Marine Corps history states that, with the exception of carrier-based attacks on July 4, 1944, "there were no carrier based raids on Chichi-Jima between June 15, 1944, and February 19, 1945," the period during which at least ten other planes besides George Bush's were shot down. Nevertheless, the log of the *San Jacinto*—classified as "secret" until recently—belies the official statement. Additionally, the Japanese High Command forbade the keeping of diaries or logs by the troops on Chichi Jima. All records were supposed to be destroyed because the events that occurred on the island were and still are a matter of national shame to the Japanese.

The apparent reason for both sides wishing to ignore Chichi Jima is that, of all the American pilots and aircrew taken prisoner there, no record exists of a single captured airman leaving the island alive. It was not only the matter of their summary executions, in violation of all international conduct concerning the treatment of POWs; it was the manner in which they were put to death.

Eleven navy airmen were shot down in the vicinity of Chichi Jima, and their bodies were never recovered, although it was suspected that some were in Japanese custody. The men were listed as missing in action. Only after the war was it learned what had happened to the downed airmen. Most of them were beheaded. A Korean laborer on the island, named Ahn, told Col. Presley M. Rixey, U.S. Marine commander of the Bonins Occupation Force, what had happened to some of the others.

Thanks to Ahn's report and a thorough investigation conducted by Colonel Rixey, twenty-one Japanese officers, including Major Matoba, were tried for these crimes against humanity. At his trial Matoba admitted that cannibalism "was a practice I had grown fond of in China." When he was sentenced to hang along with five other officers, he never even blinked. He simply yawned and then asked for a cigarette. The six were executed on Guam in 1947.

Matoba is an embarrassing memory to the Japanese, but the island of Chichi Jima is today a beautiful spot favored as a resort by the Japanese. Rusted relics of the war abound on the island: pillbox bunkers dug into the rock cliffs are still intact, rusted antiaircraft guns still point toward blue skies. The harbor is awash with sunken wreckage and tons of rusted ammunition in boxes. Just before surrendering, the Japanese defenders dumped everything into the sea.

Also in that sea is Bush's plane, his Avenger torpedo bomber with *Barbara III* painted under the cockpit. James Egan, a marine salvage expert and the project director for Ferrumar Corporation of Alexandria, Virginia, recently located its position and proposes to bring it to the surface sometime soon.

• • •

The *San Jacinto* exists now only in photographs, books of naval history, and the memories of the men who served on her. But she had achieved a remarkable record. During sixteen months of continuous combat she destroyed or damaged 712 Japanese aircraft, 22 warships, and 219 auxiliaries or merchant ships, as well as countless shore installations. She had steamed 173,000 miles without overhaul, most of the time in the combat area.

On the night of Japan's surrender she was finally detached from the fleet. As she departed from Tokyo Bay for home, the commander of the task force sent the following message: "The spark plug is not the biggest part of the machine but it is the thing which makes her hum. We will miss the leadership of the 'Little Queen,' the flagship of the Texas Navy. Our best wishes follow her as she parts company homeward bound. Well done to a gallant ship."

On its return to the States the *San Jacinto* earned five battle stars and was awarded the Presidential Unit Citation. The citation read:

For extraordinary heroism in action against enemy Japanese forces in the air, ashore and afloat in the Pacific War Area from May 19, 1944, to August 15, 1945. Operating continuously in the most forward areas, the U.S.S. San Jacinto and her air groups struck crushing blows toward annihilating Japanese fighting power; they provided air cover for our amphibious forces; they fiercely countered the enemy's aerial attacks and destroyed his planes; and they inflicted terrific losses on the Japanese in Fleet and merchant marine units sunk or damaged. Daring and dependable in combat, the San Jacinto with her gallant officers and men rendered loyal service in achieving the ultimate defeat of the Japanese Empire.

Admiral Harold Martin, commanding officer of the *San Jacinto,* who had been replaced by Capt. Michael Kernodle, was accorded the Legion of Merit.

The *San Jac* was decommissioned in March 1947 and joined the Pacific Reserve Fleet docked at San Diego. Reclassified as an auxiliary aircraft transport on May 15, 1959, she was struck from the navy list on June 1, 1970. Her hull was sold for scrapping on December 15, 1971.

As soon as Bush began his public career, his wartime past resurfaced. All over the country there were men who had served with him or known him during the war. In 1966 William Edwards saw one of Bush's campaign advertisements on television and recognized him instantly as the flier whose rescue from the sea he'd filmed from the conning tower of the *Finback.* Edwards still had the film—the navy having judged it of scant military value—and he sent it on to Bush, thinking it might be of interest to him. The other members of the *Finback*'s crew and all the surviving members of VT-51 have followed Bush's career with a special kind of pleasure: he is one of them, he shared an important period of their lives, and he hasn't changed. The quick smile is still there, as is the reassuring sense of quiet courage. He stays in touch with his old friends by handwritten letters and cards at important times in their lives.

When flying his Avenger off the deck of the *San Jac*, Bush was responsible for his own fate as well as his crewmen's. As president he is responsible for the fate of all Americans as well as that of much of the world.

Acknowledgments

A book about George Bush's wartime years would have been impossible to write without the cooperation of the President and the First Lady. During a recent interview with the Bushes, the President helped make his story more vivid, accurate, and personal while remaining genuinely modest and self-effacing. Mrs. Bush, who was serene and lovely, as I had anticipated, was equally charming and informative as she provided me with insight into her teenage romance with the man to whom she has been happily married for almost forty-five years.

It was especially difficult to research George and Barbara Bush's childhood years, but Peggy Berman of New York was helpful. Anne Sloane Morrison, who grew up with George Bush, furnished recollections of him as a youngster, as did Hope Lincoln Coombe and Pat Shiverick. That especially important period of Barbara and George's lives was rounded out for me by their siblings: George's sister, Nancy Ellis; his brothers, Prescott, Jonathan, and William ("Bucky"); and Barbara's brother, Jim Pierce. My gratitude to each of them for helping give color to events in the distant past.

Capt. Robert Rasmussen of the Naval Aviation Museum in Pensacola, Florida, made available George Bush's wartime flight log and aviation cadet training records, which were of immense value. Museum technician Jim Pressley took time out of a busy day to locate documents and pertinent books in the museum's library.

Many of my questions concerning George Bush's training as an aviation cadet were answered by his early flight instructors. James Charles Crume, Jr., who had taken young George Bush up on his first flight, recently retired as an English and art instructor at the Stewart Indian School in Nevada. James Frank McAfee, a flight instructor at Corpus Christi while George was there, retired after twenty-six years in the navy and now lives in Rome, Georgia. Edward C. Fritz, the flight instructor who once described George Bush as "eccentric," still practices law in Dallas, where he specializes in environmental issues: he is chairman of the Texas Committee on Natural Resources. Thomas B. "Tex" Ellison, a senior instructor and torpedo training officer at Fort Lauderdale, where George Bush took some early training, explained some of the technicalities of torpedo bombing. Payton "Pat" Harwell, who was in George Bush's class at Corpus Christi, set the scene on the day the graduates received their wings as naval aviators.

I am grateful for the support of the White House staff, who on several occasions cut through red tape for me and helped locate pertinent documents. Without their assistance I would have been unable to find many of the sixty-five men who either flew with or knew George Bush during the years he was a U.S. Navy pilot in World War II.

All of these men are now well along in years, but although the events recorded here happened almost fifty years ago, they still retain clear memories of their part in America's last popular war. I am indebted to all of them.

The first man I contacted, and that only because he lived within driving distance of me in Los Angeles, was Lee Nadeau, who flew as turret gunner on fifty of George Bush's fifty-eight missions and is the unofficial historian of VT-51. He put me in touch with all of the right people. He also gave generously of his time, memory, and war records while his wife, Ginny, kept us going with savory epicurean delicacies.

Other members of VT-51 who were most helpful include Lou Grab, now a retired school principal, who let me spend a full day with him at his lovely home in Sacramento, California, sharing memories of his famous squadronmate

ACKNOWLEDGMENTS

while his wife, Connie—whom George Bush nicknamed "Hot Connie"—located pertinent photos and documents.

Stanley Butchart, the only member of VT-51 who made flying a career after the war, recently retired after twenty-five years as one of the top test pilots for NASA. He interrupted some repair work he was doing "for fun" on a Lancaster, California, church bus while his wife, Miriam, baby-sat one of their nine grandchildren. Stanley, the "Mr. Fixit" of the squadron as well as one of the best hotshot pilots, spent a morning with me talking about the men of Torpedo Squadron Fifty-one and George Bush in particular.

Jack Guy, who was one of George Bush's best friends in the squadron, is still very much a part of Bush's world. He was on the Finance Committee for "Bush for President" in 1978–80, cochairman of the Georgia Finance Committee in 1983–84, and cochairman of the Finance Committee and the Steering Committee of "Bush for President" in Georgia during 1987–88. Jack gave up a Saturday to meet with me at his office in Atlanta, where he owns a seat on the New York Stock Exchange. I well remember the day; my back was in spasms. Jack went through his records, logs, and memorabilia and patiently made photocopies for me in his office while I sat in pain and watched.

Legare Hole, executive officer of VT-51, was at his home on the island of Providenciales,

B.W.I., when I arrived on one of the three PAA flights that service the island each week. Gar and his wife, "Peanut," made me feel at ease instantly. After two days of interviews with Gar, I came to understand why the other members of the squadron still look up to and admire him and why the President still considers him a good friend.

Joe Reichert, who replaced Jack Delaney as radioman-gunner on Bush's last few flights in the Philippines, shared his flight log with me as well as his personal diary.

Dick Playstead and his wife, Marge, drove from their winter home in Northport, Florida, to Tampa to spend a day with me. Now retired after nineteen years as a field representative for Boeing, Dick, one of the two squadrons' members who attended the wedding of George and Barbara Bush, had a fund of information.

Richard Lazzarevich, who was a pilot in Air Group Fifty-one, graciously came to see me while on a visit to his mother. Nat J. "Blackie" Adams, who was flying a Hellcat and saw George Bush's plane go down in smoke, now lays claim to being "the oldest living architect in continuous practice in Idaho."

Lt. William Gardner "Ted" White died when George Bush's Avenger was shot down, but his sister, Mrs. Barbara Bemis, graciously gave me valuable insight into her brother's character and background. The sisters and niece of Jack Delaney, the other crewman aboard the fatal flight, were most helpful. I particularly want to thank Jack's sister, Mary Jane Delaney, for permission to quote from her letter to George Bush after the incident. (The names of White and Delaney are inscribed on the Wall of the Missing in the National Memorial Cemetery of the Pacific in Honolulu, Hawaii.)

Donald Melvin, skipper of VT-51 and the role model for his young pilots, authored a concise history of the squadron that gave me a proper framework for George Bush's activities in the Pacific. He died recently, but his widow, Catherine, supplied answers to many of my questions.

Also deceased are Milt Moore and Doug West, the two pilots who probably saved Bush's life on that fateful September morning by keeping the Japanese at bay while Bush struggled helplessly in the water. However, their widows, Jeanne Moore and Mrs. Jacquie Forshay, provided me with insightful recollections about their late husbands.

It is interesting to note that, with very few exceptions, most of the postwar marriages among Bush and his friends still endure. Let sociologists make of this what they will; Bush's generation seems to have had more respect for their marriage vows than young people today. Perhaps their wartime experiences made them more appreciative of the value of lasting commitment and loyalty.

The chapter on George Bush's month aboard

the *Finback*, the submarine that rescued him after he had parachuted from his burning plane, would not have been possible without the help of many men. I am particularly indebted to William Edwards, the *Finback* officer who photographed George Bush's rescue from the sea. After serving his country in two wars—as a submariner in World War II and as a fighter pilot (shot down once) in the Korean War—he retired from the navy in 1967. For the past twenty-three years he has been with the New York Life Insurance Company. Edwards is a fund of pertinent anecdotes and memories; his knowledge of what was going on in the Pacific during World War II is unsurpassed. Thanks also to his wife, Margarite, for her wonderful hospitality.

Jack Peat, lieutenant (j.g.) on the *Finback*, although recovering from recent surgery, told me stories about life on board the submarine and conversations while on watch with Ensign Bush. Hugo Parkman, communications officer on the *Finback*, vividly recollected that September morning when George Bush was plucked from the sea. Lawrence Heyworth, torpedo and gunnery officer aboard the *Finback*, remembered nights he stood watch with "Ellie the Elephant."

Others of the *Finback* crew who gave me perspective on the month George Bush was aboard were Richard James Peat of Paso Robles and Daniel T. Moody of Albany, California.

ACKNOWLEDGMENTS

Naval aviator Thomas Keene, who was rescued by the *Finback* just before George Bush, told me about some of their conversations and their common despair at having to remain aboard a sub on combat patrol for a month before being returned to their respective carriers.

For the section on the activities and war atrocities on Chichi Jima, I thank Capt. Robert "Wild Goose" Strickland, USNMCR, who was the youngest pilot in Pappy Boyington's famed "Black Sheep" squadron. A thirty-year resident of Kyoto, Japan, Strickland was responsible for my making excellent contacts in Japan. Masahiro Yoshimatsu of the Military History Department, National Institute for Defense Studies, in Tokyo was instrumental in locating a Japanese report about the raid on Chichi Jima, which documents details of George Bush's misadventure over the skies of that island. John Walton, a young lawyer from America who is getting his Ph.D. in law at the University of Kyoto, translated the Japanese document. Henry Sakaida, a California *sansei* and aviation historian-writer—and one of the foremost authorities on aerial combat in World War II—gave unstintingly of his records and expertise. Jessell Savory, now a resident of Las Vegas and a descendant of the original Yankee settlers of Chichi Jima, furnished me with a history of the island during the Japanese occupation. Thanks also to Jiro Yoshida of the

Japan Zero Fighter Pilots Association, who put his considerable resources at my disposal.

I owe a special debt to the anonymous authors of the action reports, combat logs, and unit histories, which gave a dramatic chronology of George Bush's war years.

Information about the various planes George Bush flew in was provided by Don Older, who grew up loving airplanes and, despite his youth, has been a pilot for twenty-four years. He is now an instructor at Flight Safety International. Mike Green, also a flight instructor, was an LSO as well as a naval aviator during the war in Vietnam. He contributed color and helped set the scene onboard aircraft carriers. Clarke Reynolds gave me insight into the world of the aviation cadet.

The list of others who contributed their time and wartime memories is long. They know who they are, and I want to thank them.

I owe a large debt to my son Jay, an author in his own right, who helped me with research and interviews. His skill as a writer-editor makes me proud. My assistants, Tami Hill and Jody Van Dyke, faithfully transcribed long taped interviews. A writer's workday is necessarily lonely, but every morning on our long walks together Ted Mann gave me encouragement and wise advice. And to my good friend Melissa Older, thanks for being patient and understanding.

The Maureen Lasher Agency of Los Angeles initiated this project and helped with editorial suggestions and editing.

Index

Adams, Ens. Nat J.
  "Blackie," 132,
  144
Adams, Ralph, 160
Andover (Phillips Acad-
  emy), 30
Atomic bombing of Ja-
  pan, 208
Avenger aircraft, xv, 9,
  68–70, 87, 90, 98
Aviator training
  carrier landings and
      deck run take-
      offs, 71–72,
      80–81
  catapults, 90
  classwork, 48, 51–52
  final phases, 76–84,
      86–91
  flight training, 52–61
  graduation, 61–63
  photographic train-
      ing, 83

physical training, 48–
  50, 61
program design,
  45–46
reduction of training
  time, 43
torpedo training, 68–
  70, 72, 89–90

Beckman, Ens. James
  W., 166–67, 180,
  182
Bemis, Barbara White,
  192
Bernoulli's principle, 51
Bird, Ens. L. A., 132,
  162
Bombing missions
  coordination of
      planes, 88–89
  dropping of bombs,
      98–99
Bonin Islands cam-

Bonin Islands (*cont.*)
    paign, xiv. *See
    also* Chichi Jima
    mission
Boyle, Lt. J. A., 54–55
Burials at sea, 123
Bush, Barbara Pierce
    (wife)
  Bush, Dorothy, and,
    92
  Bush, relationship
    with
    aviator training,
      visits during, 50
    dating, 33–34, 35,
      40, 43
    engagement, 73–75,
      92
    first meeting,
      31–33
    honeymoon, 203
    letter writing, 35,
      67, 128–29, 174
    Maine vacation
      (1943), 72–73
    reunion during
      Bush's leave, 199
    wedding, 134, 193,
      201–03
  Bush's enlistment,
    42, 43
  childhood, 37–39
  college career, 128–
    29, 200
  concern for Bush at
    war, 181
  family background,
    36–37
  weight problem, 38
Bush, Dorothy Walker

    (mother), 24, 26,
    27
  Bush, Barbara, and,
    92
  Bush's engagement,
    75
  Bush's feelings for, 27
  concern for Bush at
    war, 181
  marriage, 20
  sports and, 28–29
  visit with Bush dur-
    ing training, 91
Bush, Elizabeth "Beth"
    Kauffman (sister-
    in-law), 201
Bush, George
  aviator training, 42–
    43, 46
    carrier landings
      and deck run
      takeoffs, 71–72,
      80–81
    catapults, 90–91
    classwork, 48,
      51–52
    final phases, 76–84,
      87–91
    flight training,
      52–61
    graduation, 62–63
    photographic train-
      ing, 83
    physical training,
      49–50, 61
    relations with ca-
      dets, 47
    torpedo training,
      68–70, 72, 89–90
  bailout at sea, 144–

49, 151, 156–58, 159–61
 Japanese account of, 151–53
Barbara, relationship with. *See* Bush, Barbara Pierce
birth, 21
boating, love for, 24
censor work, 179
Chichi Jima mission, 136
 attack, first, 14–15
 attack, second, 142–45, 149–50
 briefing for pilots, 4
 flight to Chichi Jima, 13, 14
 launching of planes, 10, 11–13
 See also Bush, bail-out at sea
childhood, 22–31
citations, 184–85, 191
"club" memberships, 186
crash landing, 81
death, thoughts of, 73
discharge from navy, 210
Distinguished Flying Cross, 184
"elephant stampede" incident, 82
enlistment, 3, 39, 41–44
faulty planes, dealing with, 108, 111, 113
on *Finback*, 160–65,

167–72, 174–75, 176, 177–81
 depth-charge attacks, 169–70
flight crew, first meeting with, 84–85
flying, love for, 55
Japan invasion, preparation for, 203–08
landing in difficult conditions, 195–96
leadership ability, 78
letter to friends, 204–06
loss of friends, 104, 111, 123, 133, 168, 174, 185, 192
Maine vacations, 24–25
money, attitude toward, 23
"mooning" incident, 122
naming of, 17
nicknames, 24, 83, 122, 130, 171
parents, relations with, 27–28
at Pearl Harbor, 98 99
Philippines campaign, 194–98
political career, 215
"Poppy" nickname, 24
public service as destiny of, 18–19
refresher flights after

Bush, George *cont.*
    shoot-down,
        181–82
  religion in his life,
        26–27, 178, 180,
        200, 209
  rescue at sea, 158,
        159–61, 219–20
  return to *San Ja-
        cinto*, 182, 183
  return to U.S. from
        Pacific, 199–200
  Roosevelt's death, 206
  Saipan invasion,
        108–09
  schooling, 23, 30–31,
        40–41
  shakedown cruise,
        94–95
  shipboard life, 126,
        127, 130–31
  siblings, relations
        with, 25–26
  sports and, 29–30,
        40–41, 105, 106,
        126
  superiors' attitude
        toward, 3–4
  Twenty Questions
        player, 3
  V-J Day celebration,
        208–09
  Wake Island inva-
        sion, 103
  wartime experience,
        legacy of, 211–13
  water landing, 113–
        15, 117
  at Yale, 213–14
Bush, Jonathan

        (brother), 21, 27,
        72, 80, 193, 202
Bush, Nancy (sister),
        21, 25–26, 30, 34
Bush, Prescott S. (fa-
        ther), 18, 214
  Bush's engagement,
        75
  Bush's enlistment,
        42, 43
  business career,
        19–20
  concern for Bush at
        war, 181
  early years, 19
  fatherhood, approach
        to, 27–28
  marriage, 20
  money, attitude to-
        ward, 22–23
Bush, Prescott S., Jr.
        (brother), 20–21,
        22, 23, 25–26, 30,
        31, 41–42, 201
Bush, Robin (daughter),
        214
Bush, William H. T.
        "Bucky"
        (brother), 21,
        181, 202
Bush family, back-
        ground of, 18–19
Butchart, Miriam
        Young, 80, 203
Butchart, Lt. (jg) Stan-
        ley "Butch," 2,
        80, 81, 96, 203,
        204
  aviator training, 81
  background, 77–78

Saipan invasion, 106, 107–08, 110

Caffey, Ens. John F., 121–22
Cahn, Lt. Comdr. A. B., 11, 12
Chichi Jima island, 136, 217
Chichi Jima mission, 136
 attack, first 13–16
 attack, second, 141–44, 149–53
 briefing for pilots, 1–8
 flight to Chichi Jima, 13–14
 Japanese defenses, 5, 137–38
 launching of planes, 9–13
 plan of attack, 7
 preparation of planes, 8
Connolly, Bill, 161
Coombe, Hope Lincoln, 25
Coral Sea, battle of, 102
Cordes, Deitrich, 123, 197
Crume, Ens. James Charles, Jr., 52, 53, 55, 56
Curley, Walter J. P., 41

Delaney, John "Del," 11, 85, 98
 bailout at sea, 145

death, 150, 168, 183–84
 Wake Island invasion, 103
 water landing, 112, 114
Delaney, Mary Jane, 191, 192–93
Dickey, Lt. Comdr. J. R., 60
Doherty, John, 158
Drinking by servicemen, 96
Duncannon shooting lodge, 30

Edwards, Ens. Bill, 158, 159, 162, 166, 170, 173, 174, 177, 219–20
Egan, James, 217
"Elephant stampede" incident, 82
Ellison, Lt. (jg) Thomas B. "Tex," 68
Estrada, Leo D., 121

Film of Bush's rescue, 158, 159, 161, 219–20
Finback, USS, 147, 153, 168–70
 daily life on, 170–81
 depth-charges used against, 169–70
 downed pilots, search for, 155–56, 158–59, 164–66
 mechanics of, 176–77

Finback, USS (*cont.*)
  military actions,
      179–80
  rescue of Bush, 158,
      159–64
Ford, Gerald R., 215
Fritz, Ens. Edward C.,
      58–59
Fuchs, Harold, 95
Fuess, Claude M.,
      39–40

Gorman, Dick, 145
Grab, Lou, 76, 77, 81–
      82, 130, 203, 204
Griffin, Lt. B. F., 111
Griswold, Jim, 164
Guam invasion, 110–
      11, 132
Guy, Jack O., 3, 76, 78,
      79, 80, 86, 94,
      105, 131, 132,
      203, 206–07
  background, 77
  Japanese fleet, at-
      tacks on, 118
  Melvin and, 87
  practical jokes,
      130–31
  V-J Day celebration,
      209

Haggard, Charles, 104
Hall, Blaine, 46
Halsey, Adm. William,
      xiii, 136
Harriman, E. Roland,
      21
Harriman, W. Averell,
      21

Harwell, Payton "Pat,"
      62
Heyworth, Lawrence,
      164, 170, 171,
      173–74, 179
Hitler, Adolf, ix
Hole, Legare "Gar," 2,
      91, 94, 95–96,
      119–20, 126
Hollowell, Ens. T. E., 117
Honke, M. M., 61
Houle, Roland "Dick,"
      82, 111, 133

Iwo Jima, battle of, xiv

Japanese fleet, attacks
      on, 117–18
Japan invasion, prepa-
      ration for,
      203–08

Kamikaze assault corps,
      189–90
Keene, Ens. Thomas,
      158, 163, 171–72,
      180, 182
Kennedy, John F.,
      70–71
Kernodle, Capt.
      Michael H., 187,
      190
Kilpatrick, Lt. M. E.
      "Buster," 1, 5
Kohler, Don, 161

Leyte Gulf, battle of,
      189–90
Link Trainer (simulated
      aircraft cockpit),
      60

MacArthur, Gen. Douglas, xiii, 187–88, 210
McIlwaine, R.D., 107
Mail call, 127–28
Marianas campaign, 102–03
Guam invasion, 110–11, 132
Saipan invasion, 106–10
Wake Island invasion, 103–04
Martin, Adm. Harold "Beauty," 93, 109, 123, 187, 203, 219
Matoba, Maj. Sueo, 138, 139, 217
Melvin, Lt. Comdr. Don, 191
Bush and, 3–4
Bush's bailout, 147, 156
Chichi Jima mission attack, first, 14
attack, second, 143, 144–45, 149
briefing for pilots, 1, 2, 5–8
launching of planes, 12
as flight instructor, 86–88
flying, love for, 6
Japanese fleet, attacks on, 118
pilots, concern for, 2–3, 6

Mitscher, Adm. Marc A., 8, 99, 119
Moore, Milton, 2–3, 86, 122, 143, 145, 202, 203, 204
Mori, Vice Adm. Kunizo, 138
Morrison, Anne Sloane, 25, 29, 34
Mussolini, Benito, ix

Nadeau, Leo "Lee," 9, 10–11, 89, 191–92
Bush, relationship with, 84–86
Chichi Jima mission, 10–11, 15
fate of Delaney and White, theory on, 183–84
gunner qualification, 91
Houle and, 133
ordnance training, 84–85
Philippines campaign, 194, 196–98
praise for Bush, 123–24
typhoon, 135
Wake Island invasion, 103–04
water landing, 113, 114–15, 117
Nighttime carrier landings, 118–20
Nimitz, Adm. Chester, xiii
Nixon, Richard M., 215

Okinawa invasion,
  186–87
Ordnance training, 84
Owen, Capt. G. T., 62

Panama City, 96
Paoletti, Frank, 10,
  97–98
Parkman, Lt. (jg)
  William "Hugo,"
  162–63, 167, 179
Pearl Harbor
  Bush's stay in, 98–99
  Japanese attack on,
    x–xi, 39
Peat, Jack, 164, 166,
  177
Peat, Richard, 171
Philippines campaign,
  187–91, 194–98
Philippine Sea, battle
  of, xiv, 111–16
Phinney, Deane, 46
Pierce, Barbara. See
  Bush, Barbara
  Pierce
Pierce, Jim, 32
Pierce, Marvin, 36–37,
  38
Pierce, Pauline Robin-
  son, 36, 37–38,
  50, 203, 214
Pierce, Scott, 37
Playstead, Dick, 87,
  105–06, 123, 131,
  190–91, 199, 202
Playstead, Marge,
  202–03
Prisoners of war, Japa-
  nese treatment

of, 138–39,
  215–16

Reagan, Ronald, 215
Reichert, Joe, 194–95,
  197, 198
Rixey, Col. Presley M.,
  216–17
Robinson, Bill, 46
Roosevelt, Franklin D.,
  xi, 206–07
Rosie the Riveter, xii

Saipan invasion,
  106–10
San Jacinto, USS
  actions during Bush's
    absence, 185–91
  attacks on, 109–10,
    112–13
  burials at sea, 123
  commissioning of,
    91–92
  construction of, 93
  daily life on, 125–31
  kamikaze attacks on,
    190
  shakedown cruise,
    94–95
  Task Force assign-
    ment, 99
  typhoon, 134–35
  wartime record,
    218–19
  See also Chichi Jima
    mission
Shipboard life, 125–31
Smith, Joe, 190
Spratlin, Lt. Comdr.
  Dean, 176

Stearman N2S-3 trainer airplane, 54
Stimson, Henry, 41
Stovall, James, 158
Submarines. *See Finback,* USS

Tachibana, Lt. Gen. Yosio, 138
Tokyo Rose, 172–73
Tomes, Wendell, 190
Truman, Harry S., 207, 208
Typhoon, 134–35

V-E Day, 207
V-J Day, 208–10
Vultee Vibrator training airplane, 58–59

Wake Island invasion, 103–04
Walker, George Herbert, 17–18, 24
Walkers Point estate, 17–18, 24
Ward, Jerrold, 94
Waring, Fred, 207–08
Warren, George "Red Dog," 35
Water landing, 112–15, 117
Waters, Francis "Tom," 79, 95, 105, 185
West, Doug, 79, 86, 143, 147, 148–49, 156–57, 181, 203, 209
Whalen, Robert, 104
White, Lt. (jg) William

G. "Ted," 141–42, 145, 148, 150, 168, 183–84
Williams, Comdr. Robert R., Jr., 155, 156, 162, 164–65, 166, 167, 176
Williams, Ted, 46–47
Woie, Carl, 205
Women, World War II and, xii, 66
World War II
  Americans' enthusiasm for, xii
  beginning of, ix–xv
  European war, ix–x, xiii, xiv, 66–67, 207
  homefront austerity and conservation, 66 67
  Japanese successes, xii–xiii, 101
  Japan invasion, preparation for, 203–08
  turning point of Pacific war, 102
  U.S. strategy against Japan, xiii–xiv
  V-E Day, 207
  V-J Day, 208–10
  women and, xii, 66
  See also specific battles
Wozencraft, Jack, 32
Wykes, Jim, 104

Yale University, 19, 213–14

Chapter 18

I made sure my sneakers were tied as I headed out the door and over to the Sun City West dog park the following evening. I had stopped by my house to change after work and grab a snack. It was still daylight but fading fast. I needed to find Cindy Dolton if I expected to get anywhere. Thankfully, she had decided to take Bundles to the dog park in the evenings again. She told me a while back she was convinced the nighttime activity with so many dogs was giving hers diarrhea. She later realized the real cause for the problem, and it had more to do with the "prizes" Bundles ate in the park than with his canine companions.

The day before, I'd read the list of the kennel club's board members to my mother. But only after being compelled to listen to the latest rumor fest about Miranda's ghost. Now it was Sue Ellen who was taking a seat on the loco train, along with Shirley and Cecilia. I kept muttering "uh-huh, uh-huh" until I was able to get my mother focused on the list. There were six names, and she recognized three of them.

"Well, of course, there's Gordon. Naturally. Hmm . . .

Marletta Mobley's obituary was just in the papers this week. Long stay in hospice. Poor woman."

"I'm sorry, Mom. Did you know her?"

"What? No. Only read about it in the paper. She was a long-term board member for that kennel club."

"What about the other person? The other one you recognized."

"Lester Folson. He used to live around the corner. Moved in with his daughter somewhere in Texas. That was at least two years ago."

"None of these other names ring a bell?"

"I can't be expected to know everyone here. Talk to Cindy Dolton."

The park was its usual frenzy of activity when I pulled up, and I was thankful I didn't have my mother's dog with me to make things worse. His penchant for amorous advances, regardless of gender, was well known in the park. People clutched their miniature breeds and hustled off the minute Streetman showed any interest in their pets. It was much easier to eke out information without him.

Cindy was standing near the side gate watching Bundles as he sniffed around, pausing occasionally to dig in the grass. "Stop that! Bundles! You heard Mommy! Mommy doesn't want your feet to get all green and dirty."

I gave a quick wave and headed right toward her. "Hi, Cindy! I was hoping you'd be here. I've got to ask you something."

Reaching into my bag, I pulled out the list of board members Nate had uncovered and showed it to her. "Do you happen to know any of these people, other than Gordon?"

Cindy took the list and read it carefully. "I knew

fingers crossed no one at the park tells my mother I went without taking Streetman. He's exhaustive, and I need to talk with Cindy Dolton. Last I knew from her, Gordon and Miranda kept a wide berth from each other. Maybe someone else knows something."

"Check that list of kennel club board members again and see if anything pops out at you. And if you do decide to go to that park, I wouldn't wear open-toed shoes."

"Eeew. Maybe I'll go tomorrow after work, and, in the meantime, I'll see if my mom or her friends recognize any of the names on the list."

"Good idea. I'll delve deeper into any Rhode Island connections. Anyway, I've got a few things to finish up before I head out to lunch with a, um . . . client. Enjoy your deli takeout."

Lunch? Client? Why the pause before "client?" Is that a nice way of him saying he has a date?

Marshall turned and went back to his office while I stood at the copier with a blank look on my face.

"Everything okay?" Augusta asked.

"Oh, yeah. Sure."

"The food will be here in twenty minutes."

Suddenly I didn't feel like eating. All I could think of was Marshall's lunch date. If it was a date.

I walked over to Augusta and whispered, "Do you know who he's having lunch with?"

Augusta grabbed the mouse and changed screens. "He didn't say?"

"No. And . . . uh . . . I was wondering . . ."

"Well, you have nothing to worry about. And you didn't hear it from me. He's meeting the deacon from St. Mark's Episcopal Church. Say, didn't I read in the paper about some thefts of artwork there? That must be what the meeting is about."

Augusta quickly shifted to another screen. "So, as I was saying, lunch should be here shortly."

"That's terrific! I'm famished."

Marletta Mobley. She was a really nice lady. I didn't know Andrew Clemson, but I heard he was nice, too."

"Was?"

"Oh yeah. He passed away last year."

"I see. Any others you know?"

"Donna Olsen moved back to Nebraska at least two years ago. What a character. Used to dress her dogs up according to the holidays. Earl Grey and Oolong."

"Earl what?"

"Those were the names of her teacup poodles."

If I ever broke down and got a pet, it'd be a cat, and I wouldn't dress it up. "What about this last name? Samson Harrington."

"Um, it sounds familiar. I'm not sure. Hold on a second." Cindy started to walk toward the benches where at least ten or eleven people were seated.

I tried to feign interest in the dogs playing and pooping, but all I could think about was getting the information I needed without having to disinfect my shoes.

"Got it!" Cindy yelled as she walked back to me.

I tried to stay put, figuring the less ground I tread on, the less chance I had of stepping on something questionable.

"Samson Harrington is alive and well. Living in The Willington. It's a senior resort complex for people with dementia or Alzheimer's. He went downhill fast, according to Brenda and Edith over there."

I glanced over at the two zaftig women Cindy pointed out. Each of them appeared to be holding small white dogs.

"Thanks, Cindy. I appreciate it."

"Tell me, why are you interested in who was on the purebred kennel club board four years ago?

They've got new board members now. Boomers who've recently moved into the community from what I've heard."

"It's a longshot, I know. But I thought maybe one of them might have had a motive to kill Miranda Lee. I heard there was some fracas over her dog not getting accepted into the club."

"Oh *that*. She threatened to sue everyone in sight, but no one took her seriously. At least I didn't think so. Most of us figured it was all a bunch of show. Anyway, that was years ago, and, as far as I know, Miranda never took any legal action."

I didn't want to say anything about the lawsuit for fear of starting a new rumor. "Um. That's kind of what I figured, but I needed to check. Anyway, thanks, Cindy. Have a good evening."

I turned and unlatched the gate to the park.

Behind me, I heard someone shouting a familiar refrain. "POOP ALERT! POOP ALERT!" Yep, if I got a pet, it would be a feline.

At least my proverbial "walk in the park" clarified one thing. None of the other former board members had come face-to-face with Miranda like Gordon did. They were either dead, gone, or too incompetent to know what was going on. So, if anyone was going to harbor a grudge, it would be Gordon. He would have had a motive. But what about means and opportunity? Unlike Cliff, who would have a reason to get Miranda on that catwalk, Gordon's movements were strictly limited to the stage. Still, he was certainly a suspect as far as I was concerned.

Driving home from the park, I noticed holiday lights. Some houses were already decorated for Christmas and their twinkling lights, bright against the desert sky, caught my eye. It was a week before Thanksgiving, and it was as if that holiday was being relegated to the minor events list, along with Groundhog Day, Earth Day, and Take Your Child to Work Day. Only in Arizona.

I checked the bottoms of my sneakers before walking into the house and kicking them off. No sense in taking chances. Then I headed to the kitchen to make myself a diet milkshake.

Two percent milk classifies it as diet, doesn't it?

Out of the corner of my eye, I saw the red light flashing on my phone. Pressing down on the small button below the screen showed who called. Big surprise. I tapped the playback button and listened to my mother's message.

"What did you find out? Was it a board conspiracy? Call me."

Not before I make my shake and take my time drinking it.

Wiping the faint chocolate moustache from the sides of my mouth, I picked up the phone and called. "Hey, Mom, got your message, and there's not a whole lot to report. Gordon's the only one who could possibly have a motive. The other board members are either dead or—"

"That's not why I called, but that's good to know. I told Streetman you'd take him next time. I'm going over to Shirley's tomorrow to try on wigs. If that director thinks I'm about to cut my hair and dye it hideous brown to play Mrs. Boyle, he's got another thing coming. I'll wear a wig. Shirley has lots of them. Besides, I'm planning on changing my hair color completely for the holidays. I was thinking of platinum with black highlights."

"Dear God. You'll look like Cruella Deville. Only in reverse."

"Phee, hair color is meant to be enjoyed. That's why the thought of bland brown will never do. Anyway, I wanted you to know I've been given the position of prompter for act two. You know why? Because Chuck Mitchenson still hasn't learned his lines and needs someone to refresh his memory. Can you believe it? Two weeks till curtain time, and he's in la-la land. It's not that I mind doing it, since I'm not in act two but, for heaven's sake, when does he plan on learning them?"

"Yeah, um, I seem to remember hearing that the other night from some of Herb's buddies. Mom, what does anyone know about Chuck? Other than the fact he goes to the same church as Cecilia. He's been off the radar, so to speak, and I'm not sure if Nate or Marshall have found out anything that would make Chuck a suspect. I'll have to check on it."

"Good. Good. Anyway, Myrna called a few minutes ago. She's in the middle of cleaning out her old file cabinets to donate them to the Sun Cities Charities. She's redoing her office area so it will double as a den."

I shook my head and wondered how long I could hang on to the phone and listen to all of this. There were only so many "uh-huhs" and "that's good" I could say.

My mother kept going. "Now I wouldn't exactly call Myrna a pack rat. But you know how it is with files. We stick things in there and never bother to look again. So, tonight when Myrna was dumping out some old theater programs from the Peoria Players, guess what she found?"

I don't know. William Shakespeare's autograph on an original playbill? "What? What did she find?"

"About a year and a half ago, Myrna went to see a production of *The Odd Couple*, directed by none other than Cliff Edwards. She saved the program. Along with a zillion other programs she's saved. And you'll never guess who was in the play. Go on. Guess!"

"Mother, I'm not playing 'Guess who was in some play in Peoria.' I want to take a shower and relax for a while."

"Fine. I'll tell you. It was Sue Ellen Blair. That's right. Sue Ellen. She played the role of Gwendolyn, one of the Pigeon sisters who dates Felix and Oscar in the play."

It was as if a bomb dropped right in the middle of my kitchen.

"Sue Ellen knew Cliff? She never let on, did she? Did he? Oh my gosh . . . I'm wondering. When did Miranda and Cliff get divorced? Never mind, I'll have Nate or Marshall check that out. Mom, this may change everything."

"Why do you think I called you?"

Chapter 19

I all but accosted Marshall when I burst into the office the next morning. He was waiting for his cup of coffee to brew and had probably had the same idea I did—arrive really early to get some work done. So early that Nate and Augusta hadn't yet walked in.

"Marshall, you're not going to believe this, so I'll get right to the point. Sue Ellen knew Cliff at least a year and a half ago. It's not a rumor. It's true. She was cast in one of his plays in Peoria. *The Odd Couple*. Myrna saw that play and kept the playbill. She forgot all about it until she started cleaning out her file cabinet. That was last night. She called my mother and well, um, there you go."

"Whoa. I'll try to absorb all of that without my morning coffee."

"I think it's ready. The light stopped flashing on the machine."

Marshall removed his cup and asked if I wanted one. After he placed the flavor I selected into the Keurig, he lifted his cup and took a sip. "Hmm. How about that. I suppose neither of them said anything because the subject never came up. Heck, there's nothing suspicious about it. It wasn't as if Cliff cast her in the part of Mollie Ralston. He didn't come on the scene until after Ellowina got food poisoning and couldn't direct the play. At least that's what my notes say."

"That's right. But think about the timing. And think about Sue Ellen. She's awfully cute and comes across as very sweet." *What the hell am I saying? I'll sabotage my own chances with him.*

"Okay, so?"

"So, if what Paula Darren told me was true, Cliff and Miranda got divorced around the same time as that play. Maybe Sue Ellen was the temptation that split them up."

"If that was the case, wouldn't she be dating him or something? I think you're going out on a limb, because, up until now, no one knew they had any kind of relationship, professional or otherwise."

"Will you look into it? Speak with Cliff. I have a hunch Sue Ellen might be behind Miranda's murder."

"What makes you say that?"

"Two coincidences too many. I think she's trying to make it look as if she's a victim when the opposite may be true. First the tungsten lamp that conveniently fell near her, then the trapdoor that Gordon fell through. Sue Ellen was insistent it was meant for her. So will you do it? Talk to Cliff, I mean?"

"Why not? It'll put your mind at ease if nothing else. The sheriff's department, by the way, isn't getting any further with the investigation either. I'm on the phone at least every other day with Bowman or Ranston. The only thing they've managed to pull up, which we've overlooked, is a rather interesting connection between Miranda and Sue Ellen."

"Connection? What connection? That day in the

theater when Sue Ellen was crying her eyes out, I asked my mother if Sue Ellen knew Miranda, and the answer was no. Sue Ellen was worried people would accuse her of killing Miranda to get the lead role. So, what's the connection?"

"They both worked at the same hospital in Rhode Island."

"At the same time? How can that be? Sue Ellen's so much younger."

"The sheriff's department was able to procure an incident report from the hospital where Miranda was employed as an RN. She was Miranda Shumway then. And get this—she was accused of negligence that resulted in the death of a sixty-two-year-old woman."

"That's terrible, but what does that have to do with Sue Ellen?"

"The report listed everyone connected with the incident, from orderlies to volunteers. Sue Ellen Blair was a candy striper at the time. At first, the sheriff's department wasn't sure it was the same Sue Ellen, so they looked into it further. Turns out our Miss Blair volunteered at the hospital as part of her high school's graduation requirement—community service. Following graduation, she had nothing to do with the medical profession. Maybe Miranda's incident scared her away."

"Holy cow! Do you think, after all those years, Sue Ellen even recognized Miranda and vice versa? Maybe Miranda's negligence somehow put a bad mark on Sue Ellen's service. That might have carried over into college applications. It could have ruined any dream career that Sue Ellen might have had."

"I'd say doubtful. Still, it's an interesting, if not puzzling, connection."

"It could also be a motive for murder. Along with a possible affair Sue Ellen could have been having with Cliff."

The outside door swung open as Augusta walked in. "Affair? Why do I always walk in late and miss the juicy stuff?"

"Good morning, Augusta," Marshall said. "You'll have to wake up with the roosters to catch all of Phee's riveting gossip."

"It's not gossip," I whined. "It's speculation."

Augusta plopped her bag on her desk and gave me a wink. "Fill me in during a break today. I love to speculate."

With that, I retreated to my office, and Marshall went to his. About a half hour later Nate popped into my office to say hi and ask how I was doing.

I looked up from my computer screen and motioned for him to grab a seat. "I think Sue Ellen Blair is our murderess, but Marshall isn't buying it. Not yet anyway."

"What makes you so sure?"

I proceeded to tell him about how Miranda and Sue Ellen's paths had crossed years ago in Rhode Island as well as the recent discovery Myrna had made about Sue Ellen's performance in one of Cliff's plays.

"Ah. Doesn't mean she was having an affair with him. Did Marshall say he was going to speak with Cliff?"

"Uh-huh."

"Then don't get carried away yet. Wait and see how that goes. As you surmised, I've given Marshall the lead role with this, since I've been so wrapped up with a case in Tucson. I should have that all tied up before Thanksgiving."

"That's next week."

Just then Augusta knocked on the door frame to my office.

"You've got a call, Mr. Williams. It's an Arthur Graven-wood. Do you want me to transfer it to your office or take a message? I told him I'd check to see if you were available."

"Transfer the call, Augusta."

Nate stood and shrugged. "That's Tucson calling, and I'd better answer."

As he walked back to his office, I realized something. Nate didn't have family nearby and neither did Marshall. I imagined they'd be spending their Thanks-giving eating takeout food and drinking beer. That thought was downright depressing. I knew Augusta had plans to go out to dinner with her canasta group. As for me, I'd be joining my mother, Shirley, and Lucinda at my mother's house.

My mother had already ordered a large turkey from the HoneyBaked Ham Company, and Shirley was bringing cornbread stuffing and sweet potato pie. Lucinda planned to bake apple and pumpkin pies. I was in charge of bringing the rolls. That, in and of itself, summed up the confidence everyone had in my culinary talents.

It was a no-brainer. As I stared at my computer screen, I knew my mother would be more than happy to have Nate and Marshall join us. It would be open season for her matchmaking as well as a chance to pry into the investigation.

I picked up the phone to call my mother before I lost my nerve. "Hi! Glad you didn't rush out anywhere yet. I need to ask you something."

"Is it about Miranda and Cliff? What else do you need to know? Are those men in your office looking into it? I'll tell you one thing, I'm going to keep an eagle eye on Sue Ellen this afternoon at rehearsal. Cliff, too. If there's something going on between them, I'll spot it. Myrna's going to do the same."

"Uh, yeah, sure. That sounds good, but that's not why I called. Listen, I was wondering . . . Nate and Marshall don't have any plans for Thanksgiving. At least I don't think they do, so—"

"You don't have to say a word, Phee. Of course they can come. Shirley always brings too much stuff, and I ordered a small ham in addition to the giant turkey, in case someone wanted something different. We've got plenty of food. Good thinking. The way to a man's heart is through his stomach."

Ugh. I hope whoever came up with that expression chokes on their dinner. "Okay. Great. I'll invite them. What time?"

"Have them come at two. We'll eat at three. Plenty of time to digest our food before it gets late."

"Thanks, Mom. It's really nice of you."

"Like I said—"

"Don't say it. Don't say it again. I'll talk to you later."

Given the fact I had already convicted Sue Ellen of murder, or at least *wanted* to do so, it seemed a waste of my time to talk with Chuck. Still, the consensus from the other players was that something was off with him. Since I didn't have any plans for the evening, I thought I'd stop by the rehearsal on my way home from work and see if I could arrange to have a few words with the guy.

It was a little past six when I walked into the auditorium. The players were almost finished rehearsing act two. I knew this, not because I was familiar with the play, but because my mother had given me a dog-eared copy of the script. Maybe she thought there were clues in there that could lead me to the killer, but Agatha Christie wasn't going to be much help.

My mother stood off to the side of the stage whispering Chuck's lines to him. It was pitiful. Too bad the play wasn't a comedy. I waited it out until the play ended and Cliff shouted, "Players down in front for notes."

"Psst! Phee! You'll get a better view up here!" How Herb was able to spot me in the dim auditorium was anyone's guess.

I tried to be discreet and motioned that I intended to remain where I was.

"What are you pointing at, cutie?"

I gave up and shouted back I had no intention of going up on the catwalk. Surprising how a voice carried in a semi-empty auditorium.

"Phee!" It was my mother. She was one of the first cast members to make their way to the front seats for the play notes. "Come on over and take a seat next to me. No one will notice."

I wasn't about to argue, because that would have been worse in terms of drawing attention to myself. I sank into the seat next to my mother. Thankfully, it was an end seat, near the outside aisle.

Slowly, the cast and crew members filled in the front rows and waited for Cliff. Chuck was seated a few rows back on the center aisle and no one was sitting near him. I didn't need to be hit over the head to make my move.

I gave my mother a nudge and whispered, "I'm going over to talk with Chuck."

Before she could say anything, I got up and cut through the empty row behind me and walked back to the center row where I plunked myself down directly behind the worst thespian I think the theater had ever seen.

Cliff was now sitting on a small stool directly in front of the orchestra pit. He had a handful of notes and didn't look too happy. "People, people, people. The play isn't a month away! It's coming at us like a freight train, and some of you have *yet* to learn your lines."

Chuck bent down his head and placed his hands over it, as if shielding himself from Cliff's words. I don't know why, but a lump formed in my throat.

Cliff continued to speak, and everyone held their collective breath. From timing to blocking, he scrutinized everything. "And let this be a clarion call to all of you. Enunciate. I repeat, enunciate. You must slow down and speak each word clearly, slowly, and carefully. Otherwise, it becomes gibberish for the audience."

Under his breath, Chuck mumbled, "I don't think I can do this."

I leaned over, tapped him on the shoulder and, in a voice as low as I could possibly make, said, "Don't be so hard on yourself."

He spun around in his seat and looked directly at me. Meanwhile, Cliff had moved to the individual scene notes, and I knew it would be a long session.

Chuck spoke softly through the side of his mouth while staring directly at Cliff. "Every time that jerk opens his mouth, I feel like punching it."

My head was practically leaning against the back of his seat. "Tough director?"

"He's had Sue Ellen in tears more than once."

"From what I've heard, that isn't too hard."

"It wasn't about the play."

"Huh? What do you mean?"

"I think they were dating."

Suddenly Cliff's voice got louder and I was afraid he might have heard Chuck and me talking. I held absolutely still and listened.

"Fluid movements. Fluid movements. That last scene looked choppy. We'll take a ten minute break and rehearse the final scene in act two."

Groans and mumbling filled the auditorium as Cliff stood and walked toward the stage manager, who was holding his own set of notes. Presumably for the crew. Quickly the stage manager yelled, "Crew only. I have a few things to go over with you."

As Chuck started to stand, I did the same. "What makes you say they were dating? Cliff and Sue Ellen."

"Um. Gosh. I don't know why I spouted off like that. None of my business. It's just that since Miranda's murder, I haven't been able to concentrate on a darned thing. I get on stage and my mind goes blank."

I didn't know what to say. Hypnosis? Meditation? A session or two with a good psychologist? Instead, I simply stood there as if my mind had gone blank as well.

Chapter 20

The crew started to fill in the seats at the front of the auditorium while the cast members who were not in the final scene made a quick escape for fear Cliff might decide to run a scene they *were* in. As I turned to the left, I saw my mother waving me over to her. I pushed both of my arms out in front and held up my hands as if I was trying to stop a train. She got the message and nodded.

Then I turned back to Chuck. "Um, about Cliff and Sue Ellen dating . . . this is really important. Um, er, well, you do know I work for Williams Investigations, so any little thing that might help us out would really be appreciated."

Chuck looked around and didn't say anything at first. I was about to plead with him again when he finally spoke.

"I don't want anyone to overhear me. I'm not a gossip monger or anything."

"I understand. But this is different."

"I know. I realize that."

Again, Chuck stood there as if he was back on stage waiting to be prompted. I decided not to rush him and waited it out. It was only seconds but it felt like forever until the guy actually opened up.

"I never saw Cliff and Sue Ellen together, other than during regular rehearsals when we were all in the auditorium. But, I did see Cliff and Miranda get into an ugly fight, and Miranda accused him of carrying on with Sue Ellen."

"Go on. What happened?"

"When we first started rehearsing, all of us were seated in the auditorium. It wasn't until later when the actors had to wait backstage. It was the end of the practice when Cliff asked Miranda to remain on stage to go over her part. All of the other actors had already left the theater. When I got to my car, I realized my keys must have dropped out of my pocket while I was sitting."

"Uh-huh, uh-huh. Then what?"

"When I walked back into the auditorium, the houselights were off, but I still found my way to where I had been sitting. Those little safety side lights stay on, you know."

Yes. Yes. Who cares about the stinking little safety lights. Come on! "So, I take it you found your keys."

"Well, yes. I had to bend down and look under a few seats in my row. And that's when I heard them. At first I thought they were running lines. I hate to admit it, but I wasn't totally familiar with the play at that point. But then, well . . . I knew it wasn't lines, because Cliff was talking about a reconciliation and Miranda said that as long as he was, oh dear, I can't really say this in mixed company."

"It's okay. It's okay. I'm sure I've heard worse."

"Miranda said that as long as he was schtupping her understudy, reconciliation was the last thing she would agree to. Then Cliff said he wasn't screwing anyone, and that when it came to screwing, she should know all about it. That's when she slapped him. Really slapped him."

It was as if I'd switched on the television to catch the latest episode of *Telemundo*. Hot, steamy, and riveting. "Wow! Er, well, that's a shame. Was anyone else around to see that? The slap, I mean."

"I don't think anyone was in the auditorium, but some of the light crew might have still been on the catwalk, and there were definitely people backstage and on the side of the stage."

"How do you know that?"

"Because I could hear voices. They carry in this theater."

"Thank you, Mr. Mitchenson, for sharing that. I'll review it discreetly with my colleagues in our office."

He nodded and slunk out of the theater. I hoped I hadn't upset him even further because that would mean he'd never learn his lines. Meanwhile, my mother stood a good twelve or fifteen feet away, waiting for me.

She had just finished talking to Myrna, who headed out the nearest exit door. "Well? What did you find out? Tell me when we get outside. They're still talking down in front."

I glanced to my side and could see the crew sitting attentively as Richard went over the run-through notes.

"You won't believe this, Mom. No one will."

"Did you have anything to eat before you came here? It's still early. Everything's open. Why don't we grab something at Bagels 'N More, and you can tell me what you found out."

"Let me guess. The other ladies are going to be there, too. Right?"

"Only Shirley and Lucinda. So, what do you say?"

"I'll meet you there in a few minutes."

If it wasn't for Bagels 'N More, I don't know what my mother and her friends would do. The place just seemed to lend itself to prolonged conversation. I was the first one to arrive, so I got us a table adjacent to the front window. Shirley spotted me immediately and rushed over, Lucinda trailing her by a few paces.

"Hi, Phee! Your mother stopped to talk with Herb in the parking lot."

"Here?"

"Oh no. The one at the Stardust Theater. Herb wouldn't be coming here at night. This is more of a morning place for him."

"That's right," Lucinda said. "Those old codgers stir up more tattletale than any of us women. Especially first thing in the morning with a cup of coffee."

No sooner did Shirley and Lucinda sit down when my mother walked in and charged toward me.

"Well? Don't keep me in suspense. What did you find out from Chuck? Why can't he remember his lines? Is it a guilty conscience? What?"

I started to open my mouth, but that was as far as I got.

My mother kept talking. This time to her friends. "Phee spoke with Chuck tonight. I was going to tell you, but there wasn't time. Something odd about that man. Too quiet. Too nervous."

"He may have a reason to be nervous," I said.

I was about to let them in on what Chuck had told me when I caught my tongue. I had promised the guy I would be discreet, and there was nothing remotely discreet about offering up information to Shirley, Lucinda, and my mother. I might as well post it publically on Facebook. Then again, I felt the need to offer up something since my mother had this innate ability to see right through me. I stuck with a piece of information they already knew. Or thought they knew.

"Uh, remember when Myrna said Miranda slapped Cliff? It's true. Chuck saw her do it. They didn't know he was still in the building."

"Lordy, Lordy. Myrna was right all along. Why did Miranda do that? What did Chuck say?"

"That he saw her slap the director." I wasn't about to get into the details. It would be all over the theater, not to mention Sun City West.

My mother motioned for the waitress with one hand and motioned for me to talk with the other. It was a talent I would never master. "There must be a reason," she said. "What do you think it was?"

I shrugged and bit my lip. There was no way I was going to let my mother keep me on the defensive. "You know, Chuck's very distraught over Miranda's death. It could be what's preventing him from learning his lines."

My mother let out a sigh. "He hardly knew her. Or did he?"

"Only from the play. Anyway, I'm sure he'll learn his lines in time for opening night."

"I should certainly hope so. Sue Ellen learned hers in a heartbeat, as well as the blocking. And she didn't have all that onstage rehearsal time like Chuck."

Lucinda stopped staring at the menu for a moment and looked directly at my mother. "Well, Harriet, maybe some people are fast learners."

I had a theory about Sue Ellen, and, thanks to what Chuck told me, I was beginning to believe she was responsible for Miranda's murder. What I desperately needed to find out was if she was having an affair with

Cliff. Sure, Marshall promised he'd talk to the guy, but I had another plan.

"Mom, can Myrna make me a copy of that program she found from the Peoria Players? I want to check out something. Maybe she can scan it and send it to my email."

I'd barely finished my sentence when all three of them started laughing.

"What? What's so funny?"

"Lordy, Phee," Shirley said. "Myrna is the last person who would know how to scan anything. She had a panic attack when her son replaced her old printer with one that scans, faxes, and copies. So, what did she do? She went around to garage sales to find an old relic that only makes copies."

I was absolutely speechless. Literally speechless. For at least three or four seconds.

"Okay, so maybe she can use her old relic, make me a copy, and give it to my mother tomorrow at rehearsal. You *are* rehearsing tomorrow, aren't you?"

My mom nodded and replied, "From eleven to one."

"Great. How about you get in touch with Myrna, and I'll stop by your house tomorrow after one?"

"Fine. But why do you need that program? What are you planning to do with it?"

"I want to see who else was in that play and find out if they know anything about a possible affair between Sue Ellen and Cliff. Those programs all show pictures of the players with little write-ups if I'm not mistaken. It shouldn't be too hard to locate someone from that cast."

"Probably a lot easier than locating that waitress. Where did she go?" My mother sat up in her seat and scoured the room.

"It's a Friday night, Harriet," Lucinda reminded my mother. "You know how busy this place gets."

Just then, the waitress, who was a few tables away, caught my mother's eye and rushed over. "Forgive me, ladies. It's been a crazy night. I've got coffees for you and some bagel crisps on the house. Whew! I can finally take your orders."

Thankfully, she remembered that my mom and her friends had to have separate checks and proceeded accordingly. I ordered the chicken and artichoke salad on a pumpernickel bagel. Everyone else opted for something that involved cream cheese.

When the waitress finally left, Shirley changed the subject from Sue Ellen to Miranda's ghost. "What about investigating Miranda's ghost? That was *not* a hologram the other night. Cecilia and I saw her rise up from the ground and hover behind that couch on the stage. Lordy, it took me hours to fall asleep, and then only when I found a red ribbon and tied it to the foot of my bed. It wards off evil spirits."

Dear God. Here we go.

Instead of trying to placate her or argue there was no such thing as supernatural spirits, I tried another tactic. "Um, you said you saw Miranda behind the couch. Hovering. Then the lights got dim."

"That's right. Cecilia and I both saw her."

"Let me ask you something. Where was she standing in relation to those trapdoors? I know there's the one in front where Gordon fell, but what about the others?"

Shirley shuddered. "I wasn't thinking about trapdoors when I saw that malevolent spirit looming in front of us."

"You think someone did this to scare the likes out

of unsuspecting women?" my mother asked. "What kind of a lunatic does that?"

"The kind who's trying to create a diversion. Look, how about instead of me stopping by your house to-morrow to get a copy of that program, I pick it up at the theater. I can be there a few minutes before one, and I'll find a way to check out the location of those trapdoors."

"I have a better idea. I mean, sure, check the trap-doors, but I think we can find out for certain if there is a malevolent spirit floating around the theater."

"Um, what did you have in mind?"

"We'll use Streetman. Dogs are known to have extrasensory perception when it comes to things like that. As soon as we're done here, we'll go home, get the dog, and take him into the theater. The cleaning crew will still be there."

Shirley wiped some bagel crisp crumbs from the side of her lips and nodded. "Your mother's right. Lordy, if Miranda's evil spirit is lurking, Streetman will know it. You and your mother can check it out and let me know."

I tried to keep my voice low. "Streetman wouldn't know an evil spirit from a piece of day-old cheese. This is ridiculous. And even on a good day, all of you know how weird that dog is. Um, sorry, Mom."

The look on my mother's face told me I might have gone a bit too far. "The dog may have his issues, I'll give you that, but when it comes to matters like this, I trust his instincts. I say we go home and get him."

"Twenty minutes."

"What?"

"That's all the time I'm going to give you. I'll agree to this little escapade, but I'm not making a night of it. I've got a busy day ahead of me tomorrow. The theater trapdoors. Remember? I like dealing with tangible things."

"Will you be bringing Marshall tomorrow?"

"What? No. Tomorrow's Saturday. Besides, he's tracking down something else on the case."

"Speaking of Marshall, did he say he can make it for Thanksgiving? And what about Nate?"

"Er, uh, well, I meant to ask them, but I didn't get a chance. I'll do it first thing Monday."

Shirley stopped thinking about malevolent spirits for a moment and caught me completely off guard. "So . . . Nate and Marshall. Do you have your pick? That Marshall is certainly easy on the eyes, but your boss isn't so bad either. Oh Lordy me! You're blushing, Phee."

I glared at my mother and then looked at Shirley. "I don't know what my mother told everyone, but I have a strictly working relationship with my boss and his partner."

Lucinda put her coffee cup down and whispered, "Maybe it's time to rethink that."

"Well," my mother said. "Phee and I had best get going if we expect to get back into the theater with Streetman."

"Call us tonight, Harriet," Lucinda said. "I don't care how late it is. I want to know what happened."

And I want to know how this even started.

Chapter 21

Streetman was wriggling and whining in the giant canvas tote my mother had placed him in. And while the tote said LIFE'S A BEACH, I'm betting the dog knew what the third word should have been. She had the tote slung over her shoulder as we walked inside the theater. Sure enough, the doors were still unlocked, and the cleaning ladies were busy.

One of them was using a large dust mop to clean the corridors, and I imagined the other one was either in the auditorium or perhaps cleaning the restrooms.

My mother shouted to the one with the mop. "We'll only be a few minutes. We have to finish up in the costume room."

"What do we do now?" I asked.

My mother looked around and sighed. "It probably doesn't matter. Let's walk into the auditorium, take Streetman out of the tote bag, and see what he does."

"If he does what I think he might do, I'm not cleaning it."

My mother ignored my comment as if I'd never said it and proceeded down the hallway until we got to the main auditorium doors. "The dimmer lights are still on. Good. We can see where we're going."

We didn't go far. Streetman walked up and down the aisles sniffing at the seats and whining.

"Does that mean anything?" I asked. "Why is he whining?"

"Darned if I know. But he does that once in a while. Whines for no reason. Well, not a reason I would know. Let's keep walking around here."

The dog kept looking up at my mother as if to say, "Can we get the heck out of here now?"

The stairwell to the catwalk was a few feet away, and my mother convinced me to carry Streetman in his tote partway up the stairs to see if he could sense anything. He didn't. And the only thing I sensed was his weight. Dead weight. He decided to lie there, limp and heavy.

"Nothing supernatural up here," I said. "Let's go onstage and backstage and get this over with."

Streetman pranced around the stage, rubbing himself against the furniture like a cat. On one occasion he sneezed and shook his head. On another he sniffed the rug that covered one of the trapdoors and tried to roll on it. As far as the other trapdoors were concerned, he ignored them. Not so much as a sniff. Then again, they didn't have smelly rugs to roll on.

"I don't think Miranda's ghost is onstage," I said.

My mother looked up as if she expected something to swoop down on us. "No, I suppose you're right. Let's go into the costume and dressing rooms. Shirley says ghosts are known to inhabit places where their spirit is at unrest."

"And you think it's the costume room? Why? Did Miranda have an issue with her costume?"

"Don't be absurd. For all we know, there could be other spirits inhabiting this place."

"Oh brother."

A few yards away, I heard the two cleaning ladies speaking to each other. Some sort of Slavic language, I thought.

My mother suddenly remembered that the dressing rooms and the costume room needed a key. "You know some Spanish. Ask the ladies if they can unlock the rooms for us."

"First of all, I know menu items, and second of all, they don't speak Spanish."

"You won't know unless you try. Go."

The ladies didn't speak Spanish. But they knew enough English to unlock the dressing rooms and the costume room for us. One of them pointed to her watch, and I nodded.

"We need to make this quick, Mom. They have to lock up and get out of here. If Streetman was going to sense a ghost, he would have done so by now."

"Give him a chance."

The dressing rooms were a bust. The dog walked in, whined, and walked out. At one point I thought he was going to leave his calling card, but it turned out he was just circling around to bite his tail.

"Pray to the gods Streetman doesn't sense anything in the costume room, or Shirley will never take a step back into this building," my mother said.

"From what we've seen so far, I don't think there's anything to worry about."

Then, everything changed. Streetman growled the second he walked into the costume room. It was a soft, low growl, but a growl nonetheless.

"Uh-oh. This isn't good," I said. "What's his problem? And please don't tell me he senses a ghost."

Shirley had arranged everyone's costumes neatly on two long racks that spanned the length of the room. Off to the back was some closet space my mom said was stuffed full of boxes and loose clothing. "It's a catchall. Shirley says once the play is over, she plans to organize it."

The dog continued to growl.

"Well, he's sensing something," my mother said. "I've never seen him so agitated."

"Maybe it's an odor on one of the costumes. Dogs have an amazing sense of smell."

"It's not an odor. If it were an odor he'd be growling at everyone he comes in contact with," my mother said.

The low growls grew in intensity as the dog inched toward the closet space. Then, out of nowhere, snarls and snapping.

"My God! She's in here!" my mother shouted. "Miranda's horrible spirit is in this room."

By now, Streetman was standing in front of the closet barking like crazy. I grabbed the doorknob and flung the door open before I had a chance to think twice. I half expected something to jump out at us. Instead, I found myself staring at old cardboard cartons and wadded up clothing stuffed into every cranny. In some instances, the cardboard looked so old I thought it was going to disintegrate.

Streetman bared his teeth and continued to growl.

"This is really weird," I said, "even for him."

I looked at the dog again. The hairs on his back were standing up and he was actually shaking. Shaking and growling.

I reached over to pet him, and he snapped. "Yikes. Maybe he smells something that reminds him of a bad experience he had."

"Or maybe it's Miranda's spirit."

Just then one of the cleaning ladies knocked on the door frame to the costume room. She took one look at Streetman and waggled her fingers.

I knew what she meant. "Mom, see if you can put him back in the canvas tote. We should get out of here."

My mother took a few steps toward the dog, but he wasn't having any part of it. He raced over to the closet and began to paw at the nearest box.

"Can you get him away?" I asked. "He's going nuts."

"He senses something."

"Um, more than likely he smells something."

Streetman continued to paw at the box, pausing only to bark and growl. At one point he lunged at it and bit the edge. The cardboard collapsed inside the box.

"I'm telling you, Mom, there's something in that box that's got his attention, that's all."

My mother tried calling the dog, but he ignored her. Selective hearing must apparently run in our family.

"That does it!" I said. "It's late, and I've got things to do." With that, I walked over to the closet, pulled out the box, and gave it a kick. "Hey, for all we know, there may be mice or worse in this box."

"Streetman's scared of mice," my mother said. "He wouldn't be acting that way. You know, Shirley said sometimes spirits can inhabit the—"

"Oh for God's sake, no one's inhabiting anything."

I reached over to open the box, but the dog beat me to it. He tore into the cardboard, and, in what could best be described as sheer madness, he ripped the thing apart, flinging the contents all over the room. All I could see were beady eyes, round black noses, and, in some cases, teeth. Streetman grabbed the nearest one and shook it like a play toy. Then he growled and shook it again. My mother was horrified.

I tried not to laugh, but I couldn't help it. "Yep, there's Miranda's spirit for you. Or should I say 'spirits'? Seems we've got mink, muskrat, and ermine. Oh, and if I'm not mistaken, isn't that some sort of beaver pelt?"

Streetman wasted no time attacking the pelts. No sooner did he grab one and shake it ferociously when he moved on to the next one. Snarling. Growling. Biting. Small clumps of fur became airborne.

"I hope the Footlighters aren't planning to do a twentieth century period play anytime soon," I said. "Your dog seems to have an issue with the wardrobe."

The fracas continued as my mother took a step closer to the dog. "Stop that, Streetman! Stop that this instant!"

I rolled my eyes. "He doesn't seem to follow commands well."

"That's because he thinks he's protecting us. He doesn't know the pelts are harmless."

"Mom, we've got to pick up those things and get them back in the box before they're no longer usable."

"I know. I know."

She bent down and grabbed what I presumed to be a dyed muskrat tail from Streetman's mouth. "Give that to Mommy. Give that to Mommy, now!"

For the next five minutes, my mother played tug-of-war with Streetman. The dog was in his glory, and I was ready to explode. Finally, I had an idea. I found an old, smelly rag in the costume room and somehow was able to substitute it for one of the costume stoles. As my mother and the dog wrestled with the thing, I gathered up the remaining wraps, some of them covered in dog saliva, and shoved them back in the torn box before stashing the box in the closet. Streetman stopped growling and whined.

"We'll bring over a new box and replace that one," my mother said as the dog sniffed around the room. "And not a word about this to anyone. As far as Shirley and Lucinda are concerned, Streetman's venture was inconclusive. Understand?"

"Oh, believe me, I'm not admitting to anything. Although we probably should get those things dry-cleaned. It must have been the musty odor that attracted him in the first place, because those stoles are processed."

The poor dog was exhausted by the time he was plunked back into the canvas tote and carried to the car. He didn't make a move until my mother plopped him on the couch and fussed over him, muttering "my brave, brave little man." Then she looked at the floor and shrieked. "Teeth! There are teeth on the floor!"

"Oh my gosh," I said. "He must have pulled them off one of the stoles and kept them in his mouth."

My mother walked to the kitchen, got a paper towel, and removed the teeth. "Don't tell a soul about this. Understand?"

"Believe me, it's not going to come up in any conversation I'm about to have." *Now and well into the next decade.*

"Good. Good. So, maybe you'll have better luck with those trapdoors tomorrow. And don't forget, be sure to find out if Nate and Marshall can make it for Thanksgiving."

"No problem. I'll tell them to bake a pie for you and trap an animal for the dog."

Chapter 22

If it wasn't ghosts, it was my love life. Or lack of it.
How I survived dinner last night and that awful experience at the theater was anyone's guess. In my wildest
imagination, I never pictured the dog going berserk
over some animal stoles. And now I was faced with a
worse scenario—Thanksgiving with Nate, Marshall,
and the lunatic fringe. Well, it wasn't too late to avoid
it. After all, I hadn't invited the men yet.

As I placed my Jamaica Me Crazy, a Wolfgang Puck
favorite of mine, into the Keurig, I had second thoughts.
On the one hand, I didn't want anyone to feel uncomfortable at my mother's house, especially if she or her
friends started dropping not so subtle hints about
how I was available for dating. Then again, I felt badly
that Nate and Marshall would be alone for the holiday. In the end, guilt trumped comfort, and I decided
to offer up the invitation on Monday. Meanwhile, I
spent Saturday morning dusting, vacuuming, and
tackling a substantial pile of laundry. It amazed me
how much dust could permeate the door seals and
windows to leave a fine film of red specks all over.

Still, it was a far cry from dealing with those brutal Minnesota winters.

I jotted off a quick email to Kalese, who was feeling pretty low she wasn't able to spend Thanksgiving with me. At least she had made plans with some of her teacher friends and was looking forward to flying out here for Christmas. Then I grabbed a strawberry yogurt for lunch and headed over to the Stardust Theater. It was twelve-twenty.

It wasn't as if I expected to find a shimmery dress on the floor beneath one of the trapdoors, but I needed to see just how feasible it would be for someone to pull off a stunt like that. All they'd need was a semi dark room and someone with a decent wig. Shirley and Cecilia's imaginations would (and in this case, *did*) fill in the rest.

Without a background in stagecraft, I was left to Google searches and the scant recollections I had when I was in a school play back in high school. What I discovered during my late nights on the computer was that there were literally countless different kinds of trapdoors used for all sorts of theatrical purposes, the most sophisticated being the ones in those illusion shows like David Copperfield. I seriously doubted Sun City West had shelled out the money for an automated system, especially since the theater was built in 1978 and designed to hold simple community events and performances.

Then there was the issue of the "trap room." Apparently the trapdoor opened into a small room beneath the stage. What I learned was that many college and university theater departments had their trap rooms as part of a ground floor that could serve any number of purposes from classrooms to storage areas. I figured the one I needed to scope out at the

Stardust would be more like a dark storage area in a sub-basement. And, not surprisingly, I was right.

My timing was spot-on when I got to the auditorium. The director had just completed his notes for the cast, and the stage manager told the crew to arrive a half hour early to the next rehearsal for their notes. My mother was seated down front on the center aisle, and I headed her way.

Myrna saw me first and rushed over. She grabbed my arm and ushered me into a seat before speaking. "Harriet has what you need. You know . . . the program."

"It's okay, Myrna. You don't have to whisper. There's no one around us."

"Do you think Sue Ellen's our killer? She doesn't strike me as a murderess."

"She knew Cliff before doing this show. I want to find out if they had a prior relationship that wasn't limited to the stage. Maybe someone from the production of *The Odd Couple* will know that."

"So you think she and Cliff were in cahoots to get rid of Miranda?"

"Uh, no . . . not exactly. I mean, I don't know. That's what I need to find out, and please don't say anything to anyone."

"Oh you can count on me. Only your mother knows about it. And Cecilia. And Lucinda. And . . ."

Oh what the hell! Why not come out and announce, "Phee is trying to find out if Sue Ellen and Cliff were once an item."

My stomach started to rumble as I thanked Myrna and walked toward my mother, who was a few feet from me, heading up the aisle.

"I've got the program, Phee. Quick, stash it in your bag before anyone sees you."

"My gosh, this isn't *The Man from U.N.C.L.E.* No one cares if you're handing me a piece of paper."

"You never know. Here. Take it."

I slipped the program into my bag and watched as the cast and crew filtered out of the auditorium.

"Listen," I said. "I need to check out what's below those trapdoors. Any chance you or someone you know can show me without making too much of a scene?"

"Hold on. I'm pretty sure Wayne can. He did the set construction, and they were always going down into the storage area."

Next thing I knew, my mother belted out, "Wayne! Are you still here?" I swore it echoed off of the walls.

Wayne was above us on the catwalk with a few of the other men and shouted back, "What do you need?"

It was followed by, "I can't tell you out loud," which produced a bunch of caterwauling from his buddies.

"Hang on, Harriet, I'll be right down."

My mother hustled Wayne into a corner by one of the exits and told him I needed to see what was below the stage. Since he had no idea why on earth I would need to do such a thing, my mother had to fabricate something. It was better than rehashing what Shirley and Cecilia thought they saw. Wayne would've dismissed that as a waste of his time.

"Phee was here the other day when Cliff said he was going to make sure those trapdoors stayed locked. She told her boss she'd check on that."

Wayne shrugged and motioned for us to follow him. "Whatever you do, don't pull on those side curtains. Don't even shove them back. They're as old as the hills, and some of the grommets are coming loose from the top. Can't get them fixed in time for the show."

I kept my hands to myself as we walked backstage to a small door near stage right. It wasn't locked, and as soon as Wayne opened it, he flipped on the lights—small, dim wall lights that reminded me of the staircase to Dr. Frankenstein's lab.

"Be careful," he said. "The stairs down to the basement are steep."

"I'll wait here," my mother announced, "to make sure no one turns the lights off on you."

Wayne walked in front of me and waited until I reached the bottom step. I was standing in a large rectangular room also dimly lit with wall lights. Most structures in southern Arizona don't have a basement. But this was a theater and its builder, Del Webb, must've seen a play or two in his time. Plays that needed trapdoors.

"Just so you know," Wayne went on, "I carry a flashlight in my pocket. Can't be too careful around here. Come on. I'll show you where the trapdoors are."

My eyes were getting adjusted to the semidarkness, and an exit sign hung directly across from where I was standing.

"Where does that go? The exit, I mean?"

Wayne swept his flashlight across the room in a grand gesture. "Secondary exit. It's an even steeper staircase that leads directly outside around back, where the Dumpsters are."

At the mere mention of the word "Dumpster," I cringed. My first experience in dealing with murder in Sun City West had me Dumpster diving in front of a large senior citizen apartment complex. I had no desire to try it again.

"So, um, where are the trapdoors? All I can see is this dark room."

"Watch your feet. Two of the doors are directly in front of you, and they have automated step-ups."

"What?"

Wayne flashed the light in front of me, and I could see what appeared to be wooden boxes on the floor.

"Look straight down. Each of those has a button in the middle. When you climb on the box and step on the button, the box starts to rise until you're on the stage. Step on it twice, and it goes down. It's automated, like I said, but really old school. When they use these trapdoors, they're supposed to put doggie gates around them so the actors and crew know where they are."

"Doggie gates? You've got to be kidding me."

"Hey, I didn't build this. It was state of the art in the seventies. It's a mechanical crank system. Not a whole lot different from the original ones in the eighteen hundreds. Still has to be oiled and cleaned so it doesn't get stuck."

"What about the other trapdoor? The one Gordon fell through?"

"That one's a few feet behind you, and it's not automated. It's just an opening for scenes where the actor has to disappear in a hurry. That huge foam padding against the wall has to be placed under the trap so no one gets injured. Lucky for Gordon it was there. Of course, now that the trapdoors are locked from top and bottom, it's not a worry."

"Do you know who moved the foam padding?"

"Nope. Probably Cliff or Richard when they made sure the trapdoors were locked."

Wayne made a point of flashing his light under each of the doors so I could see that the eye pin door latches were secure.

"Wayne, do you know the last time these doors were used in a show?"

"Gimme a second. I need to think about it."

While Wayne stood there looking at the doors, my eyes finally allowed me to see what was against the walls. It was a veritable treasure trove of furniture, mirrors, and miscellaneous hardware, not to mention a small rack holding some costumes. The whole area struck me as the perfect hiding place for spiders, scorpions, and God knows what else.

"Got it," he said. "It was a few years back. Ellowina directed *A Christmas Carol* and had the ghosts appear through those trapdoors. That's why some of the costumes are down here. Too risky to have the actors wear them as they walk down the stairs. Since it's Arizona, we don't have to worry about mold. Anyway, the trapdoors haven't been used since, and I should know since I've been working for the Footlighters since two thousand eight."

"So, who keeps the mechanisms from seizing up?"

"Daniel in building maintenance is supposed to, but, between you and me, I doubt it. Usually falls to the play director, and even if their play isn't using the trapdoors, the director checks on them for future use. At least Ellowina did. Not sure it's something Cliff's going to do since he's only temporary for this play. I'll be glad when Ellowina returns for the spring production. I heard she was recuperating at her niece's place in Surprise."

"It's a good thing she has a niece who can take care of her. Pretty nasty thing, food poisoning . . . Um, before we go back upstairs, I've got another question. Why on earth is there a chemical storage cabinet down here? I can see the primary color codes on the door."

"It's a regulation from the county. Has to be locked, too. Since we use chemicals from time to time, we're required to store them properly. They inspect the buildings at prearranged intervals. We've got another cabinet upstairs in a separate closet near the dressing rooms."

"I see. Uh, out of curiosity, who has the keys, and what kind of chemicals are in there?"

"We bought some cheap padlocks from the hardware store, and the keys are hanging in the maintenance closet near the dressing rooms. I know for a fact we've got lubricating oils for the machines, cleaning oils, and solvent. Also chloroform."

"Chloroform? Why that?"

"It's a great solvent and cleaning agent, especially for old stage machinery. That is if you can stand that sweet, pungent odor. Even with a mask you can smell it."

"But don't you have to worry about passing out? Isn't that what kidnappers use in all the movies?"

"Yeah. In the movies. But in real life, all it will do is make you woozy. Someone would have to hold a soaked cloth over the victim's head for hours, I suppose, not seconds."

"My gosh, Wayne, you're a wealth of information and—"

"PHEE! WHAT'S TAKING YOU SO LONG? ARE YOU ALL RIGHT?" My mother's voice bounced off the stairwell walls and could be heard well into the basement.

"BE RIGHT UP! WE'RE FINE! Guess we should be heading up, huh? My mother's having a hissy fit."

"Yep."

Wayne walked ahead of me, his flashlight casually swinging from his arm. Even though we didn't need it to find our way to the stairs, it gave us a decent amount of extra light.

I walked past the piles of old furniture and bric-a-brac, glancing over at the rack of clothing. An elaborate velvet cape with a white faux trim hung there and I figured it had to be a costume for The Ghost of Christmas Present. Dangling on the hanger next to it was a cane that I presumed was meant for Scrooge, and some sort of silvery pointers that looked like wands. Then my eyes moved to another costume and I froze. It was a long, gray, shimmery dress and not something from Dickens.

"Wayne! Wait a second. Who else in the cast and crew knows about this basement area and the trapdoors?"

"Miranda, for one. She was always snooping around. But most of the time she was busy bothering the guys on the catwalk. Had a real thing about being noticed on stage."

"Who else?"

"Far as I know, that's it, except for Cliff and Richard. Oh yeah. And Sue Ellen."

"Sue Ellen?"

"It was a while back. Miranda was still alive. Look, I'm not one to go spreading rumors. It was probably nothing. I was backstage. Stayed late to fix a wobbly chair leg for the prop people. Nearly jumped out of my skull because I heard voices. Who did I see but Cliff and Sue Ellen coming up from the basement. They didn't see me, and I got busy real quick with the chair leg. Like I said, it was probably nothing."

Wayne held the door open for me, and I found myself staring right at my mother.

"My God, Phee. I thought you fell in a pit or something. The cleaning ladies are locking up."

I turned to Wayne and thanked him again before giving my undivided attention to my mother.

"Well? Did you find what you were looking for down there?"

"Oh yeah. Shirley and Cecilia saw an apparition all right, only this one is still breathing. Wait until we get outside, and I'll tell you about it."

My mother all but shoved me through the exit in order to find out what I had discovered in the basement.

No one would be able to hear me from where we were standing in the parking lot, but, to play it safe, I kept my voice low. "It's more than a coincidence that the shimmery outfit Shirley and Cecilia's ghost was wearing happened to turn up in the basement, on a rack of clothing that the actors use when they have to make quick changes before rising up through the trapdoors."

"What kind of deranged person would do a thing like that? Dress up to look like Miranda so they can give someone a heart attack? Oh no. OH NO! Do you think they were trying to kill Shirley or Cecilia?"

"No, no. And whatever you do, don't tell *them* that. I think there's got to be some real evidence that points to Miranda's killer, and it's right here in the theater. No one's going to find it if all these distractions keep pulling them away."

"Hmm. You may be right. It pains me, but I'm not going to say a word to Shirley or Cecilia. Let them believe it was a ghost."

"Yeah, my sentiments exactly. So, when's the next rehearsal?"

"Monday afternoon."

"I'll let Marshall know about what I saw. If he needs to stop by during rehearsal, I'm sure he will."

"What about you?"

"Unless there are bodies on the floor, I need to stick with my accounting."

"I'll call you after rehearsal."

"What else is new?"

Chapter 23

I realized my nights at the condo pool were numbered, even though the water was heated. At sixty degrees, the air temperature felt as if it had arrived from the Arctic Circle. Still, I didn't hesitate for a second when my friend Lyndy called later that evening and asked me to join her. Spending the afternoon searching for clues at the Stardust Theater had really wiped me out, and I couldn't imagine a better way to relax than to be in the water.

Meeting Lyndy when I first moved to Vistancia was the only breath of normalcy I'd had. Like me, she was dealing with some rather peculiar relatives in Sun City West and knew exactly what I was up against. Now, months later, as we clung to pool noodles and gazed at the mountains in the distance, it was Miranda's murder we were talking about and not our weird relatives.

Lyndy tossed her noodle over the edge of the pool and swam toward me. I was treading water in the shallow end, one hand on my noodle, the other flailing around in a halfhearted attempt to get exercise. I stopped splashing as she got closer so I could hear what she was saying.

"I'm surprised the sheriff's department let them continue with the play, considering one of the cast or crew members is probably the killer."

"Yeah. That's what I thought, too, but I figured they'd rather keep everyone right under their noses. That way they've got all the suspects in one place. And if the killer is one of them, maybe he or she will make a stupid move. Besides, they've got a sheriff's deputy on duty for rehearsals."

"You must have your own idea by now as to who the murderer is. Am I right, Phee?"

"I've got a theory. Lots of smoke and wind, but nothing substantive. In fact, I had planned on doing a little sleuthing on my own, but I'm having second thoughts."

"What do you mean?"

I looked around and made sure we were the only ones in the pool. "I have an idea it might be a cast member who was in another play with the same director. I even got a copy of that playbill from one of my mother's friends."

"Does your idea mean you've got a motive?"

"I think this woman was having an affair with the director and found out the guy wanted to get back together with his ex-wife, so—"

"So your suspect eliminated the competition. That makes sense in a tabloid sort of way."

"It does, doesn't it? Murdering the ex-wife isn't uncommon."

"Not in movie plots, anyway."

"Ugh. Nate and Marshall keep saying the same thing, but my gut feeling tells me I'm right. Anyway, I was going to check it out for myself but, by doing that, I would be going behind Marshall's back."

"Ouch. That's not good."

"I know. Especially since he promised he'd confront the director about the alleged affair."

"Or make-believe affair, if you're not right."

"Or if the director lies in order to cover it up. That's where my new information comes in. I have the names of the cast members who were in the play with my suspect. One of them is bound to know if the woman in question was having an affair with the director. Those things are kind of hard to keep under wraps."

"That's what you were going to check out?"

"Uh-huh. But in retrospect, I'm going to hand it all over to Marshall first thing Monday."

Lyndy and I finished our swim, toweled off, and raced back to our collective houses.

The next morning we met to hike at Lake Pleasant, something we had planned to do once the fall weather arrived. Thankfully, it was one of those glorious days in the southwest when the humidity was gone and the temperature was in the high seventies.

Lake Pleasant Regional Park was less than a half-hour's drive from Vistancia. In addition to two marinas, it had numerous hiking trails and was home to wild donkeys. The first time I hiked there, I was startled when they crossed my path. Now I treated it like the dog park, only there was no one to yell, "Poop alert!"

By early afternoon, Lyndy and I were exhausted. We stopped at the Lakeside Grill on the way home, stuffed ourselves with burgers and fries, and swore we'd diet the next day.

Lyndy ran a napkin across her chin and smiled. "So

you're absolutely sure you're not going to contact one of those Peoria cast members about the affair?"

"I'm tempted, but, like I said yesterday, I'm handing it over to Marshall. With directions."

"Directions? I thought *he* was the investigator."

"I'm handing him the cast list for *The Odd Couple*. It's basically an all-male cast, with only two women, and my suspect is one of them. It makes perfect sense to interview the other female cast member. Not to sound sexist, but if my person-of-interest was having an affair with the director, it would be more likely for her counterpart in the play to know what was going on."

"You should be the investigator, Phee. Seriously."

"I'll just be glad when the killer is finally caught. My mother is a nervous wreck, and her book club friends are one step away from adding Valium to their daily diet."

"Yeesh. Sounds brutal. When can I buy a ticket for the show?"

"Seriously? You want to see *The Mousetrap*?"

"After all of this? Of course."

"According to my mother, tickets go on sale tomorrow. They'll have a small window in front of the theater entrance, and sales will run from nine to two. Of course, you can get tickets at the door, too, or I can pick one up for you."

"Given the whole murder thing, they may be performing for a full house. Can you get me a ticket for opening night? Actually, make it two. I'll bring my aunt."

"I should bring you a headset that connects to the lighting crew. It would be more entertaining."

By the time I got home, all I wanted to do was

plop down on the couch and close my eyes. Between swimming last night and hiking this morning, I'd had enough exercise to last me the entire week.

The light on my answering machine was flashing and the callback number looked sort of familiar, but I couldn't place it. I pushed play and waited.

"Phee, it's Nate. Sorry to bother you on a Sunday, but it's important. I left a message on your cell but it must be turned off."

I quickly called him back. "Nate! Oh my gosh. Are you all right? Is Marshall all right? Is—"

"Everyone's fine, kiddo, but the office is under water, so to speak."

"What?"

"Yeah, I got a call from the fire department. There was a water main break, and our office, along with a few others, got flooded. Most of the water's been pumped out, and we've got a service crew coming in first thing tomorrow to deal with the carpeting, but I could use some help moving the paper files into plastic cartons. At least the small workroom is tiled so we can move the computers in there. Augusta's already on her way, and Marshall went to Home Depot to get the containers. He should be back soon."

"Sure thing. Give me thirty minutes and I'll be there. Do you need anything?"

"Yeah. The body of a twenty-year-old."

I laughed as I hung up the phone and raced to throw on a clean shirt. I figured my jeans would have to do. When I got to the office, Nate, Marshall, and Augusta were already working. Marshall gave me a quick wave before turning his attention back to the stack of containers.

Nate greeted me as well. Surprisingly, his voice was optimistic. "Thanks, Phee, and welcome to 'Water

World.' The floor's damp and the power's off until morning, but we've got plenty of daylight for the next few hours. SERVPRO is going to be moving our file cabinets and desks, so we need to get all of our paperwork into containers that we'll store in my car and Marshall's. Marshall and I have already moved the desktop units into the workroom. Then tomorrow night we should be able to get everything back in order. What a mess."

"Does the city know what happened?"

Augusta looked up from her desk. "Old pipes is what happened."

"She's right." Nate picked up a giant Rubbermaid bin and headed to his office. "Apparently this stuff happens more often than not, according to the fire chief. Once we get organized, I'm going to have Augusta scan all of our file documents and put them on CDs. Should have done that before."

"Too bad we can't have the carpeting torn up and tile put down."

"Not as long as we're tenants, I'm afraid. At least the owner is paying for the cleanup."

"Well, I'll get started in my office. I shouldn't be too long. Most of the business records are already on CDs."

"Wish I could say the same for the investigative reports," Marshall said. "Some of these are longer than a Russian novel with all of that intrigue. Hey, and speaking of clandestine activities, I pulled off one of my own. I purposely ran into Cliff Edwards on Saturday night."

"How?"

"I found out where his favorite watering hole was and happened to stop by. Turns out you may be right. Hard to say. That guy is a regular Lothario. I don't know what it is about theater directors, but I must be in the wrong business."

"About Sue Ellen . . . what did he tell you?"

"Not much. He was real cagey, which made my suspicion barometer hit the top. I have a feeling he was seeing her."

"I know how you can find out for sure. Well, maybe not for sure, but sure enough."

I then proceeded to tell him about Myrna and the playbill she had from *The Odd Couple*. It was all starting to make sense, and this time Marshall agreed with me.

"So, you want me to look up the lady who played one of those bird sisters?"

"Pigeon sisters. I said Pigeon sisters. According to the program, her name is Maeve Fletcher, and she played Cecily opposite Sue Ellen, who had the part of Gwendolyn. I've got a copy of the program at home, and the best part is, they've written little blurbs about all the actors. You know, their background, where they work . . . all that stuff. It was only a year or so ago so it shouldn't be too hard for you to find her. She was with the Peoria Players. They're a much younger crew than the Sun City ones, so she's probably still alive."

As soon as I said that, I bit my tongue. I hated to be so maudlin about some of the senior population, but with information about mortuaries and funeral arrangements arriving in the mail every other day, it was hard to ignore.

"Done deal. You can relax. It looks like we won't be in the office tomorrow anyway, so call me when you get home and read me the info. I'll take it from there."

If ever I felt like giving him a hug, that was the moment. Then, out of the blue, something occurred to me. Something I'd been putting off—Thanksgiving.

It was four days away, and I needed to offer up the invitation. "Before I forget, I need to ask you and Nate something." I motioned for him to follow me into Nate's office.

I don't know why I felt so nervous, but I did, and the words rushed out of my mouth. "I know it's really late notice, but if you're not doing anything, I mean, have any plans for Thanksgiving, my mother would love to have you join us. Not just us. Shirley and Lucinda are coming, too. I already checked with Augusta, and she's got plans with her canasta group. So, um . . . it would be the six of us."

I'd seen pictures of prisoners being led to the gallows who looked cheerier.

Nate glanced at Marshall. "That's so nice of your mother, Phee. Really. I'm not sure what Marshall's plans are, but I've got an aunt in Sierra Vista, not too far from Tucson. It's my mother's sister, and she's in her eighties. I promised I'd spend Thanksgiving with her. Then I plan to stay in Tucson. I've got a few things to finish up on a case down there. Thank your mom for me, okay?"

I nodded and prayed for another water main break to send torrents of liquid across the room. *I wonder what excuse Marshall will come up with?* I held my breath and waited. *Who knows? Maybe he's got a relative floating around somewhere in Arizona, or worse yet, he found a girlfriend.*

Marshall gave me a smile. "Wow. Gee. That's so unexpected and nice of your mother to think of me."

"So you'll be able to make it?"

"Um, actually no."

Here it comes. The long lost uncle.

"Since I don't know too many people yet, I contacted

St. Vincent de Paul in Phoenix. I'm going to be working at their shelter all day feeding the homeless."

Talk about unexpected.

"Oh, Marshall, that's a wonderful thing to do." *Yes. Feed the needy. Just don't find a girlfriend.* "Well, I'd better keep moving my stuff into those boxes."

I made a quick retreat and didn't emerge until every single one of my paper files and the contents of my desk were safely packed. When I finally stepped back into the main office, Marshall and Nate began to load the boxes into their cars. Marshall had also purchased one of those small folding hand trucks so none of us would get a hernia moving the stuff.

Nate offered to take us out for pizza, but the consensus was we were all too tired. Augusta put a sign on the door explaining we would reopen on Tuesday and changed the message on the answering machine. Thank goodness the phone had a battery backup. She also phoned Nate and Marshall's Monday appointments and rescheduled.

As Augusta and I headed out the door, Marshall said, "Don't forget to call me when you get home, Phee, and give me the information on the Pigeon woman."

"Someone from the play, huh?" Augusta asked when we were out the door.

"In a roundabout sort of way, yes."

"Tell me about it on Tuesday."

I laughed and headed to my car, the entire time thinking about Marshall feeding the homeless at St. Vincent de Paul. I was beginning to develop an even bigger crush on the guy.

It was already dusk when I unlocked the door to my casita and stepped inside. I was in one of my "might as well get this over with" moods and immediately walked over to the kitchen counter, where I'd stashed the playbill, along with some other miscellaneous flyers and takeout menus.

The write-up on Maeve Fletcher was sweet and succinct. She was originally from Idaho, married with two grown children, and had her own small business—"Gifts-on-the-Go"—in the historic district of Glendale. According to the article, she was "no stranger to theater, having performed in numerous community venues."

It would be simple enough. All Marshall had to do was drive to the historic district in Glendale and take it from there. He'd get to her store, hand her his card, and hopefully walk out with the information he needed. I, on the other hand, wouldn't be able to stop myself from ogling the knickknacks, cutesy gifts, and whatever else her store offered up. And if that wasn't bad enough, it would take an act of God to haul me away from the historic district.

I'd been there once with my mother, and we'd spent a full day perusing Victorian tearooms, French boutiques, artist studios, pastry shops (okay, we didn't just peruse those), and all sorts of clothing stores from handmade to designer. The area encompassed a large square known as Caitlin Court, and each shop, painted in a different pastel color, was its own little house. Yep, Marshall would be in and out of there in no time.

I picked up the phone and made the call.

He answered on the first ring, taking me by surprise. "Hey, Phee! That was quick."

"Um, yeah. I wanted to get this information to you before I got busy with something. I won't keep you.

You must be zonked out from all that packing and moving."

"I'm beat. but I'll live. Hold on a sec. Let me get a pen so I can write it down."

I glanced at the program and reread Maeve's write-up. As soon as Marshall got back on the line, I read it to him.

His groan took me by surprise. "Oh no. Gift shop. In a historic district, no less."

"Um, is that a problem for you?"

"Depends on how small and how cramped her dainty little shop is going to be. I'm always worried as hell when I get dragged into one of those places that I'm going to knock over an entire shelf of breakable figurines, or, worse yet, expensive breakable figurines."

Uh-oh. Sounds like he's familiar with those stores. But who drags him there? Hopefully his mother or grandmother.

"Sure you're okay with this?"

I swore the guy would probably have felt more comfortable walking through a construction site or even a sewage-processing plant.

"Yeah. I'll be fine. Oh, I meant to tell you something and completely forgot with all the stuff going on at the office. Remember when I told you the sheriff's department found a connection between Miranda and Sue Ellen?"

"Yeah. Back in Rhode Island at some hospital. The negligence thing involving Miranda. Why?"

"Because something about it kept bothering me. I think there's more to it, but with the HIPAA privacy laws, even the police will wind up with a watered-down version. So, I called the only person I knew who could work his way behind a smokescreen and come out smelling as clean as a whistle."

"Don't tell me you called—"

"Uh-huh. Rolo Barnes. Cyber sleuth extraordinaire. You remember Rolo, don't you?"

"Remember him? I had to buy him a brand new Cuisinart over a year ago when he tracked down some routing numbers for Nate and me. He was on a juicing diet. What kitchen gadgetry will he need now?"

"I have no idea. Last I heard he was on the Paleo Diet."

"Like in Paleolithic? Geez, doesn't he realize cavemen had really short lifespans? I mean, *really* short."

"Yeesh. I wonder if he thought of that. Doesn't matter. I'm sure there's some sort of high-end kitchen appliance that goes along with his new diet, but whatever it is, it'll be worth it, especially if he connects Sue Ellen with an ironclad motive for murder."

"But that was so long ago," I said.

"You know what they say about revenge."

"Not as much as they say about jealousy. The more I toss this over in my mind, the more convinced I am about the reason Sue Ellen killed Miranda. It wasn't the part in the play she wanted, it was the director."

"Don't get too ahead of yourself, Phee. Sue Ellen isn't the only one with a motive. There's still that lawsuit with Gordon over Miranda's foo-foo dog and the volatile stage relationships she had with Stanley, Cliff, and Ellowina, not to mention any residue from her prior involvement with Len."

"It's worse than a soap opera, isn't it? It's like everyone who crossed paths with Miranda had a motive to kill her."

"Motive or not, keep in mind they needed means and opportunity too. Miranda was killed on that catwalk, so it wasn't as if someone with Herculean strength dragged her body up those stairs after they murdered her."

"I'm guessing Gordon or Len could have over-powered her up there, but she was pretty evenly matched with Sue Ellen."

"The deputies think she was taken by surprise, and I tend to agree. That gave her killer the advantage. He or she could have pushed Miranda backward and then used her own necklace to strangle her before winding those electrical cords to make it look like an accident. The real conundrum is figuring out who took advantage of the opportunity."

"Took advantage?" I asked.

"Miranda's body was found on a Tuesday after-noon. She was last seen alive by cast and crew at the end of the rehearsal the day before. No one, not even her friend Paula, saw her leave the theater, but every-one assumed she must have. Paula had driven Miranda to rehearsal that day but figured she got a ride home with Cliff since she'd been doing that lately."

"That guy doesn't miss a beat, does he?"

Marshall made some sort of "hmmph" sound. "Ac-cording to my notes, the lighting crew stayed late to readjust some spotlights because Ellowina had tried something different and Cliff was making adjust-ments. The guys all left together and headed over to Curley's. A few of the actors were still milling around, so no one knew for sure who the last people out of the building were. I'm guessing the cleaning ladies and, of course, Miranda's killer."

"You think Miranda went up on that catwalk to readjust the spotlight and—"

"The murderer was probably watching Miranda's movements after the rehearsal and stayed out of sight long enough to surprise her on the catwalk. They had the perfect opportunity."

"What about Shirley's teal tunic on Miranda? How do you explain that?"

"I've seen that tunic, and it's long. Deputy Bowman showed it to me. Shirley won't go near it but according to my notes, it was left in plain sight in the costume room. Someone could have grabbed it to use as a disguise in the dark and sneak up on the catwalk."

"And pretend to be Shirley? She's the only person of color on this production."

"In the dark, on that catwalk, it wouldn't have mattered. I've been up there, and you can't see anyone's face clearly. Maybe in the new modern theaters with better low-level lighting, but not in this place. No way."

I had to admit, he made a good point. One that got me thinking. "Um, Shirley, Sue Ellen, and even Paula are all about the same height and weight as Miranda. Oh my gosh. Come to think of it, so are Len and Gordon. And in the dark . . ."

"Yeah. I know. Opportunity. Listen, it's getting late and you must be tired, too. I'll see what I can find out from Maeve if I don't break anything in there first. I'll talk to you on Tuesday. Enjoy your day off tomorrow, courtesy of some old pipes."

"Thanks, Marshall. For doing this. And don't worry. I'm sure that shop has glass coverage."

I threw on some old sweats and fixed myself a cheese and tomato sandwich before conking out on the couch, something I'd intended to do hours ago. Nothing feels as good as napping on the couch. With a full day off tomorrow, I could take care of all of those annoying little errands that I'd been putting off, from grocery shopping to getting my car washed. The thin red film of dust that coated the windshield had bothered me weeks ago. Now it had become really annoying, and using the wipers only made it worse. The good news was I didn't have to deal with putting on snow tires or stocking up on lock defroster.

As I started to adjust the pillow cushions before reaching for the remote, I suddenly remembered I needed to tell my mother that Nate and Marshall wouldn't be able to make it for Thanksgiving. *Thank goodness.* No way was I about to leave myself open for the barrage of questions my mother would have regarding their unavailability, so I did the cowardly thing. I picked up my iPhone and sent her an email. Then I grabbed the remote, clicked on the TV, and watched as the local news came on. Damn.

The water main break in Glendale was the hot topic. I switched to another station, and it was similar footage. It didn't take a seer to figure out what was about to happen next. The only question I had was how long it was going to take. Two minutes? Five? Maybe ten? I leaned back and glanced at my cordless phone, still nestled in its charger. Sure enough, the tip turned red and the ringing began.

"Hi, Mom. I guess you saw the news. By the way, I sent you an email. Nate and Marshall made other plans for Thanksgiving."

"You should have called me right away about the flooding. Herb has a Shop-Vac you could use. He loaned it to Louise once when her bathtub overflowed into the living room. Of course, now she's replaced the carpeting with tile."

"Uh, thanks, but it's beyond a Shop-Vac. Anyhow, it's all taken care of. Nate has one of those restoration teams coming in tomorrow, and we went there this afternoon to move files and stuff."

"So you've got the day off tomorrow . . ."

I held perfectly still, waiting for my mother to finish her thought and praying she didn't have some bizarre errand she wanted me to run.

Her voice sounded practically ecstatic. "Thank goodness. I've been wracking my brain trying to find someone who could help Eunice Berlmosler with the ticket sales. Clarisse Evans, you don't know her but she's on the publicity and ticket committee, has to stay home and wait for her exterminator. Termites. Well?"

No, no, no! Clarisse Evans's termites are not going anywhere. One day isn't about to make a difference.

"I'm sorry, but I've got to get caught up on my own errands."

"This would only be for an hour. One hour. It's not going to kill you, and you'd be doing Eunice a great favor. Ticket sales are from nine to two. I, myself, would have offered to help, but we're rehearsing from ten to two. Besides, she needs coverage at noon. Come on."

"One hour. Tell her one hour. That's all she's getting from me."

When I got off the phone, the thought of putting on snow tires didn't seem so bad.

Chapter 24

Eunice Berlmosler practically gushed all over me when I arrived at the Stardust Theater's small ticket window a few minutes before noon on Monday. She was a petite woman in her late seventies or eighties and, for some reason, reminded me of a suffragette.

"Thank you so much, Phee, for helping out. Your mother told me how you're tracking down Miranda Lee's murderer."

"Um, actually, I'm—"

"Terrible thing. Murder. And leaving the body up on the catwalk like that. Frankly, I give the entire cast and crew credit for going on with the show. And with a new director, too. Poor Ellowina. Her plays were of the highest quality. I heard she was recuperating at a relative's house. Anyway, let me show you the tickets. We take cash, check, and credit cards."

"Credit cards? Really?"

"Why, yes. If we didn't take credit cards, we'd lose lots of sales. The Footlighters have a special tablet and this little square device."

"I know how to work those. I was just surprised you took credit."

Eunice showed me the tickets and cashbox.

"There are four performances in all. Fridays and Saturdays starting the week after Thanksgiving. Red tickets for the first weekend. Blue tickets for the second. All tickets are the same price. No special seating and don't let anyone tell you otherwise. Believe me, they'll try. And they'll come up with all sorts of excuses, too. The handicapped seats are in front and in back, as well as some marked ones on the aisles. First come, first seated. Oh, and before I forget, no pets. Some people actually try carrying their dogs in tote bags. Can you imagine?"

Oh yeah. If my mother wasn't in the play, Streetman would have a front row seat.

"Won't you be selling tickets here as well?"

"Oh no, dear. I've got to take a batch of flyers to the recreation centers and the businesses on Camino del Sol. I'll be back to pick up the remaining tickets and the cashbox. I've already sold thirty-one tickets, and it's only the first morning. Of course, most tickets are sold at the door."

She thanked me again and headed to the parking lot. And while Eunice told me all about the tickets and the payment methods, she forgot to inform me about the kind of questions I would be fielding, beginning with the first person who approached the window. It was a gray-haired woman wearing a red polka-dotted blouse and black polyester pants. I smiled and gave her a nod.

The woman crinkled her brow and leaned in to the ticket booth. "Can you tell me what this play is about?"

I proceeded to explain it was an Agatha Christie murder mystery, but, apparently, that wasn't enough.

"Are there musical numbers? I like singing and dancing."

"No. No music. This is a drama. It's a very famous play."

"That's right. You said murder, didn't you? Is it very gory?"

"No, it's not."

"I'll have to think about it."

So much for my first customer.

The next people to approach the ticket window came fifteen minutes later. A man and a woman. In a rush. They bought two tickets, paid cash, and left. As they walked away, the man said, "If it's a snoozer, I'm falling asleep, and I don't give a crap if I snore."

Then, about ten minutes after that, a smart-looking woman in her fifties came up to the window and extended a credit card. "I'm from Grand."

I wasn't sure if it was an announcement, a proclamation, or small talk, so I nodded and waited for her to continue. I later found out from my mother that the people who live in Sun City Grand have a tendency to announce it with great flourish. This woman was no exception.

"The stage manager is my uncle, and my mother would never forgive me if I didn't see the show."

"It's a good one. I think you'll enjoy it." *If Chuck learns his lines, and no one else is murdered.*

I swiped her card, thanked her, and told her to have a nice day.

Staring at the parking lot, I saw people heading to the craft rooms that were adjacent to the theater. No wonder my mother liked it here so much. No time to be bored. I had managed to get my car washed in the morning but needed to go food shopping as soon as Eunice returned. Snatching a pen and small pad from my bag, I started to make out the list I'd planned to do last night. I was so engrossed, I didn't notice the two white-haired ladies standing in front of the window. Both were sporting autumn décor sweatshirts.

"Excuse me," said the one with the pumpkin patch on her shirt, "we'd like to purchase tickets for opening night."

With that, she handed me a twenty-dollar bill. Exact amount.

"Sure, here you go." I handed her the tickets and watched as she gave one to the other lady and put hers in her small purse.

"Did Ellowina come back to finish directing the play?"

I shook my head. "Ellowina? No, I believe she's still recuperating from food poisoning."

"Yes, I knew about that, but I was sure I saw her at Costco's in Phoenix a few days ago."

Then the other woman spoke. Green sweatshirt with dancing turkeys. "I told you it wasn't her, didn't I?"

"It sure looked like her."

"Well, it wasn't. And what would Ellowina be doing in the hardware department? At a Phoenix Costco's, no less?"

"How am I supposed to know? Especially if it wasn't her. Besides, we were there, and we don't live in Phoenix."

"The only reason we were there was because we were visiting Uncle Murray. And you were the one who said you wanted to know if the Phoenix Costco was better than the one in Peoria."

Then she turned back to me. "My sister and I have

seen all of Ellowina's plays. She's an outstanding director, especially with her family background."

"Family background?"

"Yes, yes. The newspaper did an article about her a few years ago. Her mother was a thirties stage actress, and her father was a set designer for theaters in New York and Boston. Funny that she became an English teacher. I imagine her parents guided her down that path to avoid the uncertainties of the theater. Ellowina's father passed away not too long ago, but her mother died unexpectedly when Ellowina was just coming into her own as a teacher. I heard somewhere she never got over it."

The green sweatshirt sister interrupted. "Enough already. The ticket lady doesn't want to hear all of that."

I shrugged and smiled simultaneously. "That's okay. It was pretty interesting."

"Well I'll tell you one thing," the pumpkin patch sweatshirt went on. "I'm not saying I'm happy Ellowina got food poisoning, but at least it meant she wasn't the one who had to deal with one of her cast members getting murdered."

"Oh, and I suppose it was all right for the other guy?" green sweatshirt asked.

"I didn't say that. It was awful all around, but Ellowina's a very sensitive woman. That's all I'm saying."

Just then, a burly man wearing a buttoned-down shirt and shorts made a beeline for the ticket booth and shouted, "I need four tickets for opening night!"

The two sisters thanked me and stepped aside so I could handle the transaction. They stood there talking to each other before yelling out a thank you and heading for their cars.

When I was done handing the tickets to the man, I

looked at the tablet to check the time. One forty-two. So much for working one hour. Eunice showed up twenty minutes later, apologetic for being so late.

"That's okay," I said. "I was glad to help out." Then, I suddenly remembered I was supposed to buy three tickets as well, one for me and two for Lyndy. I ran them through my debit card before leaving Eunice to close out. I had barely gotten three or four feet away when she said, "Aren't you going into the theater? The rehearsal should be about over."

"No. I've got to get going. I'm running late. Uh, again, it was nice meeting you."

I took off like a high school sprinter hoping to make the track team. If I needed to know anything about what went on at rehearsal, I was positive it would come directly from my mother.

No sooner did I get into the car, fasten my seatbelt, and turn on the AC when my cell phone rang.

My God! The woman doesn't waste a second, does she?

I slid the arrow and took the call, not bothering to check the number. "So, how bad was it? Chuck forget his lines again?"

"What? It's me. Marshall."

"Marshall. I'm sorry. I thought it was my mother. What's up?"

"I didn't want to wait until tomorrow to fill you in on my little encounter with Maeve Fletcher. I still can't believe I walked out of there without breaking anything. I've never seen so many teeny little glass fig-urines in my life. And one whole section of animals with wings on them. Seriously. Pigs. Horses. You name it. I all but broke out into hives in that place. But, the good news is Maeve was more than willing to offer up her observations."

"Was I right? Was I right? Sue Ellen and Cliff *were* having an affair."

"Whoa. Get a grip. And uh, yeah, you were right. At least as far as Maeve was concerned. Said she saw Sue Ellen and Cliff locking lips on more than one occasion when they didn't think anyone else was around."

"I knew it. I knew it. She has to be the one who murdered Miranda. Can you confront her and get her to crack?"

"Get her to crack? I'm not exactly Philip Marlowe, and it isn't all that easy. I'll need more evidence, so I'll be speaking with the sheriff's department and backtracking the timeline. We'll see where that takes us."

"But you *do* think it could be her? Don't you?"

"Quite possible. Yeah. I'd be more inclined to worry if it wasn't a motive like love or revenge. I don't think anyone in the cast or on the crew has anything to worry about. Even if Sue Ellen is the one playing all these little games with cryptic notes and ghost-like vanishing acts."

"Speaking of which, it's been pretty quiet lately. Oh, bite my tongue."

"By the way, if it turns out you're right, then who takes over for Sue Ellen?"

"Paula Darren. She knows all the lines. She's the prompter for the first act. She and my mom both have to continue prompting during the performance in case Chuck backslides. And get this—Herb is the understudy for two of the men's roles."

"What about the other parts? Don't tell me it'll be one of the deputies who's had to babysit."

"No, they do a 'flip-flop.' It's kind of common in the theater, from what I've been told. Main characters learn one other character's role in case they have to switch around."

"As much as I want to catch the killer, I'd be more inclined to wait until closing night, or I might really wreak havoc with that play."

"Closing night? That'd make for one hell of an encore."

"Anyway, I'll see you first thing tomorrow. The carpets won't take long to dry, and the service company will be there way before we open to put back the furniture."

"Sounds good. Thanks, Marshall."

I ended the call and pulled out of my parking spot. Cast and crew members were working their way out of the main entrance. Without wasting a second, I headed straight for the parking lot exit and didn't bother to glimpse at the rearview mirror.

Chapter 25

I never thought I'd be so happy to sit at my desk as I was the day after Thanksgiving. It had been a relatively quiet week, compared to the frenetic ones I'd been experiencing. Even Thanksgiving Day at my mother's wasn't as godawful as I'd expected.

Shirley appeared to be more relaxed since there weren't any more ghost sightings at the theater. She attributed it to the fact that Cecilia had filled an entire spray bottle with holy water when her priest wasn't looking and spritzed that water generously throughout the stage, auditorium, and dressing rooms in the Stardust Theater. Cecilia even talked Bill into taking what was left and spraying it into the air on the catwalk.

Lucinda thought the whole thing was a bunch of poppycock (her words) and told us as much when she wasn't gorging herself on everything in sight. The best part of the day was that no one pressured me about my love life. Instead, they fabricated all sorts of scenarios involving Miranda, Sue Ellen, and even Paula Darren. The screenwriters for *The Bold and the Beautiful* would have been proud.

"It's too bad you have to work tomorrow," my mother said. "The three of us are meeting Myrna and Louise at Home Goods tomorrow morning, and then we're going to Arrowhead Mall for winter fashion shopping."

I couldn't imagine anything worse. This wasn't a crew that would have responded tactfully to such questions as "Does this make me look fat?" or "Does this make me look old?" I simply smiled and explained that we had to catch up at work due to the water main break.

Now, sitting comfortably at my desk, I was about to do exactly that. At least until Marshall gave a quick rap on the door frame and stepped in.

"Unbelievable. Absolutely unbelievable. The sheriff's department called to let me know they plan to arrest Stanley Krumpmeyer for Miranda's murder."

"Stanley? They've got it all wrong. All wrong!"

"I'm driving over to their posse station in Sun City West right now. Funny, but up until I moved to Arizona, I'd always thought posse's disappeared with the cowboys. Having a citizen patrol that's connected to the county sheriff's office is a real boom for the community. Anyway, Deputy Bowman agreed to fill me in. All he would tell me over the phone was that, in retrospect, they shouldn't have allowed everyone to stay seated together in the auditorium when they questioned the cast and crew."

Small gurgling noises seemed to take over my throat, and all I could do was nod. How could I have gotten this wrong? Stanley Krumpmeyer? It didn't make sense.

"So, I'll keep you posted. Nate's flabbergasted, too. He's with a client right now. Feels as if we've been blindsided on this one."

Marshall was out the door before I got my voice back. Robotically, I went through the weekly accounts and updated the billing, but my mind kept going back to Stanley. If it was a horserace, he'd be the longshot.

"Are you all right in there, Phee?" It was Augusta. "It's been over three hours, and you haven't gotten up once for a break. In fact, Nate shouted out a 'good-bye' as he headed off to see a client, and you never even heard him."

"Oh gosh. I'm sorry. I've literally had to force myself to concentrate on work because the police are about to arrest the wrong suspect, and there's nothing we can do at this point. Poor Stanley."

"Is that the suspect? Stanley?"

"Uh-huh. Stanley Krumpmeyer, whose only claim to fame is the broadcast club and now, of course, this. Miranda's murder. Only he didn't do it. I'm positive it was Sue Ellen."

"The sheriff's office wouldn't be arresting him if they didn't have evidence, would they?"

"That's what Marshall's going to find out. If there was evidence, what on earth did we miss?"

Augusta crinkled her nose and stood still for a moment. "Planted evidence."

She emphasized the word "planted" before continuing. "In most of the murder mysteries I've read or seen, the killer usually plants evidence to incriminate someone else."

"That's got to be it. I bet that's exactly what Sue Ellen did. But I wonder how . . ."

"Wouldn't wonder too much longer. Look out the window. Here comes your answer now, and if my eyesight is good, he's brought us lunch."

I knew it was Ray's famous meatball subs without

even bothering to check out the large box Marshall had carried inside.

"My treat, ladies! I had to pass Ray's on the way here and couldn't resist. We've got to have soda in the fridge. I'll grab some cans and we can eat in the back room. It doesn't look as if they're knocking the doors down to get inside. Not with all those sales going on today."

We both thanked him as he handed us the subs to carry while he took care of getting the drinks. A few seconds later, we were all gathered around the small table in back.

Augusta had barely unwrapped her sub before poking me in the arm. "Aren't you going to ask him? It's been bothering you all morning."

"Augusta's referring to Stanley's impending arrest. I had to tell her. She's following this case, too."

Marshall grinned as he popped the tab on his soda. "I figured as much. Well, I won't keep you in suspense any longer. It doesn't look good for Stanley. Bowman and Ranston went over the notes they made on the day Miranda's body was found and had some more questions for a few of the cast and crew members. Instead of a repeat performance at the theater, they called those folks into the posse station for questioning."

"It couldn't have been any of my mother's friends, or I would have heard about it. Heck! I would have been asked to escort them like the last time something like this came up."

"Bowman's faxing me a complete set of notes, but this is what I've gotten so far. A few days before the murder, Miranda and Stanley were having one of their usual spats involving upstaging, and I guess Stanley lost it. He was heard saying, 'what I wouldn't give to put my hands around your neck and squeeze the last breath out of you.'"

Augusta reached for a napkin and wiped some of Ray's famous tomato sauce off of her chin. "He's an actor. Of course he'd say something like that if she ticked him off."

"That wasn't the most incriminating part," Marshall replied. "The timeline was. The medical examiner was able to pinpoint a fairly accurate time of death, and it coincided with the hour immediately following a late rehearsal that only involved a few of the players."

"And Stanley was one of them."

"I'm afraid so. And that's not all. Two of the people that the deputies spoke with said they saw Stanley follow Miranda up to the catwalk as they were leaving the theater. I imagine Miranda wanted the lights adjusted to suit her, and Stanley had other ideas. They probably had a big row, and he gave her a shove. Enough to knock her down before actually strangling her."

I had all I could do to contain myself. "Wait a minute. Wait a good minute. Why didn't those two alleged witnesses say something on the first day?"

"Bowman and Ranston asked them the same thing. The answer was pretty simple. They were afraid to say anything because Stanley was sitting right there, and if all of a sudden he got carted away, he might have figured out who turned him in."

"So now what? When do they plan on arresting him?"

Marshall glanced at his watch. "I think they already have."

If I could read anything at all in Marshall's expression, it was a combination of astonishment and genuine sadness.

"You don't think he did it, do you?"

"It's too easy. Something's missing. I feel as if it's right in front of me and yet I can't see it."

"The only thing that's right in front of you, Mr. Gregory, is your sub, and you've hardly touched it."

"I know, Augusta. I know. I guess I'm not that hungry. I'll save it for later. I need to put a call in to Phee's mother and let her know what's happened. I really feel awful about this."

"Well, you can feel good about one thing," I said. "My mother's out Black Friday shopping, so it'll be you and the message machine. Until, of course, she returns the call . . ."

We thanked Marshall again for lunch and watched as he headed into his office. I knew he was beating himself up over this, but I also knew he was as persistent as Nate when it came to tracking down the truth. I didn't expect Stanley to remain behind bars for long.

The phone was ringing the minute I got home and unlocked the door. Thinking it might be Marshall with some new information, I picked it up immediately, only to find myself flinching at the sound of my mother's voice.

"Herb just called. I had to hear it from Herb! Stanley's been arrested for Miranda's murder, and Herb is now playing the part of Christopher Wren. That's like having Andy Devine play the part of Butch Cassidy. I don't know what's worse. The play's going to be a disaster. I never figured Stanley for a killer. Honestly. This is going to devastate the broadcast club. And who knows what it will do to our ticket sales."

It was typical Harriet Plunkett—all over the place with me at the other end unable to get a word in.

"Calm down, Mom. Didn't you get Marshall's message?"

"I haven't checked my message machine. I walked in the door, put my packages on the couch, and, by the way, there were lots of bargains at T.J. Maxx. I bought Streetman the cutest little winter sweater."

"No way! The dog has a better wardrobe than most of us. Anyhow, Marshall called to let you know about the arrest. It came out of nowhere."

"I'll say it did. Stanley was the last person I'd suspect. Not that I blame him. She probably pushed him to a breaking point. At least we can all relax now. We don't have to look over our shoulders anymore. Did the deputies find out why on earth he took Shirley's tunic? Phee? Are you listening?"

It was like an electric shock. The tunic. If the witnesses said they saw Stanley following Miranda to the catwalk, then what about the tunic draped over her arm? No one mentioned seeing Stanley carry it up there.

"Mom, I've got to make another call. I'll get back to you later tonight."

"Call me before *Blue Bloods* comes on. I like to watch Tom Selleck."

Who doesn't?

My fingers were fat and clumsy as I raced to dial Marshall's cell number. *Come on. Come on. Answer it.* I jumped in as soon as Marshall said hello.

"I knew something was wrong, Marshall. I knew it. Shirley's tunic. Did any of those so-called witnesses say a word about Stanley carrying that fringy, teal tunic up the catwalk? If not, how do you explain how it got draped over Miranda's arm?"

"My God, Phee. I can't believe I missed it. I must be

slipping. Unless he went back up later to put it there, but that makes absolutely no sense. It had to be someone using it as a disguise. Like we talked about before. I've got to call the sheriff's office. It won't change anything since they're convinced they've nabbed the right guy, but it will certainly muddy the waters for them."

"Good. Make it as murky as possible, or Sue Ellen will be getting away with murder."

As things turned out, the tunic didn't seem to matter to the sheriff's department. Monday morning came, and Stanley was still stuck in the Fourth Avenue Jail in Phoenix, awaiting his arraignment. I had only seen that place once; it was when I first moved here and my mother and I got lost downtown looking for the art museum. As I recalled, the four-story brick structure with bars on its windows reminded me of a post-war warehouse. Dark and depressing.

Rehearsals had also taken on that tone, according to my mother, who was now phoning me at least twice every night in case she forgot to mention something the first time. Her major complaint, aside from the fact Chuck was starting to "backslide," was her observation that Herb was really not well suited to play the role of Christopher Wren.

"At least Herb knows the lines. That's a start, Mom, isn't it?"

It was Tuesday night, and I was in for a long discourse.

"You know who would make a good Christopher Wren, don't you? Marshall. Marshall would be perfect in that role."

"Don't you dare even suggest it. I swear you'll make him leave the state."

My mother went on to tell me the rehearsals were now timed run-throughs, and, to make matters worse, Cliff had become so obsessive about having the play meet the expected running time of one hundred and forty minutes, that the cast and crew were about ready to stage a mutiny instead of a play.

"He's like a madman if it goes even one minute over. The only saving grace is the fact that all those weird little disturbances like the air-conditioning going wacko, the smell of Shalimar, and those hateful little messages have stopped. And I'll tell you what I'll be thankful for—when this play ends and we can go back to reading about murders."

"Disturbances. The disturbances have stopped."

"Yes, that's what I said."

"If you ask me, that's because Sue Ellen got what she wanted and there's no need to keep the charade going. Darn it. I wish I could prove she did it. This is so unfair. So, only two more rehearsals, huh?"

"That's right. One tomorrow night and dress rehearsal on Thursday. You know you're always welcome to sit in."

"Uh, that's okay. I'll be there for opening night. Marshall and Nate plan to attend, too, plus my friend Lyndy and her aunt."

"Good thing you bought tickets. I heard it's a sellout."

"Marshall and Nate's tickets were comped. Along with a few for the sheriff's department. That was before they arrested Stanley. The Footlighters probably wanted to make sure there was enough security in case, well, you know."

"All I know is the same thing you do, Phee. They've got the wrong man. And poor Streetman. This has been very upsetting for him, too. He keeps looking for that set of teeth he absconded with the other night."

"You threw them out, right?"

"Of course. Thank goodness that fashion statement went out in the thirties. I'd have to hide my wardrobe from him."

Chapter 26

If Wednesday was the proverbial "calm before the storm," then Thursday was an honest-to-God tempest. It started the minute I got into work. Marshall broke the news that he'd heard from Rolo Barnes. Nate was standing a few feet away at the copier, and Augusta was just coming in the door.

"Before you get all worked up, Phee," Marshall said, "keep in mind this isn't enough to have Stanley released."

I was nodding so fast I probably resembled one of those Bobblehead dolls. "What did he find out? What? What? Come on, tell me."

"What did *who* find out?" Augusta tossed her bag on her desk and motioned with her arms as if she was coaxing a preschooler to recite the alphabet.

Marshall took a long breath and looked directly at us. "A sixty-two-year-old woman by the name of Lenora Billings died of asphyxiation because her oxygen tank wasn't replaced in time. The nurse on duty was none other than Miranda Lee, or, I should say, Miranda Shumway at the time. She was accused of negligence, but there was some discrepancy since

Miranda claimed it was her candy striper who did the reading for that tank."

"I didn't think candy stripers were allowed to do those things," I said.

The sound of Augusta clearing her throat was like a freight train blowing through town. "Hells bells. I had a niece who was a candy striper, and she did whatever the duty nurses told her to do."

Suddenly, everything clicked in. "Oh my gosh. That candy striper was Sue Ellen Blair. Right?"

Marshall clasped his hands and nodded. "Yep. 'Fraid so. Although no charges were filed, Miranda was let go and Sue Ellen lost her community service."

"I said that! All along, I said that."

Marshall had this sheepish look, and Nate appeared equally culpable as I continued.

"I bet Miranda set her up. That's a bona fide motive for murder and much better than Stanley losing his temper. Heck, Herb's buddies are always losing their tempers. Every other day they're yelling and arguing up there on that catwalk, yet none of them are pushing or strangling each other."

"I'm kind of agreeing on this one. Not getting credit for community service wasn't all Sue Ellen lost," Marshall said. "The incident went on her record, and she was never able to secure the scholarship money she needed to go to a four-year university. Instead, she had to settle for community college before taking an entry-level job for a department store. Rolo really did his homework on this one."

For a minute, I almost felt bad for Sue Ellen. She was only a kid when it happened. "What about Miranda?"

"According to Rolo, she eventually married a very wealthy Leonard Milestone."

"And a very dead one," Augusta added. "Phee told me about their honeymoon in the Andes."

Nate flashed me an odd look before turning his attention to Augusta. "My goodness, what hasn't Phee told you?"

"I . . . I . . ."

"Never mind," he continued. "It doesn't matter. What does matter is that Sue Ellen probably held a lifelong grudge against Miranda, and when she found herself face-to-face with the very woman who had shattered her dreams, she wanted to get even."

I all but shouted at both men. "Can't one of you call the sheriff's department and have them bring in those people for questioning again? Maybe one of them saw Sue Ellen lurking around."

Marshall walked toward me, put his arm around my shoulder, and spoke softly. "I made the call to them as soon as I got Rolo's message. They'll get back to me."

How long is his arm going to stay around my shoulder? Two seconds? Five? Does it mean anything? Why am I thinking about Marshall's arm when it's poor Stanley and that duplicitous Sue Ellen I should be concerned about? I took long slow breaths, partly because I was still reeling from the arm thing and partly because I needed a minute to think before I spoke. "What did Stanley tell them? Surely he didn't confess."

Marshall nodded in agreement. "He swore he never laid a hand on Miranda. Len and Chuck were leaving by the back corridor when he decided to have it out with her. He admitted to following her up onto the catwalk because he was sick and tired of her shenanigans. Said he read her the riot act and then left. She was still standing in front of the large elliptical light, according to Stanley."

Nate picked up the papers he was copying and paused before looking directly at Marshall. "Are you thinking the same thing I am, buddy?"

"That the sheriff's department might wait till opening night before they decide to bring in Sue Ellen?"

"Yep. Should be a real fiasco. Much as I hate watching stage dramas, this is one I intend to see from start to finish."

"You might want to have Phee add a line item to our budget for Rolo's next piece of kitchen gadgetry. He's on that Paleo Diet now."

Nate's mouth opened slowly. "Don't tell me. Worse than juicing?"

Marshall and I nodded, all the while trying not to laugh.

"That's not all, Boss," Marshall said. "Rolo's not done yet. Said he wanted to keep digging."

"Sounds like we'll be refurbishing his kitchen by the time he finishes. I'll need to get a credit line at IKEA."

Just then the phone rang and Augusta picked it up. "Phee, it's your mother."

"I'll take it in my office. I'm sure I'll need to be seated."

My mother dispensed with the greeting and charged ahead as I leaned forward and booted up my computer.

"It's official. It made the front page of the *Sun City West Independent.* Stanley Krumpmeyer is being charged with murder."

"He hasn't been found guilty, he's just been charged, and I think that might change."

"Why? What did you find out?"

"I can't get into it right now, Mom, but Nate and

Marshall are following other leads. Look, I've got to get back to work."

"One more thing and I'll let you go. Eunice Berl-mosler called a few minutes ago. The programs arrived."

The tension was building in my neck so I tried rolling it from side to side, but it only made it worse. "Good. Good. Programs . . ."

"I'm not done. She's pitching a fit because Stanley is listed in the cast and it's too late to get the programs reprinted. Plus, the Footlighters don't have that kind of money."

"Tell her to do what they do on Broadway. Someone walks out on stage and announces 'the part of so and so is being played by blah-blah-blah.'"

"I suppose that's what she'll have to do. Anyway, Shirley has worse problems."

"What worse problems?"

"Finding period clothing to fit Herb. That gut of his is making it impossible. He'll look like Tweedledee in a woolen vest and even worse in a cardigan."

"I'm sure Shirley will think of something. Look, I've really got to go."

"Call me if you hear anything. Dress rehearsal is from one to four today. Curtain is at seven tomorrow evening."

"Got it."

I tried not to think about Eunice's programs, Herb's bulging waist, or my mother's annoying calls. Most of all, I tried not to think about Sue Ellen and the fact that she might get away with murder. Instead, I focused on the office billing until my stomach started rumbling and I took a short break to grab a taco at Quick Stop.

Augusta used her lunch hour to run errands, and, frankly, I lost track of Nate and Marshall. Hadn't even noticed when they left the office. Both of them had other cases to deal with, even though they were giving this one a fair amount of attention.

At approximately one-fifteen the phone rang, only this time it was Myrna. "Phee, I think you should get over here as soon as you can."

"Oh my gosh. Did something happen to my mother?"

"No, no. She's with Sue Ellen. Trying to get her to stop crying. There was an envelope taped to the hanger that holds Sue Ellen's costume. Inside was a note that said 'Appointment with Death.' Whoever wrote it is obviously familiar with Agatha Christie's mysteries."

"Whoever wrote it is obviously familiar with how fast Sue Ellen can break into tears."

"Shirley swears all of the costumes were on the rack and lined up perfectly when she left the day before and none of them had notes attached."

"People are in and out of that theater all the time. It would be hard to pinpoint who could have snuck in."

"That's not all."

"What? There's more?"

"Sue Ellen was shaking when she read the note, but she didn't start crying until she looked at the shoes she'd be wearing in the play and saw another note taped to one of them. It was a worse message."

"What could be worse than referring to an appointment with the grim reaper?"

"A note that said 'Your pitfall awaits before the curtain closes for good. Watch your back. Too bad you can't stay out of the spotlight.'"

"Oh brother. First the stupid notes that you and Mom got, then the lipstick on the mirror, and now this. Whoever's behind this wanted to create a stir even before the play started. Why? Who the heck knows. Look, I don't think the same person who wrote the notes and did that little number with the lipstick is the one who put these messages on Sue Ellen's costume."

Myrna gulped a breath, and I went on.

"If you ask me, Sue Ellen Blair is a far better actress than anyone realizes."

"You're not saying she put those notes there herself, are you?"

"That's exactly what I'm saying. It would be real easy for her to slip them on the hanger and shoe when no one was looking and then play the role of the frightened little victim."

"I'm not so sure, Phee."

"Why?"

"Because she's threatening to walk off the set. That's why your mother is with her now. Trying to convince her not to. But it will be tough. Sue Ellen and everyone else still believes the real killer hasn't been apprehended."

"What about Paula Darren? Where's she?"

"Backstage studying Sue Ellen's lines."

"Isn't that convenient. What about the menacing notes?"

"The deputy sheriff on duty took them, but they won't be any help. They were printed from a computer like the other ones, and the font was Times New Roman. Good grief. Even my seven-year-old grandson could do that."

"Look, I don't know what help I'm going to be if I come over. In fact, I'd probably be in the way. I'm sure my mother will be able to convince Sue Ellen to stop crying and get on stage."

My mind instantly flashed back to Mankato when

I was ten and had the worst case of stage fright ever for our fifth grade play. It was only when my mother threatened to come to my school every day and eat lunch at my table that I overcame it. She couldn't possibly come up with something like that for Sue Ellen so she'd need another tactic.

"Let's hope so, Phee," Myrna said. "Let's hope so. OH MY GOD!"

"What? What's happened? Are you all right?"

"I'm fine, but the lights went out. All of them. Everyone is yelling."

"I'm calling nine-one-one."

"Don't! It's okay. The circuit breaker got tripped. That's all. I can hear Bill and Wayne now. Daniel, the maintenance guy, went to fix it. Cliff's screaming for everyone to stay where they are. Like we're about to move around in the dark. Idiots we're not."

Dear God, do not let those lights come on only to have another dead body appear. "I'm going to wait on the phone with you, Myrna, until everything is back to normal."

"That could take a few minutes."

"That's okay."

I made small talk about all sorts of things while my mind conjured up images of dead bodies on rafters, dead bodies lying across the stage, and dead bodies hanging from ropes that dangled over center stage.

"The lights are back on. Everything's fine."

"Are you sure?"

"I think so. Cliff is having us do a sweep of our immediate area."

"I'll hold."

In the background, I recognized Bill's voice. It was impossible not to. I could hear him bellow, "Ain't no stiffs up here. Unless you count Kevin. His back is seizing up."

I also heard Wayne telling everyone he was going to check the basement under the trapdoors.

"Myrna, call me back if anything out of the ordinary happens, okay? And please tell my mother I'll stop by her house after work."

"I know some say Stanley is the killer, but let me reiterate it's not the feeling most of us have."

"Is the buddy system still being used?"

"Sort of. But it's real difficult now that we're in dress rehearsal."

"I understand. Thanks for calling."

Part of me wanted to drive right over there and scope out every single corner of the place. Who was Sue Ellen fooling? Instead, I called Marshall on his cell, told him what had happened, and before I could ask him to check it out, he announced he was on his way over there. Honestly, what wasn't there to like in that guy?

About an hour and forty-five minutes later, Marshall called back, and I was totally unprepared for what he had to say.

"I know how the killer did it, Phee. I know how he or she killed Miranda. It was carefully calculated, not spur of the moment. I showed the deputy on duty what I had found, and he's placing a call into his office."

"How do you know? What did you find?"

"I did the same thing you did. I checked out the electrical panel and the basement area."

"With Wayne?"

"No, Wayne was on the catwalk with Bill and Kevin making some final adjustments so I had Daniel do it."

"The maintenance guy?"

"Yeah."

"You don't suspect him, do you?"

"Not in the least. No motive whatsoever. He's been employed for the past nine years and everything about him is clean. The deputies did a complete check on all the employees. Anyway, I had him open both chemical storage cabinets for me. The one upstairs and the one by the trapdoors in the basement."

"Why? Wayne said it was just paints, chemicals, and solvents."

"I know. But I remembered something that people were complaining about. Especially Shirley. She was convinced Miranda's ghost was haunting the theater because the aroma of the perfume Miranda wore was lingering in the air. Someone was doing that on purpose and what better place to store perfume than a locked chemical cabinet."

"So you found it? The perfume, I mean."

"Oh yeah. Sickening sweet. If you or Augusta came in wearing that stuff, we'd have to fumigate."

As soon as he said that, I was relieved I gave up that scent when I was sixteen.

Marshall continued. "So, like I was saying, the upstairs cabinet only had paint, but behind the cans of solvent and chloroform in the downstairs cabinet I found a few small spray vials of perfume, only the label said 'parfum.'"

"That's because perfume would have cost a small fortune. The scent is the same only it's toilette water."

"Figures."

"Seriously, it's real easy to spray, especially something so tiny that could be held in someone's hand without being noticed. So, how did they do it? How did they murder Miranda? You said you figured it out."

"The killer planned this ahead of time, knowing

Miranda would be up on the catwalk. He or she stored those vials of perfume, or whatever you call it, in the basement chemical cabinet. Then, the night of the murder, they got down to the basement, unlocked the cabinet, took a cloth, soaked it in the chloroform, which does carry an aroma but only up close and personal, and headed to the catwalk. They also made sure to take one of the tiny perfume bottles with them."

"What about Stanley? He admitted to following Miranda up there. Wouldn't he have noticed anything?"

"Not really. The auditorium was dimly lit and the killer waited it out until Stanley left. Then they made their move, using that teal tunic of Shirley's to throw people off in case they were spotted in the semidarkness."

I leaned forward and readjusted my chair, hoping Marshall wouldn't hear the squeaking noise. "Okay, I'm following you. Then what?"

"Once they made sure Stanley left, they walked up the catwalk. Miranda most likely assumed it was Stanley and probably didn't pay any attention. Anyway, our killer was able to get close enough to Miranda to wave that chloroform cloth under her nose. Probably came up from behind her."

"Wayne told me a whiff of chloroform wouldn't be enough to make someone pass out."

"He was right. It wouldn't. But, given even the slightest sniff, it would make someone woozy, and that's all our killer needed to carry out the deed. With Miranda stunned momentarily, the killer got in a good shove. That explains the bump on the back of Miranda's head. She fell backward and hit her head on the catwalk."

"But I didn't think that's what killed her."

"It wasn't. Remember the ligature marks on her neck?"

"Yeah."

"Well, with Miranda on the floor of the catwalk, probably dazed from hitting her head and inhaling chloroform, the killer was able to strangle her with the necklace she was wearing. Fortunately for our killer, although not Miranda, the victim made it real easy by wearing that necklace. Of course, I'm pretty sure the killer would have grabbed one of the nearby electrical cords if Miranda wasn't sporting that nice piece of jewelry."

"What about all those electrical cords found tangled over the body?"

"Real easy. The killer did that after the fact. To make it look as if Miranda did it herself somehow. Even managed to find one with a frayed end and put it in Miranda's hand while draping the other one over the edge. The tunic was the finishing touch."

"Holy cow! All of that from looking into a chemical storage cabinet?"

"Hey, I paid attention in my criminal justice classes. Listen, my theory puts a new perspective on this, so Bowman and Ranston are on their way over here."

"What's everyone else doing?"

"They're still rehearsing."

"Sue Ellen, too?"

"Far as I know."

"Wow. I'm stunned. And frankly disappointed I didn't come up with a theory that actually had some evidence. Although, if we think the killer is Sue Ellen, how would she know about the chemical storage cabinets? And where the keys were? I would have thought only the stage manager, the director, and seasoned lighting and construction crew members would be aware of it."

"That's true, but, according to the stage manager, a complete tour of the entire theater was provided for any cast and crew members interested. Four people signed up—Len Beckers, Paula Darren, Miranda Lee, and Sue Ellen Blair. He said the women just wanted to 'go along for the ride.' Only Len seemed genuinely interested. Even requested a copy of the lighting instrument schedule."

"Golly, that's more information than I would want."

"Look, I'll give you a buzz later. If it's real late, I'll try you at home. Unless, of course, you've made plans to go out."

What kind of leading statement is that? Does he want to know if I'm dating? "Um, er, yeah, that's fine."

Chapter 27

I spent the remainder of the afternoon wondering if the sheriff's department would be releasing Stanley and arresting Sue Ellen. I got the answer when I arrived at my mother's doorstep at a little past six. It was already dark outside.

The minute she opened the door, I got an earful. "Sue Ellen is as free as a bird. Skated out of rehearsal like Scarlett O'Hara's maid on her way to fetch that doctor."

"Aren't you going to let me in?"

"Oh, I'm sorry. Come on in. Streetman's still under the couch. The doorbell upsets him sometimes. Are you hungry? I can take something out of the freezer."

"NO! I mean, no, I'm not very hungry. I'm only going to be here a minute or so. Did you get my message from Myrna I'd be stopping by on my way home?"

"Yes, but she didn't say anything about dinner."

"I wanted to make sure everything was all right. It sounded like absolute chaos at rehearsal."

"No, that was minor chaos when Myrna called you.

Absolute chaos was when those investigators from the sheriff's department came back."

"You mean Deputies Bowman and Ranston?"

"I've got news for you. The Marx Brothers would have been less intrusive. Those two were all over the place. Impossible to have a run-through. I thought Cliff was going to pitch a fit. Anyway, you know the old saying, 'Lousy dress rehearsal, great play' or something like that."

"What about Marshall? Where was he?"

"Trying to keep Bowman and Ranston from walking across the stage. For heaven's sake, I can't imagine what evidence they thought they'd find on stage."

"Mom, I know those trapdoors are secured, but be careful tomorrow night, okay?"

"The stage manager and Wayne are going to check them before the curtain goes up."

"What about the deputy on duty? Where's he going to be?"

"Circulating. That's what they said—circulating. Sure you don't want anything to eat?"

"No, I need to get home." *So I can trounce on Marshall's call the second I hear the phone ring.*

"The ladies are meeting for breakfast in the morning. You know you're always welcome to join us."

"I'll join you tomorrow night to celebrate the opening night performance. You *are* celebrating, aren't you? It's kind of a theater tradition, as far as I know."

"It's a reason for Herb and his crew to drink more beer at Curley's. Same for the men in the cast. The rest of us are going to the Homey Hut. We even invited Paula."

"Okay. The Homey Hut it is. Talk to you later, Mom. I've got to run."

I was out the door and at my car before she had a

chance to offer me dinner again or insist I stay and wait for the dog to greet me.

Friday morning started out as poorly as Thursday. It seemed like the minute Nate walked into the office, his phone rang with an emergency call from his aunt in Sierra Vista. He barely had time to make himself a cup of coffee when he had to dart out of there.

"Augusta, if I have any appointments today, please call, apologize, and reschedule. Marshall can pick up the slack if need be. He knows what's going on."

Then he walked over to where I was standing. "Listen, kiddo, I'm really sorry about this, but I have to go down to Sierra Vista. Seems like my aunt fractured her hip yesterday and is in the hospital. She waited until now to call me. Looks like it will just be you and Marshall for opening night."

"Oh my goodness. I'm so sorry about your aunt. Will you be staying there long?"

"Only overnight. Then I'll be returning with . . . holy crap, I can barely spit it out . . . Mr. Fluffypants. My aunt will be in rehab so she needs someone to watch him."

"Her cat? You're taking care of her cat? That's so sweet of you."

"Cat? Hell no. I wish it were a cat. Mr. Fluffypants is her African Grey parrot. He has the temperament of a two-year-old, and he bites. Say, are either of you any good with birds?"

I clenched my teeth, and Augusta shook her head violently.

"I'll pass on this one, Mr. Williams. As far as I'm concerned birds belong in two places—flying in the air or in the oven with lots of stuffing."

"I'm with Augusta. Sorry, Nate. I'd feel awful if it got loose or anything . . ."

"The two of you can stop worrying. I guess I'd better get used to the darn thing. They live forever, and she's probably going to leave him to me in her will. But that stupid bird better not expect to be coddled like that Munson woman's bird. One of your mother's book club friends, Phee. You remember? The car lights disturbing its sleep? My God, of all things to leave someone in a will."

"Who's leaving who in their will?" Marshall had stepped out of his office and was heading straight for the coffeemaker.

"You don't want to know," I said. "Unless you have an affinity for birds."

Marshall glanced at Nate, who was trying not to laugh as he spoke.

"Listen, all of you, I've really got to head out. And don't look so alarmed, Phee. I'm sure everything will run smoothly tonight. The sheriff's department hasn't decided whether or not to put Sue Ellen in custody, so I doubt there'll be a scene at the theater."

Marshall nodded as Nate took a few steps toward the door.

"Don't worry," I said. "We'll be fine. Good luck with your aunt."

Once Nate had left the office and Augusta had returned to her work, I moved closer to the coffeemaker, where Marshall was just finishing up.

I wondered if he could detect the uneasiness in my voice. "I don't know about you, but I'm pretty convinced it's Sue Ellen. Iron clad motives but nothing tangible. Do you ever get the feeling there's something right under our noses, but we can't see it?"

"I feel that way on most of my cases. It means we're

getting close. Anyhow, I plan to be at the theater no later than six-thirty."

"I'll be there even earlier. I heard the seats fill up fast. Look for me in front, will you?"

"Sure thing. And stop worrying. Look, I know the cast and crew are really on edge. Last thing anyone needs is for you or me to become unglued, okay?"

"Okay."

Unglued? I had no intention of becoming unglued.

I left the office promptly at five with Augusta practically throwing me out of there.

"Go home, Phee. Get something to eat and relax for a few minutes. You're wound up tighter than the actors. I'll lock up."

Marshall had left an hour or so earlier, with a few work-related stops to make before meeting me. I figured he'd eat at a fast-food place on the way, since we wouldn't be getting out of the theater much before ten. With my stomach in knots, I settled for two slices of toast with apricot jam and a cup of tea, before opening my closet to pick out something to wear.

Granted, it wasn't exactly a date, but it was a theater performance. No sense letting the few long skirts and dresses hang there until Goodwill called. I selected an ankle-length, sleeveless blue sheath with a matching shrug and adorable, strapped, wedge heels. After all, I didn't have to walk across a stage or climb over anything. I just had to get to my seat without tripping.

My hair looked absolutely perfect with the highlights, and the subtle makeup I applied looked decent. I added blue lapis earrings to the mix and was ready to head out the door. Ready, until the phone rang. This time I knew better than to let the answering machine get it.

"Phee! It's Lucinda. I'm glad I caught you. I'm backstage. Shirley is running all over the place like a madwoman. Sue Ellen's white blouse is missing. Missing. Shirley thought you might have one we could use. You're the only one we know with a respectable bust. So, do you?"

A respectable bust? What the heck's that supposed to mean?
"Uh, yeah. I do. More than one. White, off white, ecru . . ."

"Good. Bring two. Just in case. When you get into the auditorium, walk up the side steps to the stage and go directly in back to the dressing rooms. No one will stop you."

"How's my mother holding up?"

"Like a trouper."

"Good. I'll see you in a bit."

It was really weird for part of Sue Ellen's costume to go missing. I imagined the blouse was on a hanger with another piece of clothing over it, and, in all the excitement of opening night, Shirley didn't notice. I folded my short sleeve ecru blouse and the three-quarter length white one before slipping them into a plastic bag and heading out the door.

Traffic was light on the local route that connected me to Arizona State Road 303 and Sun City West. I turned up the radio and began to relax. That was when my cell phone rang. With one hand on the wheel and the other reaching down to the cubby where I stashed the phone when I drove, I had second thoughts about picking it up. Arizona law carried a hefty fine for motorists who drove while distracted, and answering a cell phone fit that category. I let it ring.

Five minutes later it started again. There was a small

shopping center a mile or so down the road, so I pulled over to see who it was. Two voice mails and both of them from my mother. The message was basically the same. "Phee, there's been an accident on the 303 and Grand Avenue. Don't use the highway, or you'll get stuck. Must be a bad accident because our deputy on duty had to leave."

I backtracked and took an alternate road that seemed as if it was dotted with traffic lights every few feet. At one particularly long light, I took my chances and hit the resend button. My mother must have had the phone in her pocket because she picked up immediately.

"Mom, got your message. Can't talk. The light's about to change. I'm on my way."

"Good. And it's a good thing Nate and Marshall are coming. We won't have the deputy sheriff here or the other one that they were going to send tonight. Of all nights for someone to have a car crash."

"Yes, when they found out it was opening night for your show, they said, 'Gee, let's have a car accident instead.'" I pounded my forehead with my left hand and waited for the light to turn green. "Only Marshall will be coming. Nate had to go to Sierra Vista. Long story."

"Only Marshall? He'd better be armed. He does carry a weapon, doesn't he?"

"Cut it out. Everything will be fine. Light changed. Got to go." I put the phone on mute and instead of returning it to the cubby, I put it in my bag.

The parking lot in front of the Stardust Theater was filling up as I pulled in. Luckily, I managed to secure a spot not too far from the entrance. Once inside, I handed my ticket to the usher at the door and walked briskly down the aisle toward the steps to the stage. Lucinda was right. No one stopped me.

The stage was dimly lit, and there were people bustling all around on both wings. I knew where the backstage door was and walked through it toward the costume room, trying not to think of the last time I was in there. The door was ajar, but I knocked anyway. Shirley stopped talking the minute she saw me.

"Hi, Shirley!" I said. "I got Lucinda's message. Hope one of these fits Sue Ellen."

I handed her the plastic bag and looked around. Herb was the only other person in there, hurrying to grab his costume. He muttered something about indigestion and took off.

"You're a godsend, Phee. Lordy, I don't know what could have become of that blouse. Sue Ellen's in the dressing room getting her makeup on. I'll bring these to her."

"Is my mother there, too?"

"I think so. Do you want me to check?"

"No, no. I'll see her after the play. I'd better get to my seat. By the way, someone left a hammer and some wire on the floor in the hallway back here. I almost fell over them."

"Darn that Wayne. He was supposed to pick up after himself. The couch broke. Cliff noticed it as soon as we got here and hollered for Wayne to fix it. Just like a man. Leaving all his messy things lying around. I'll get to it myself as soon as I give these blouses to Sue Ellen."

As I walked down the steps from the stage, I eye-balled the theater. Eunice was right. It was a sellout. Lucky for me, Lyndy and her aunt were about six or seven rows up from the stage and had saved me two seats on the aisle. I hurried over.

"Don't ask," I said, my rear end barely touching the cushion. Then I realized Marshall wouldn't see me if I was seated, so I turned around and scanned the audience. No sign of him. So much for six-thirty. I began to think he got caught up in that accident and blamed myself for not phoning or sending him a text.

Lyndy introduced me to her aunt, a small woman with a grip that could crush a steelworker. Both of them had programs, but I'd been in such a hurry to get to Shirley, I hadn't stopped to pick mine up.

"I'll be right back. I've got to get a program."

By now there were few seats left in the room, and Marshall was nowhere in sight. I walked to the main auditorium doors and asked the usher to give me two programs in case they ran out before Marshall arrived.

Once back at my seat, I took my cell phone from my bag to see if there had been any contact from Marshall. Sure enough, a text was waiting. With Nate in Sierra Vista and the deputies out on call for that road accident, I really wanted Marshall to get here ASAP. As luck would have it, that wasn't about to happen. According to his text, his car battery died, and he was stuck waiting for emergency service. The only saving grace was that my mother knew none of this. As far as she was concerned, he was armed and at the ready.

Chapter 28

Fidgeting in my seat, I stared at the closed curtain. To ensure no one would sit in the extra spot Lyndy had secured, I moved closer to the aisle, leaving a space between us.

"Marshall's car battery died," I whispered as I leaned over. "He's stuck somewhere waiting. It's a long-term rental, so after this he'll probably be looking to buy a car."

"I don't know that it makes a difference out here," Lyndy whispered back. "Car batteries seem to die without warning. At least where I come from, the car would struggle to turn over and that's how you knew. But here, geez whiz. One minute you're driving and the next thing you know, you're not. I think it's the heat. I read someplace that it causes the fluid in the battery to evaporate."

I was about to say something when the lights in the theater started to dim and a spotlight appeared in the center of the stage, forming a perfect circle on the dark curtains. A woman came out from stage left, walked toward the light, and spoke. It was Paula Darren, dressed from head to toe in black. Black mock turtle top, black pants. For a second, I was taken back, but then I remembered stage crew members always dressed in black so if they needed to walk on stage with a prop or something, they wouldn't be as conspicuous.

Paula's voice was sharp and clear without the need for a microphone. "Good evening and welcome to the Footlighters' presentation of Agatha Christie's *The Mousetrap*. For tonight's performance, the part of Christopher Wren will be played by Herb Garrett."

With that, she turned and walked back the same way she had come. Seconds later, the curtain opened and the play began. Absently, I rolled my program and Marshall's into a tight coil and clasped it in my hand.

Act one was going off without a hitch. At least from my perspective. No lost lines. No fumbling. Chuck must have gotten it together after all. Everyone's acting seemed smooth and, above all, captivating. I had to admit I was equally impressed with my mother's performance as the ill-tempered Mrs. Boyle.

Unlike rehearsals, there was barely a sound emanating from the catwalk. Bill and Kevin were supposed to be up there in case one of the elliptical lights had to be adjusted. For a brief second, I thought about Miranda's body and something Len Beckers had said about the position of her head. Tilted back like a Greek tragedy. An offhanded remark, but still . . .

If Marshall had made it to the theater, I had no way of knowing. He might have taken the first seat he could find since it was dark and it would be too annoying for him to hunt for me down in front. I'd need to wait until intermission to know for sure. Left with no other alternative, I leaned back and watched the performance. When the curtain closed at the end of the first act, the applause was thunderous. I stood and scanned the auditorium for Marshall. No sign of him. On a hunch, I checked my phone again. Sure enough, another text.

"Still waiting. Hope to make it by act two."

I was staring at my phone when Lyndy tapped my elbow. "That was a fabulous first act. I didn't realize your mother was so talented. Do you mind letting us through? We need to use the restroom before the next act begins."

"Oh, sure."

I stepped aside and let Lyndy and her aunt into the aisle, along with three other women. There was no way I was going to attempt using the ladies' room. With my luck, act two would begin, and I'd find myself midway through the waiting line. I'd hold my bladder, even if it meant crossing my legs.

With the houselights on and most of the theater emptying into the hallway, I thought it might be a good time to take a look at the program. I started to unravel the coil when Eunice approached.

"Phee! I thought that was you. Isn't this a marvelous performance? I must say, if act two goes as well as act one, it will be one of our best."

Then, as if to substantiate what she'd said, Eunice began to expound on every play the Footlighters had performed since the discovery of dirt. *Arsenic and Old Lace, Barefoot in the Park, Our Town, You Can't Take It With You, A Christmas Carol* . . . The list was never ending, and I struggled to appear interested. Thankfully, the lights blinked on and off, warning the audience the play was about to resume in five minutes. The next series of blinks would be for two. Sort of a theater standard from what little I knew.

"Oh my, Phee! Have we been talking that long? I'd better get back to my seat."

As she turned and headed up the aisle, Lyndy and her aunt returned, followed by the three ladies seated next to them.

All of them must have had the same idea I did because they, too, were opening their programs. The cast list filled an entire page, followed by head shots and short biographies for each of the players and crew members, similar to the program Myrna had shown me from the Peoria Players.

My eyes darted immediately to my mother's photo and her write-up. Frankly, Sarah Bernhardt paled in comparison. I all but choked. Then I scanned the other pictures and write-ups. The cast was listed alphabetically. As I started to read from the top of the page, it was as if a mule had kicked me in the stomach. In less than a second, I realized the awful mistake I had made. Sue Ellen wasn't the killer. She was about to be the next victim.

One word in the program gave it away. Marshall and I had all of the other pieces except this final clue. Now I was staring right at it and had to think fast. Oddly enough, my hands weren't shaking but my ankles were. It was the sudden frightening revelation that set off the bizarre tremors in my body.

Next thing I knew, the lights were blinking. The two minute warning. Lyndy and her aunt were still studying their programs. I reached into my bag and pulled out my phone. It was the fastest text I had ever sent, and I prayed Marshall would get it in time.

"KILLER CATWALK BASEMENT HELP"

Then I put the phone back, leaned over and handed my bag to Lyndy. Where I was headed, the phone and bag would only get in my way. "Can you hold this for me? I've got to go."

"Sure. That long waiting line's probably gone by now. You won't miss much."

That's what you think.

Those messages Sue Ellen had found on her costume hanger and in her shoe were more than threats. Now I found myself struggling to remember exactly what they'd said. Something about death before the curtain went down, or was it something about staying out of the spotlight? I wasn't sure, and now my hands were shaking along with my ankles.

The doorway to the catwalk was between the two entrance doors that led into the theater, and I couldn't afford to waste another second getting there. As I started up the aisle, the lights went out and temporarily blinded me. By now my entire body felt like the proverbial leaf in the wind. I heard the curtain open behind me, and one of the players began speaking.

Fortunately, a small shim held the door open and a dim light emanated from the narrow slit. The stairs were those awful grated ones and, to make matters worse, they were circular. No wonder Miranda was killed on the catwalk. No one in their right mind would drag her body up here.

My feet felt wobbly in heels, and I cursed under my breath for wearing them. In addition, my long sheath dress was catching on the side rails.

Please don't rip. Please don't rip. I actually look decent in this dress.

Bill spotted me immediately as I stepped onto the catwalk. I put my finger over my lips with one hand

and motioned for him to come closer with the other. Behind him, I saw Kevin sitting on a small stool.

Keeping my voice to barely a whisper, I tried to explain. "Whatever you do, don't put the spotlight on Sue Ellen unless someone else is in it with her."

I didn't give Bill a chance to respond.

"And don't let anyone up here, no matter what they tell you. Miranda's murderer wants to kill Sue Ellen before the final curtain."

Bill all but pressed his mouth to my ear. "Up here? Like shoot her or something?"

Maybe. Maybe. I was never too good at deciphering cryptic messages or riddles, for that matter. "Geez, I hope not. Who knows?" I was beginning to ramble and needed to focus. "Remember, block the entrance to the catwalk and keep Sue Ellen out of solo spotlights."

"Cripes. *Now* you guys figure it out?"

He motioned for Kevin as I turned and started down the stairs. One step and I knew I was in trouble. It felt as if I was going to tumble forward. For some reason the ankle straps on my heels weren't offering any support. Maybe it was the difference between walking up the stairs versus down. Holding onto the railing, I managed to turn around and walk back up.

Leaning on the catwalk's side rail, I took my shoes off and slipped the straps over my left arm, leaving my right hand free. Bill and Kevin were both preoccupied, looking over a large sheet of paper that must have been the instrument schedule.

I returned to the auditorium in a matter of seconds. Act two was underway, with its main character unaware of what was in store for her. If the killer wasn't planning on the catwalk, that left the basement. I had to get backstage and downstairs in a hurry. The trouble was, I couldn't very well go tromping up the side steps to the stage like I did when I delivered those blouses to Shirley. I had to find another way backstage.

I remembered the door Wayne had shown me. The one that went directly to the basement. I had to reach it and get down there before Sue Ellen found herself lying on a hard stone floor with the killer inches away. The mattress padding that had saved Len Beckers was probably nowhere in sight.

Unfortunately, my mind kept blocking me from figuring out how to get to the back foyer behind the stage. I forced myself to slow down and reason things out.

As I stood in the main hallway, with the entrance doors to the auditorium behind me, I knew I'd need to take one of the side corridors that ran parallel to the auditorium. But which one? Maybe it was because I was right-handed that I chose the hallway on that side and ran as fast as I could. My feet were probably black with dirt, and the floor felt greasy and cold.

Terrific. Do they spray this place for scorpions and spiders? If not, those things are most likely under my feet. My bare feet because I hate wearing hose!

The wall on the left, which faced the outside of the building, had giant posters featuring past plays. Maybe Eunice could walk down memory lane here. I didn't pause to read the titles. As I got to the end of the corridor, I saw two doors. I grabbed the first one and pulled. Locked. Taking a deep breath and trying not to panic, I grabbed the next one.

Luck was on my side because it opened up to a small, dimly lit foyer, but something wasn't right. If this was backstage, there should have been people milling about. I heard voices, so I had to be in the general vicinity, but it was anyone's guess where I'd landed.

By now, my heartbeat sounded like a tribal drum. To top it off, my throat felt as if it was about to close up. Straight ahead was another door, and like *Alice in Wonderland*, I reached for the knob and gave it a pull. This time I knew exactly where I was standing. The costume room was off to the left, and the door to the basement was only a few feet from me. I all but scared Shirley to death as I rushed into the costume room.

"Shh! Don't say a word. I'm going downstairs to where the trapdoors are. Find Wayne and have him follow me."

I started to race out when I had a second thought. "Tell Wayne to grab that hammer and the roll of wire he left on the floor out there. Tell him to bring those. We don't have much time. Hurry."

Shirley must have seen the desperation on my face or maybe it was in my voice. It didn't matter. She took off running as I got to the basement door.

I had no idea how far along the play was or how many scenes were left until it was too late for Sue Ellen. But to kill her in the middle of the play? I doubted that would happen. That meant it would probably happen at the curtain call. Sue Ellen had the lead. She would be taking the first solo bow in the spotlight. I tried not to think about it.

The only voices I heard were the ones coming from the stage. The crew knew better than to speak while a performance was going on. My hand shook as I closed the basement door behind me and took a step down. Someone had turned the dim wall lights on. Barefooted, I made little noise.

I moved slowly, petrified to breathe. Had Marshall

gotten my text? If so, was his car battery replaced, and could he get here before the curtain call? Bill had asked if I thought the killer intended to shoot Sue Ellen, and, truthfully, I wasn't sure. It was all in the interpretation of those notes. Yet something told me the killer had a different venue in mind and had prepared for it when the play was first cast.

I took another step and listened carefully. Nothing. The air itself was holding its breath. I was certain the killer was down there and tried telling myself they weren't interested in me. *Yeah, right.*

The muted voices from the actors seemed surreal as I kept going. My eyes were getting used to the semi-darkness, but I wasn't sure exactly where the stage was in relation to the basement. Behind me, the door to the stairwell opened. Thank God!

"Wayne," I whispered, "did you grab the hammer and wire?"

There was no response. I asked again. This time the teeniest bit louder.

I thought perhaps he didn't want to speak out loud on the off chance his voice would carry to the stage.

"It's okay," I said. "I'll stand still until you reach me."

The dry dirt smell that permeated the basement suddenly changed. I caught a whiff of sweet, sickening perfume and knew in that second it wasn't Wayne who'd followed me to the basement.

Spinning around, I hurled a shoe, but my aim was off and it bounced against the railing before thudding to the floor. At least it gave me time. I moved quickly in the darkness, bumping into the racks of clothing against the wall. I tried to steady myself with my free hand but fell backward, taking the velvet cape with the white faux trim with me. I also took something else—the sharp silver wand that was hanging with the costume.

Thank you, Ghost of Christmas Present.

Scrambling to my feet, I waved the wand in front of me, but I wasn't fast enough. The sickening sweet smell was directly under my nose, and I forced myself to stop breathing long enough to ram my elbow into the person who was about to murder Sue Ellen and possibly me. I must have caught them off guard because I could no longer smell the chloroform. They had dropped the cloth and reached for another weapon. In a matter of seconds, I was on the receiving end of Ebenezer Scrooge's walking cane.

The small wand and wedge heel shoe I was holding were no match, but my legs were. I dropped the wand and shoe as I delivered a kick to the shin that was so strong I actually felt the vibration. Then I darted toward the open area, where I was certain the trap-doors were located. If I had only seen that program when the show started, I could have anticipated this. Now I knew for sure.

Cloaked completely in black, it was easy for the killer to get below the stage without being noticed. No one would have batted an eye. The darkness obscured what the clothing did not. I should have realized it was real easy for someone so familiar with the theater mechanics, the play, and the timing to know the exact moment to make a move. Now it was my turn. I kicked again, this time forcing the killer to tumble backward toward the wall. The scant light was enough to reveal her face, and, although we had never met, I knew who she was.

"One murder's enough, Ellowina. Killing Sue Ellen isn't going to make a difference."

"Who the hell are you?"

"I'm Phee Kimball, Harriet Plunkett's daughter."

"If you know what's good for you, you'll step aside."

"I can't do that." *What am I thinking? Of course I can step aside. This woman is a crazed maniac killer. What the hell am I doing?*

Her voice was coarse and raspy and the tone devoid of any emotion. She was on her feet and inches from me before I knew it. My only recourse was to keep her talking long enough for the play to end. I couldn't let her reach that trapdoor and unlatch it. Sue Ellen would fall and break her neck. And where the heck was Wayne? Or Marshall, for that matter? How long did it take to change a car battery?

Ellowina was still holding Ebenezer's cane. She hadn't intended to use it as a weapon, only a device to lift the screw lock and slide open the trapdoor. Suddenly, everything began to make sense. When Wayne showed me those latches, they were too close to the wood to be unhitched without someone getting a ladder and doing it by hand. But if the latches were switched with the kind you found on those old door locks, then all someone would need was a long stick or cane to lift them up.

It finally hit me. Now. When it was too late. A real investigator would've figured this out the minute they laid eyes on those latches. The apparition that shook the senses out of Shirley was old Ellowina herself. She was the ghost. It was the perfect pretense for her to get into the basement in order to switch out the locks. No wonder she drove all the way into Phoenix to get new locks. She couldn't risk being spotted around here. That lady who bought the tickets from me was right all along. It *was* Ellowina she'd seen in the Phoenix Costco.

Too bad my grand epiphany wasn't going to do me any good. But I figured stalling might. "You never did have food poisoning, did you?"

"My, aren't you a quick study. No, I didn't. But I sure could act, so I faked it. Even if it meant dealing with a colon cleanse and drinking salt water and ipecac solution. No one questioned it. Then I got a little rumor going about the salmonella. Rumors work well here, don't they?"

"But you couldn't be seen here, could you? Not in daylight, anyway. So the rumor about staying with your niece must have been the one thing that was true in your string of lies."

"Yes. And how fortuitous she owns a car that looks exactly like Miranda's. It came in handy on one of the nights I happened to be in the theater. And happened to notice Shirley's clutch bag in the costume room when everyone left. I knew she'd be back."

"Scaring Shirley and Cecilia wasn't enough? You had to scream through Curley's parking lot as well?"

"I'm surprised you didn't mention the perfume. I thought that was a crowning touch. Cost me enough to dose the tires with that stinking Shalimar. It worked, didn't it? I couldn't wait to get to the nearest car wash once I got back to Phoenix."

"Wasn't murdering Miranda enough? Sue Ellen has already paid the price."

"I wouldn't say that. She's still breathing. More than I can say for my mother. What they did was beyond reproach. They destroyed a family. *My* family."

"Don't make it two murders, Ellowina. Stop while you can."

"How did you know it was me?"

"I didn't. Not until tonight, when I read your full name—Ellowina Billings Bice."

"If you know what's good for you, you'll leave. I planned this a long time ago. When I first saw Sue Ellen in *The Odd Couple* playing the role of Gwendolyn, I knew it was her. She looked exactly the same as she did when she was a teenager. And I thought, 'How does she get to be so carefree and happy?' Not anymore."

"What about Miranda?"

"That was easy. I saw her perform at Sun City Grand a month or so after I spotted Sue Ellen. That cinched it. I'd never have another chance like this again. I made sure to find their emails and send them invitations to try out. I'd cast one in the part and the other as her understudy. Aren't you going to ask why I selected *The Mousetrap* in the first place?"

I would have asked her to recite Macbeth's famous soliloquy if I thought I could keep her talking. "Okay, why?"

"Like I said, I planned this a long time ago. I knew how superstitious your mother's friends were, and I had to have them take part in my production. Why do you think I selected an Agatha Christie mystery play? I knew her book club couldn't resist."

"You were the ghost on the stage that Shirley and Cecilia saw, and now I know why. Once you had killed Miranda, you had to come up with another way to murder Sue Ellen. You had to test out your theory with the trapdoors. So you disguised yourself with a teal tunic that looked like the original. In the dark, anyone would think it was Shirley."

Directly overhead a sudden vibration hit the room.

Applause. I paused to look up, and that was my mistake. Ellowina jabbed the cane right into my stomach and took off as I fell to my knees. I heard her running up the stairs.

"You didn't think I'd go this far not to have a backup plan, did you?"

I started to open my mouth when everything went black. She had turned off the lights and closed the door.

Chapter 29

Pitch black. I had never really understood the expression until that moment. The theater basement was devoid of any light. Not that it mattered. I was in too much agony from that jab to my stomach. It felt as if she'd punctured more than one vital organ. I stood up slowly, the pain radiating to my back.

Above me, the cast was taking its bows, and Ellowina Billings Bice was about to execute her Plan B. Whatever the heck that was. I started to piece together all sorts of scenarios, rejecting each one.

Loose light fixture? No, too uncertain. Overloading the fog machines with too much liquid nitrogen? No, she'd kill everyone. Poisonous flowers for Sue Ellen? Only in the movies. What? What? The answer was lodged somewhere in the back of my mind, and the more I pressed myself for answers, the harder it was for me to think.

By now I was standing, but it was like playing Blind Man's Bluff. I didn't need anyone to spin me around; I was already disoriented. Disoriented with a shooting pain that ran from my navel to my tailbone. I pictured myself in the emergency room with some medical assistant filling out a form.

"Can you please describe the shooting pain you feel, Miss Kimball?"

Shooting! My God! That's what Ellowina was going to do. She was going to shoot Sue Ellen. Shoot her in the back. Wasn't that something the note said? It didn't matter. The synapses in my brain inexplicably retrieved the conversation I'd had with Randolph Tilden Jr. when I confronted him in the parking lot that Sunday.

Randolph had described how formidable and capable Ellowina was. He'd also mentioned running into her at some shooting range a while back. It didn't mean anything to me at the time, but it sure did now. It meant one thing—Ellowina had a gun. Okay, maybe two things—Ellowina had a gun and she intended to use it.

Those side curtains would make the perfect hideout. Especially for someone dressed in black, who knew how to slip behind the stage unnoticed and exit the same way.

Standing still wasn't going to solve anything, so I picked a direction and walked straight ahead, my arms outstretched. The worst thing that could happen was I'd bump into a wall. So what? Next thing I knew, my hands touched something smooth and metallic. The chemical cabinet. It was on the same side of the room as the stairs. All I had to do was press the palm of my hand against the wall and move forward. One step at a time.

I could feel the grit on the soles of my feet and tried not to think about it. I kept moving. It wasn't too late. *I* wasn't too late. The audience was still applauding. Just then a hazy flash of light illuminated the stairs. Someone was opening the door.

"Ain't no one down here, Shirley. Place is dark. Want to see for yourself?"

It was Wayne's voice. I yelled up to him, but the only sounds that came out of my mouth were small, croaking ones.

"Lordy, no. I'm not going near that basement. You take another look."

"I did. There's no one down there."

I tried yelling again, but it was as if someone had cut my vocal cords. Instead, I made a fist and pounded on the staircase railing. The metal echoed like nobody's business and caught Wayne's attention.

"Who's down there?"

He opened the door all the way and flipped on the lights.

"Phee! What are you doing in the dark? Hey, are you hurt?"

My voice was barely audible as I reached the top of the stairs. I practically forced myself to speak louder.

"Ellowina's got a gun. She's going to kill Sue Ellen."

"I'll get the houselights on!"

"No. She's backstage. Turn the stage lights off and keep the curtain closed."

Wayne raced to the light panel as Shirley started screaming, "Lord preserve us now!"

The cast must have taken its final bow because the audience began yelling, "Encore! Encore!"

I kept telling myself over and over again no one shot blindly in the dark. No rational person anyway, and Ellowina was pretty darn rational. As I stared at the backdrop curtain, I tried to figure out which wing she was in. Both were close enough to the basement door, but only one was near the outside exit by the garbage bins. That had to be Ellowina's escape route.

She was on stage left and armed. I wasn't sure how

long we'd be able to keep the stage and the players in darkness as the audience clamored for an encore. Seasoned actors knew that when the lights were out on stage, they needed to stay perfectly still. But this was a community theater, and who the hell knew what any of them could be thinking.

My throat felt as if someone had ripped out the vocal cords. The only good news was the pain in my gut was subsiding in proportion to the adrenaline surging through my body. I took a step forward when someone spun me around by the shoulders. It was Cliff Edwards, the director.

"What are you doing on the stage? Behind the actors, no less?"

Small gurgling sounds emanated from the back of my mouth, barely above a whisper. "Ellowina Bice is behind those side curtains over there waiting to fire a shot at Sue Ellen. Does that answer your question?"

Cliff immediately started yelling, "All of you. Exit stage right. No open curtain. Exit stage right. Follow the glow tape. HURRY!"

Unfortunately, the players weren't so easily convinced, and it was total pandemonium with everyone shouting at once.

"THE AUDIENCE WANTS ANOTHER CURTAIN CALL!"

"I INTEND TO TAKE ANOTHER BOW!"

"THIS IS PREPOSTEROUS! WHO CLOSES THE CURTAINS ON THE CAST?"

"WILL SOMEONE OPEN THOSE CURTAINS?"

"ENCORE! GIVE THEM AN ENCORE!"

The next voice I heard was Marshall's, and it resounded like a cannon as he stormed across the stage, ushering everyone out of there.

Then Cliff continued to yell, "Exit stage right! NOW! All of you into the greenroom and don't say a word."

People pushed. People shoved. People grumbled. But at least they left the stage. All but one—my mother.

"Phee! Why are you on the stage? What's going on? What's the big rush to get us off the stage? The audience loved us."

"It's just a precaution," I lied. "I'll talk to you in the greenroom. I need to see Marshall for a minute."

"Fine, fine. This better not happen tomorrow night." My mother tromped off the stage muttering and spewing, unaware of her proximity to Ellowina and oblivious to the fact that her daughter was standing barefoot on a filthy stage.

The side curtains were on guiding tracks and when drawn together created folds that were easy to hide between. Other than the glow tape, the only other light on the stage came from the foyer. It was enough for the cast to make their move, but apparently not enough to see where Ellowina had placed herself.

"Sorry, Phee," Marshall whispered. "I should have been here."

"It wasn't your fault. At least you didn't miss the finale."

Wayne was a few feet away from us at the light board. There was no need for him to shout in order to be heard. "Hey. We've got to turn the houselights on and let the audience out. Show's over. Can't keep them in the dark. Richard called nine-one-one from his cell phone and skirted out one of the back exits. He overheard everything from where he was standing. He's going to head back to the auditorium from the main entrance to prevent anyone from going backstage. I'm turning on those houselights now."

Marshall's voice was surprisingly calm. "Understood. Do it."

He tapped me on the shoulder and pointed to stage right. "Go into the greenroom. It's not safe for you here. And by the way, where's that deputy sheriff on duty?"

"At a traffic accident on Grand and the 303. Must be a bad one."

"Aargh. Glad I didn't take that route. Okay, okay, get going. Any crew members you see, get them into the greenroom."

Cliff must have already spread the word when he evacuated the cast because there was no one in the foyer backstage or down the corridor. The only other crew members were on the catwalk and would probably hang around up there until everyone had left the theater.

I crossed the stage and walked past the side curtains, same as everyone else did. Only everyone else didn't get grabbed by the neck. Strong fingers pressed into my flesh, and I froze.

"Don't you dare make a sound," Ellowina hissed. "This gun's got a full magazine."

With a hand around the front of my neck and a cold metal cylinder pressing against my temple, I couldn't have made a sound if I wanted to. I stood absolutely still. The lingering scent of sweet chloroform was impossible to ignore. It must have gotten onto Ellowina's hand when she held that cloth. I tried not to inhale.

Her voice was soft, barely above a whisper. "If you don't want to join Miranda, you'll do as I say. Walk directly into the corridor and open the greenroom door. If it's locked, knock and tell them who you are. Tell them everything is okay. When they open the door, tell Sue Ellen the sheriff's deputy is outside and needs to speak with her. Do you understand?"

"Uh-huh."

"My gun will be aimed directly at you once you start walking. Don't try anything stupid."

I could hear the audience emptying out of the auditorium. A cacophony of voices and shuffling feet.

"Stand still," Ellowina said. "We've got plenty of time while the audience leaves."

She didn't have to tell me twice. I stood there for what seemed like hours. Finally, the noises dissipated from the auditorium and Ellowina gave me a slight shove. At least the gun wasn't about to go off on the side of my head.

I figured Marshall would hear me if I screamed, but I was afraid Ellowina would have a knee-jerk reaction and shoot me. I kept quiet. The stage was dark, but the dim light in the hallway, along with the glow tape, was enough for me to make my way over to the greenroom. Ellowina wasn't taking any chances. She had the gun pressed against me as we navigated through the tight maze of side curtains. Only Marshall remained on the stage as far as I knew.

I heard his footsteps but they sounded as if he was moving in the opposite direction from me. To the corridor maybe? That was where one of the light panels was located. It didn't matter. Even if he was two feet away, it might as well have been the Atlantic Ocean. There was nothing I could do. As far as he was concerned, I was already out of there and in the greenroom.

Just then, my foot stepped on some sort of strap, and the next thing I knew, a metal pole was leaning against my leg. One of the poles from Randolph's skis. Someone had left that prop against a wall, upside down no less, and it got jostled when I stepped on the hand strap. If I had been walking any faster, it would have fallen. I wasted no time grabbing it, trying to figure out how far up the metal point was.

When I was fairly certain I had a good grip, I took a breath, leaned back, and plunged the tip of the ski pole into Ellowina's thigh. It was enough to catch her off guard. The gun dropped to the floor, and I kept poking that pole into her. My scream was probably heard in four counties.

"HELP! MARSHALL!"

Another voice followed.

"LIGHTS UP!"

It was Wayne's voice and, in an instant, the stage lights came on. Ellowina's gun was a few feet from me, and I tried to nudge it with my bare foot. Like a madwoman, she gave me a push and lunged for it, but, instead of grabbing the gun, she inadvertently yanked on the side curtain. The very curtain Wayne had warned me to keep my hands off. Something about loose grommets.

Suddenly I was on the floor, suffocating under a dusty velvet blanket.

Ellowina's not going to kill me. The damn dust mites are. I couldn't help but wonder when was the last time they cleaned that thing.

I was so busy trying to get out from under the weight of the curtain that I momentarily forgot Ellowina was trapped in there with me. She, unfortunately, didn't forget, and began to kick at me with all of her strength. I kicked back. Each thrust tore my sheath dress a bit more. Of all nights to wear something formfitting.

She had another advantage, too. Her shoes were heavy suckers, and my ankles were getting the worst of it. I was about to do the one thing that my mother never would have condoned while I was growing up—pull her hair.

What the hell, Mom. It's my only chance.

As my fingers wrapped themselves around Ellowina's closely cropped hair, someone else's hands brushed against me. I figured it had to be Marshall trying to get hold of Ellowina. He and Wayne had managed to pull the curtain off of me and that crazy director. In the blink of an eye, Marshall had one arm around Ellowina's waist and the other holding his service revolver to her side.

I got up on my elbows and started to hyperventilate. My dress was in shreds, my body bruised, and my face covered in dirt and dust. So much for trying to impress a guy.

Marshall didn't say a word as I struggled to stand up. He was still holding Ellowina by the waist and pointing his weapon at her.

"I found a spool of wire if you need to tie her up," Wayne said. "Got a hammer, too."

"That won't be necessary." Marshall turned to Ellowina. "Will it?"

Then he looked at Wayne. "Open the front curtain. Those deputies should be coming in any second."

"It's about time!" Bill's voice reverberated across the empty auditorium. "Best damn scene in the whole play and you had the curtain closed."

I was still staring at my dress, tears rolling down my cheeks. Worse still, my hair felt as if it had been electrified.

Marshall turned his head from Ellowina and looked at me. "Are you all right, Phee? Did you get hurt? And why are you barefoot? You could have stepped on a nail or something."

"I . . . I . . . oh, never mind."

While I was struggling to catch my voice Bill bellowed

from the catwalk, "Hey, you guys! Some broad's been running all over the place looking for Phee Kimball. Something about a handbag. We told her to go backstage, but that was before all hell broke loose."

My hands immediately flew to my hair, and all I could feel was frizz. "I, um . . . I guess I'd better go to the greenroom. It doesn't look like Ellowina's going anywhere."

Marshall was standing perfectly still, his gun at her torso. "Tell the cast and crew they need to stay there until the deputies arrive, okay?"

"Yeah. Fine."

Lyndy was waving to me from down the hallway as soon as I left the stage.

"Whoa! What happened to you? It looks like you've been in a fight with a street gang. Did you fall or something? I've been looking all over for you. I figured you ran into Marshall, and the two of you sat in the back of the auditorium for the second act."

"Don't I wish. And compared to what happened, the street gang sounds like a walk in the park."

Lyndy's mouth dropped when I gave her the details. "Yikes. No wonder you look like hell. Are you all right? Do you want me to drive you home?"

"No, I'm fine. Listen, the deputies are about to arrive, so you'd better hurry before you get caught up in this. I'll catch you later."

"Oh gosh. I'd better hustle. My aunt is waiting out front and probably getting twitchy. I'll call you tomorrow. Oh, and tell your mother it was a great performance."

Lyndy took off just as the deputies got to the stage. The thudding of their feet on the wooden floor reverberated as I approached the greenroom.

Cliff had had the common sense to lock the door. Unfortunately, no one was about to open it, no matter how hard I pounded. Finally, I took the phone from my bag and dialed my mother's cell number. I had remembered something about her telling me she kept the phone in the greenroom, "just in case."

"Phee! Why are you calling me?"

"Because no one will open the door! That's why. Open the greenroom door! It's okay."

In retrospect, I should have been more explicit. I should have said, "Open the greenroom door, but don't let anyone out." I didn't, and what followed was worse than a Black Friday Sale at Best Buy.

Everyone charged out at once. The cast, the crew, and the two cleaning women who knew enough English to hide when they heard someone use the word "killer." I supposed it was the last time they'd volunteer to clean the theater after a show, even if it meant time and a half.

If there was one thing to be thankful for, it was the fact that this was a relatively small cast. Had it been *The Music Man,* more than one of us would have been trampled to death.

"Wait! Don't! Hold up! Wait!" I shouted.

It was futile. I got jostled, tousled, and bumped as the actors raced back on stage, probably hoping to eke out any final bits of applause.

Herb was the worst, nearly knocking me over as he ran downstage. "Sorry, cutie, my fans await."

What awaited instead was an empty auditorium, with the exception of Ellowina being escorted out by two county deputies. Marshall and another sheriff's deputy were busy tagging and placing her gun in a Ziploc bag. I got out of Herb's way as the other actors and crew members filled the stage. Everyone was staring at Ellowina's silhouette as the house lights dimmed.

Next thing I knew, Paula let out a shout and charged down the side steps, running toward the deputies. I wasn't sure if she was screaming, "Why, why, why" or "Die, die, die," but it didn't matter. Within seconds, she jumped on top of Ellowina and pounded her. Paula was flailing her arms as one of the deputies tried to stop her.

It wasn't going to work. Even with her hands tied, Ellowina still managed to kick everyone in sight. She was so forceful she nearly knocked over one of the deputies. Above us, Bill and Kevin laughed hysterically.

"Hey, down there! No one told Kevin and me there was a third act!"

"Phee!" It was my mother's voice directly behind me. "Were you alone on stage with that crazy woman?"

"Um . . . er . . . which one?"

"Well, not Paula. Ellowina. Who do you think? The deputies are arresting Ellowina. Why didn't you tell me ahead of time? You left your poor mother on stage like a sitting duck with a homicidal maniac lurking around."

"She isn't . . . I mean, I didn't . . ."

I was so preoccupied arguing with my mother that I barely realized Marshall had joined the melee. He had Paula by the waist and was dragging her away from Ellowina and the deputies.

Behind me Sue Ellen was crying. Not soft, simpering cries but loud, nasal sobs that, for some inexplicable reason, made Bill and Kevin erupt in more raucous laughter.

"It's not funny, you two!" Myrna shouted.

"Sure is from here," was the reply.

Chapter 30

It took the better part of an hour to get everyone calmed down.

Sue Ellen wouldn't stop crying, and Paula kept yelling at Marshall, "You have a gun. Why didn't you use it?"

Good thing I wasn't the one with the gun, or I might have bopped it over her head.

Since the three deputies had left with Ellowina, it was up to Marshall and me to break the news that the original director was the one who had murdered Miranda and planned to kill Sue Ellen at the end of act two. But the hardest part was getting everyone to sit down in front.

"Wayne," I shouted. "Can you turn up the house-lights?"

"We just turned them off."

"Well, turn them on again. Marshall and I need to speak with everyone, and we need some light."

One by one, the actors and stage crew moved to the front seats.

About the same time my mother noticed I was barefoot. "Where are your shoes, Phee? Why are you walking around barefoot? You could step on something. Worse yet, you could pick up a fungus from these floors. Who the heck knows the last time they were cleaned."

"A foot fungus is the last thing I'm worried about now. And my shoes are in the basement."

"What were you doing in the basement? Oh . . . don't tell me. Don't you dare tell me you were alone with Ellowina. What's the matter with you?"

In the meantime, Shirley had slipped back to the costume room to bring me some green elf slippers. They were the only shoes she could find in a hurry. With my hair sticking straight up in a frizz ball, my dress torn, my eye makeup running down my cheeks, and now the green slippers, I looked like something out of Dr. Seuss. And not one of his adorable characters, either.

The cast and crew were still filling in the seats when, out of nowhere, Chuck Mitchenson said, "Hey, how do we know she was acting alone? She could have an accomplice. And they could have another gun, for that matter."

"Gun? Someone's got a gun?" It was Cecilia, who was still standing on the stage. At the mention of the word "gun," everyone began to squirm in their seats and a few people ducked or slunk below.

"No one's got a gun!" Marshall shouted. "We're positive she was acting alone. No gun!"

Lucinda, who'd been relatively quiet during the entire ordeal, stood up from her second row seat and held up an aerosol can. "I have bug spray! That's right. Bug spray. If anyone makes a move, I'll use it."

"Lordy, stop that." This time it was Shirley. "Ain't no bugs to spray, Lucinda, and smelly air won't stop a gun."

More shrieks were followed by a loud blast.

"A GUN! SOMEONE'S GOT A GUN!"

The noise ripped through the auditorium like Air Force One on takeoff. Only, it wasn't a gun. I found out later it was Kenny, who'd accidentally hit the sound effects button on the panel board as he was making his way from backstage. It didn't matter. Full and total panic ensued.

"GUNS! EVERYWHERE!"

"SPRAY THE BUG SPRAY, LUCINDA!"

"DON'T YOU DARE!"

"DUCK! DUCK AND COVER!"

"IT'S NOT AN AIR RAID DRILL!"

Some people tried to get out of their seats while others tried to get under them. Above us, Kevin and Bill were doubled over laughing and snorting.

Finally, Bill shouted in a voice that could wake the dead. "HEY, YOU CHOWDERHEADS! THAT WAS THE STUPID SOUND EFFECTS MACHINE! KENNY HITS THAT THING ALL THE TIME. LAST WEEK WE GOT A SERENADE OF YOWLING CATS. THERE'S NO DAMN GUN!"

Who would have thought Bill Sanders, of all people, had the voice of reason?

But he did, and for what it was worth, it got everyone to stop panicking. Long enough to sit still and wait for Marshall and me.

"This is worse than combat duty," Marshall whispered as he walked down in front. "And how did you know it was Ellowina?"

I kept my voice real low. "From the program. Her name. Billings Bice."

"Yeah, about that . . . Rolo left me a text message while I was waiting for the emergency road service. Remember when I told you he wanted to probe further? Guy's like a damn bloodhound. Anyway, he found out that Leonora Billings, the lady who died of asphyxiation, had a daughter by the name of Ellowina, and he looked her up. I tried calling Bowman and Ranston but got their voice mails. Anyway, the rest is . . . well . . . you know."

"Do you need a microphone?" Wayne asked as Marshall and I stood between the front row and the stage.

We shook our heads in unison.

"Go on," I whispered. "You're the detective. They'll listen to you."

Marshall was clear and succinct. He explained that Ellowina was caught attempting to murder Sue Ellen and that there was reasonable evidence to indicate she was the one who killed Miranda Lee.

"Good! Now, can we get out of here? Curley's is going to close soon and I need a drink," Herb said.

He was followed by the rest of his pinochle buddies. Each one grunting about needing a beer.

Myrna, who happened to be sitting next to Herb, pounded him on the shoulder. "Not so fast. We need details. Lots of details. I want to know Ellowina's motive. I want to know how she did it. The first murder, that is. Because Sue Ellen is still with us."

As if to prove Myrna right, Sue Ellen began to hyperventilate, only to be escorted out of the auditorium by Cliff. He had his arm around her waist and kept telling her everything was going to be all right. Would their flames of passion, so obvious during *The Odd Couple*, going to be relit?

Marshall spent the next five minutes reassuring Shirley and Cecilia that Miranda's ghost wasn't haunting the place.

Lucinda spoke up, too. "See? I told you! I told you so."

Bill exited the catwalk and sat three rows back.

A perfect spot for bellowing. "Why did the old biddy off Miranda? That's what I'd like to know."

He wasn't the only one asking that question. Before Marshall or I could explain, the cast and crew offered their own explanations, each one wackier than the one before.

Finally, in a fit of exasperation or maybe even desperation, I yelled, "Revenge! Revenge for Ellowina's mother. Miranda and Sue Ellen caused her death."

Everyone gasped at once. A full two seconds of absolute silence. Some were better at it than others.

Kenny stood and waved his hands in the air. "I say we go to Curley's and drink to Ellowina's deceased mother."

"Yes! Let's drink to that and anything else," Wayne called out. "Give me a minute to finish telling Harriet something first."

Marshall shrugged, and we were about to call it a night when my mother sprang from her seat, stepping over knees, legs, and feet to get to her only daughter. "My God, Phee! Wayne just told me you were fighting with Ellowina. Following her into the basement wasn't enough for you? No wonder you look so disheveled."

Then she turned to Marshall. "And what took you so long to nab that crazy Ellowina?"

"It's not his fault," I said. "His car battery died, and he didn't get to the theater until the end of the second act."

"The end of the second act? You mean you missed the play? The hell with Ellowina. I expect the both of you to be at tomorrow night's performance. No excuses. And, as for your boss, there are two more performances next weekend, and I expect him to be at one of them."

"Now, can we get a damn drink at Curley's?" someone yelled.

Richard, who had managed to prevent the audience from swarming backstage after the performance, looked as unkempt as I did. Apparently dealing with a belligerent crowd wasn't part of his usual duties as stage manager.

He waved his hand in the air from where he was seated and made one announcement. "Curtain goes up tomorrow on time. Business as usual. Be here promptly at six. Whoever gets to Curley's first, order me a Corona."

Randolph, Gordon, and Len shouted out that they would take a raincheck. The rest of the men charged out of there in record time. All but one--Wayne. I begged him to go downstairs to retrieve my wedge heels. He took one look at my feet and acquiesced. Just then, two deputies came in and asked for Marshall and the stage manager. Apparently they needed to search the premises, starting with the projection booth and catwalk, to be sure Ellowina hadn't stashed any weapons. They also informed me I would be needed for questioning in the morning. So much for sleeping in.

My mother and the book club ladies decided to stick around in the costume room. God forbid they miss some tantalizing tidbit, like someone finding another weapon. The two cleaning ladies were so shaken up they refused to stay another minute and swore they'd be back in the morning to tidy up. Cliff and Sue Ellen were long gone, so that only left Paula. She was sitting downstage, her legs dangling over the apron into the orchestra pit. I actually felt bad for her.

"I'm sorry about your friend," I said.

"Not many people liked her, and I suppose I can understand why. Miranda had a certain edge to her and a way of pushing people to their breaking point. She did that with Len Beckers, you know. Told him she was going to let the world know he wasn't the man he pretended to be unless he took one of those little blue pills. It was catty and mean, but Miranda was ticked at him for one reason or another."

"Wait a minute. Hold up a second. Are you telling me Miranda was about to tell the world Len was impotent?"

"Not necessarily impotent but a lackluster and unpredictable performer." Paula leaned back and stretched, her neck straining to go farther. "Sorry. I feel as if my body is in knots from the neck down."

Suddenly I remembered something. It was insignificant at the time, but not anymore. I jumped up, told Paula I understood how she felt, and scrambled to find Marshall before it was too late. I raced to the foyer behind the stage and nearly knocked into Wayne, who had just come up from the basement with my heels.

"I'm looking for Marshall and the deputies."

"Don't you want your shoes first?"

"Oh my gosh. Thanks, Wayne." I grabbed my heels, started to put them on and then thought otherwise. Heels would slow me down, and my feet were already as filthy as could be.

"If you see Marshall on your way out, tell him I'm looking for him. And the deputies, too."

"Sure thing."

I would have seen them if they were in the auditorium or backstage, and I would have heard them if they were still on the catwalk or in the projection booth. That left the dressing rooms and costume room. Both were across the hall from where I was standing.

Tell Monty Hall I am taking what's behind the door on my left.

"Have you seen Marshall or the deputies?" I stared straight at Shirley. "Quick! Tell me."

"Lordy, honey, slow down. You're running like the devil's on your tail."

"He might be. I need to find them."

My mother all but shoved Shirley to the side of the doorway. "Now what? Don't tell me there's another murderer on the loose. Sophie Vera Kimball, you slow down and tell your mother what's going on. Do we need to lock ourselves in here and dial nine-one-one?"

"No, he's not after you."

"Oh Lordy, another killer's about to strike. Lock the door, ladies. Someone find me my cell phone. Better yet, shut the lights. He won't see us in the dark."

Normally Shirley moved at a leisurely southern pace. But, in that instant, she was like Jesse Owens at the starting block. In a flash, we were in total darkness.

I tried to keep my composure as I yelled, "Turn those lights back on. The killer's not in the building."

My mother was relentless. "So there *is* another killer. I knew we weren't safe. Who is it, Phee? Who? Who?"

"You're sounding like that stupid owl commercial. Look, until Marshall and the deputies check it out, I really don't want to make accusations."

"You don't want to make accusations? You've got us locked up in the dark, scared to take a breath, and you don't want to make accusations? What's the matter with you?" My mother's voice had reached a fever pitch, and it reached Marshall, who was at the far end of the hallway.

"It's okay. We'll be right there, Harriet. Turn on the lights."

Seconds later, Marshall, Wayne, and the two deputies walked into the costume room, their gazes all fixed on me.

"I don't think Ellowina acted alone, and I think I can prove it."

One of the deputies crossed his arms and leaned back. "Go on. We haven't got all night."

I was so worked up that it amazed me I was able to be coherent. "Bill was the first person to find Miranda's body. He said there was a stiff on the catwalk or something equally crude and to the point. But someone else had another description. They said her head was tilted poetically back and that she upstaged everyone by looking like a Greek statue. Only the killer would have known that or said that. Why? Because they positioned her, and it wasn't Ellowina. Ellowina got out of there as soon as she thought Miranda was dead. She even said so."

I tapped my feet as the words rushed from my mouth. "Here's what I think happened. Ellowina used the chloroform to make Miranda woozy and fall. Miranda hit her head, but that didn't kill her. Ellowina used Miranda's necklace to strangle her, but she didn't succeed. Even the coroner's report said as much. Said it was inconclusive. Possibly a combination of a drug-induced state and strangulation. Miranda was still alive when Ellowina left the catwalk."

The sheriff's deputy who had crossed his arms now shook his head. "You're going to have a hard time proving that."

"I don't think so. There was one piece of evidence everyone overlooked—the crumpled instrument schedule lying next to the body. It was the old schedule. The original one. Other than the play director, the stage manager, and the lighting crew, only one other person had a copy, and it must have fallen out of their pocket when they got near the body."

"So you think they were working in tandem with Ellowina?"

This time it was the other deputy, and I was the one who shook my head.

"No. Stanley was the first person up the catwalk that day. He and Miranda had words, and he left. Ellowina was waiting it out, unseen in the auditorium. She did exactly what she confessed to doing—catching Miranda off guard with the chloroform- and Shalimar-soaked cloth, then giving her a shove and finalizing it by using Miranda's own necklace to strangle her. But here's the rest of the story . . ."

"Goodness, Phee," Myrna said. "You sound like Paul Harvey."

"Who?"

"She's too young to remember Paul Harvey," Lucinda said. "He used to have a wonderful radio show called *The Rest of the Story*."

My mother had reached her apex; she turned to Lucinda and shushed her.

"Anyway," I went on, "Ellowina never realized she dropped the cloth when she went to strangle Miranda. She may have been so intent on getting out of there that she didn't think about it. Remember, no one found the cloth; the only evidence of chloroform and Shalimar was from the medical examiner's office. That cloth is long gone. The killer wasn't stupid enough to toss it out in the theater and wouldn't have had time to go around back to use the Dumpsters, so they had to take it home. A good forensic team would be able to find evidence of the solvent and the perfume in their car."

Marshall took a step toward me and picked up where I left off. "So, what you're saying is you believe

Ellowina wasn't alone in the auditorium. Once she left, the real killer, who had been watching from below, used that opportunity to pick up the fallen cloth and finish the job."

"Yes. That's what I'm saying. That's what I said, or meant to say. We figured out Ellowina's motive was revenge. Our killer's motive was, well . . . self-preservation."

"Huh?" Marshall looked perplexed. "You'd better explain."

"When Ellowina left the auditorium, the killer made his way to the catwalk, where Miranda was still breathing. Placing and holding that cloth over her face for more than a few minutes ensured she wouldn't be breathing anymore. Murder by chloroform takes time, and that was something our killer had. No one else was around. Stanley had already left, and he probably figured the other two guys who were backstage did the same. Only one of them didn't."

My mother motioned with her hand for me to speed things up. "Which one, Phee? We haven't got all night."

"I've cracked the murder of the year, so please hold on for a few more seconds. So . . . um . . . as I was saying, there was only one person who had an instrument schedule, a motive, means, and an opportunity, and that was Len Beckers. The means was the cloth that literally fell into his lap. The opportunity came when he was heading out of the theater and went through the auditorium. That's when he saw the attempted murder take place. He didn't plan on killing Miranda, he just took advantage of a situation that presented itself, especially since he had a motive. Miranda was about to destroy his reputation. I didn't know about the last part until I spoke with Paula a little while ago. Then I pieced everything together."

Everyone gasped at once, but only my mother realized the true consequence. "Dear God. Who are we going to get to play the part of Mr. Paravicini at such late notice?"

Louise elbowed her way toward me. "I want to know what dirt Miranda had on Len's reputation. What was it? Tax fraud? Embezzlement? Tampering with the bowling scores? What? What was that witch holding over his head?"

"Um . . . er . . . I'm really not comfortable speaking about this in public. Defamation of character and all. Um, uh . . . can you give me a minute alone with Marshall?"

Before anyone could say a word, I walked out of the room and motioned for Marshall to follow. I was certain my mother would be eavesdropping on the other side of the door, so I took a few steps and whispered, "I'm really uncomfortable having this conversation, but Miranda was going to tell everyone Len was impotent."

"Ouch. That's a motive if I've ever heard one."

"You're not going to tell them in there, are you?"

"And have to get into that sort of a conversation with your mother's friends? Hell no! Plenty of time to speak privately with the deputies. By the way, great sleuthing. I'm just sorry you had to take the brunt of Ellowina. I feel awful about that."

Awful enough to throw your arms around me like they do in all those romance novels? "I'll be fine."

"Want me to drive you home? We can always swing back for your car tomorrow."

Yes, yes. Drive me home. Swing back. Stay overnight. "Um, er . . . I'll be fine. Honest."

"Okay. If you say so. We'd better go back in there."

The door wasn't fully open when a veritable inquisition from the cast and crew ensued.

"So what was it? Cheating clients?"

"Bigamy! I'll bet Miranda found out he has more than one wife."

"Running a pyramid scheme?"

"Bootleg liquor?"

"Bootleg liquor? This isn't prohibition."

Marshall ran his fingers through his hair and took a breath. "If you must know, it was over some sketchy business dealings. We'll look into it."

Myrna made a *tsk tsk* sound and poked Louise. "Is that all? I wanted to hear something juicy. Something riveting."

"Sorry to disappoint you, but that's about as exciting as it gets." Marshall gave me a wink and walked over to confer with the deputies.

While the women continued arguing amongst themselves, my mother sat in one of the chairs against the wall and sighed. "This is so anticlimactic. Such a letdown."

I pulled another chair over and put on my shoes. "I wouldn't say that. We caught the perpetrator and the opportunist. I'd call that a really good night."

"Only one of them is in custody. For all we know, Len Beckers could be on his way to South America. That's where all those criminals go."

"That's ridiculous. Where do you dredge up this stuff?"

Just then the two deputies left the room, and Marshall walked toward us.

"They've sent a car to Len's house. Not much we can do now except head home and make sure the theater is locked up."

Wayne held up a ring of keys and smiled. "No worries. I'll be more than happy to do that."

Chapter 31

The next morning, Stanley was released from the Fourth Avenue Jail, relinquishing his cell to Len. According to Marshall, who had been in close contact with the sheriff's department, Len confessed to finding Ellowina's cloth on the floor of the auditorium and going up to the catwalk to see if Miranda was still alive.

"You're not going to believe this," Marshall said when he phoned me around eleven, "but Len told the deputies he only wanted to make sure Ellowina finished the job. He said he thought Miranda was already dead, but didn't want to take any chances, so he tilted her head back and held the cloth over her mouth. You were right all along."

"So now what? It's going to be impossible to find out who really killed her, isn't it?"

"Both of them will still be booked for murder in one capacity or another. Murder, accessory to murder, attempted murder . . ."

"Now you're sounding like the reading list for my mother's book club."

"Oh . . . speaking of which, I need to send your

mother a complete investigative report. She hired us, after all, and paid the introductory fee."

I choked back a laugh. "Have you spoken to Nate about this? Does he know what happened?"

"I called him as soon as I got home. Didn't want him to turn on the television and be surprised. The news is running on all the local channels."

"Oh my gosh. I never turned the TV on. Kinda slept late, made breakfast, took a walk. Wow. Headline news. Did anyone mention my name?"

"No, nor mine. Deputies Bowman and Ranston were given credit for breaking the case."

"Oh brother. If that doesn't top the cake."

"Don't worry about it. Happens all the time. So, about tonight. Your mother expects us to catch the full performance. What time should I pick you up? Better yet, let's go out to eat first. Okay? I've been dying for a decent steak."

"Sounds good to me. The curtain opens at seven, so we'd better join the geriatric crowd and eat by five."

"As long as we don't get into that habit. Pick you up at four-thirty."

I'd barely ended the call when my phone rang again.

Surprise. Surprise. My mother. "I would have called you sooner, but I've been on the phone all morning with Shirley. She got a call first thing from Cliff and you're not going to believe this."

"If it's about Stanley—"

"Of course it's about Stanley. He's been released from jail and intends to walk himself on stage tonight in his role of Christopher Wren. Yeesh. Where does that leave Herb? I'll tell you where it leaves Herb. He's got to become Mr. Paravicini to replace Len."

"Um, okay. Does he know the part?"

"Of course he knows the part. That's not the problem. Shirley is going out of her mind."

After years of navigating through my mother's thought processes, I'd gotten pretty good at it. "The costume, huh?"

"Herb's big gut, that's what. Where's Shirley going to find a three-piece suit to fit him?"

"Doesn't Herb have any suits?"

"No one wears a three-piece suit in Sun City West unless they're on display at a mortuary."

"Hey, you've answered your own question. Have Shirley call the local funeral parlors. They must have buried lots of overweight men."

"Good idea. I'll talk to you later."

The phone call ended as fast as it started.

Then Lyndy called, and I kept her on the line for at least forty-five minutes. "You tackle a killer and uncover another one. Holy cow! You really should be a detective."

"I like bookkeeping. And accounting."

"And Marshall?"

"Yeah, that too. But like I've mentioned before, it's awkward. Working in the same office."

"Awkward until he kisses you smack on the lips. Then you'll have to come up with another word."

I wished he would kiss me smack on the lips. I'd come up with a whole damn dictionary.

That night, Marshall and I enjoyed a terrific steak dinner at the Texas Roadhouse, followed by a sold-out performance at the Stardust Theater. Apparently, news of the recent arrests sent ticket sales booming. We went backstage to congratulate the players and caught a different kind of performance. Herb's.

"No one told me this suit was used to dress a corpse before cremation!"

"Uh-oh." I inched my way closer to Marshall. "Looks like Herb just found out the suit came from a local funeral home and not Men's Wearhouse."

Shirley and Cecilia tried to placate him while the rest of the cast forced themselves not to laugh.

Herb continued ranting. "There's a special tag on the inside collar. It says Mencke's Funeral Parlor. This isn't funny. I don't know why all of you think it's all right to dress someone in something that was previously worn by a corpse."

"Hey," Marshall said. "At least the suit looks better vertically."

I gave my mother a hug and promised her Nate would be in the audience the following weekend.

That night I got my kiss from Marshall, but it wasn't exactly a full-blown, hot, on-the-lips ordeal that would make my palms sweat and my pulse race. Still, it was a start. I had invited him back to my place following the performance and made us some coffee to go with the apple strudel I'd picked up at the local bakery. In retrospect, I should have offered him wine, and lots of it.

We were sitting next to each other on the couch, reliving the entire *Mousetrap* fiasco, from Shirley's ghost to Herb's oversize waist. I caught a faint whiff of that crisp apple scent that seemed to take over every time Marshall got near me.

Then, without warning, he leaned over and gave me a hug. "You have no idea how awful I feel about your encounter with Ellowina. When you were tangled in that curtain. I can't believe that happened while I was only a few yards away. One second I was on the stage, and the next I was in that small corridor by the lighting panel."

"It's okay. Don't beat yourself up. It's not as if it was broad daylight. Those side curtains obscured everything."

"Yeah, but a gun to your head? I'd never forgive myself if anything happened to you."

"Well, it didn't. I'm still breathing."

"Keep it that way." Then he leaned over again, put his arm around me, and planted a soft kiss on my cheek while squeezing my shoulder.

"Phee," he continued, "there's something you need to know."

Here it comes. Here it comes. He's gay. He's in a relationship. He's gay, and he's in a relationship.

"Part of the reason I took this job was because I knew you were here. I've always liked you. Maybe now we can get to know each other outside of work. Um, that is, if you feel the same way."

Maybe it was the earnest tone in his voice and the way his eyebrows seemed to rise up, but all I could do was nod.

"And, by the way, I thought you looked particularly adorable with your hair all mussed and those splotches of dirt on your face."

"Adorable? I looked like one of The Three Stooges."

"Yeah, I happen to be a big fan of them, too. What do you think? Are you okay with this?"

Okay? I'm over the moon. "Is it going to be a problem with us working in the same office?"

"Not unless I decide to toss all of the paperwork off your desk and throw you on it like they do in those sappy movies."

"Do that and Augusta will have a coronary."

"She'd be followed by Nate."

We started laughing and it felt wonderful. The evening ended with a sweet peck on the cheek and another hug. Later, as I drifted off to sleep, I swore I could detect the unmistakable aroma of an apple orchard in the fall.

Two weeks later I had breakfast with my mother and the book club ladies at Bagels 'N More. Myrna, Cecilia, Lucinda, Shirley, and Louise were there, plus three snowbirds who'd recently returned for the winter—Constance, Riva, and Marianne. More would be arriving in January. Like usual, everyone was talking at once.

"There were two killers on the set?"

"I'm telling you, Arizona has gun laws for a reason. We all should be packing heat."

"Don't use the word 'packing.' I still have five suitcases to unpack."

"This is the last time I'll ever take part in a theater production!"

"I want to read about domestic murders, not witness them."

"You didn't witness the murder. All you saw was the body."

"Someone saw a dead body?"

"And a ghost."

"There was no ghost. Ellowina staged that."

Suddenly Shirley shushed everyone. "Lordy, that clever murderess staged enough goings on to make sure we all had high blood pressure. It was Ellowina who monkeyed with the air-conditioning and the trapdoors so someone would fall. And Ellowina who took the lipstick and wrote that message on the mirror.

And don't let me forget she perfumed car tires and the catwalk to make like Miranda's Shalimar-scented spirit was stalking us. But there was one thing she didn't do. She didn't turn the power off. So there!"

Lucinda waved the waitress over and tugged at Shirley's sleeve. "The power goes off all the time. It's that darned electric company, not a ghost."

"I'll have to give that Ellowina credit for one thing," my mother said. "Good planning. She started with those cryptic notes and wouldn't stop. We could all learn a lesson from her."

"Yeah," I said, "don't mess with the Booked 4 Murder book club."

Everyone started to laugh when, all of a sudden, another member burst through the door with such a grand entrance that half the place turned to look. It was my Aunt Ina, back from her vacation in Malta. Her long braids were woven with red and black ribbons and piled on top of her head like the Queen of Spades. A bizarre faux fur wrap covered most of her body, if only to give her reason to toss it off and throw it over an empty chair, revealing a long peasant dress in assorted shades of crimson and burnt orange.

"Hello, everyone! Did you miss me? Our flight got in late last night from Toronto. Louis is still sleeping, but I couldn't wait to see all of you. I knew you'd be here. Here's the best part—I've brought my book list with me. Don't make a single decision until you read this list. Murder mysteries in Malta. I'll have copies for everyone. I imagine it was a boring fall without me, but not to worry, Ina Stangler Melinsky is back."

The waitress had left a full pot of coffee on our table, so I poured my aunt a cup. "As long as Agatha Christie isn't on that list, I think you'll be fine."

"Agatha Christie? That reminds me, before we left for Malta, Louis bought two rows of tickets for the ASU Gammage Theater in Tempe for their midwinter production. Our treat for the book club. They're doing *The Mousetrap.*"

"Put the tickets up on eBay, Ina," my mother said, "or you'll be voted out of the club immediately."

Don't miss the next Sophie Kimball Mystery,

BOTCHED 4 MURDER

by J.C. Eaton,
coming in January 2019
to your favorite bookstores and e-tailers.

And in September 2018, J.C. Eaton has

CHARDONNAYED TO REST,

the next WINE TRAIL MYSTERIES book
available from Lyrical Press
and your favorite e-tailer.
Please turn the page for a preview!

Penn Yan, New York

Catherine Trobert, owner of Lake View Winery, brushed her honey-blond bangs away from her eyes with one hand and leaned across her chair to pat my wrist with the other. We were the first ones to take our seats at the semimonthly Women of the Wineries meeting held at Madeline Martinez's establishment, Billsburrow Winery. It was the week before Labor Day, and everyone was anxious for the fall winery events to begin.

Well, not everyone. I certainly wasn't. I was anxious to hear from my script analyst regarding the screenplay I had submitted for review. I was under contract with a Canadian film company that specialized in TV romances. Managing my sister's winery for a year while she and her husband, Jason, were off chasing after some elusive bug in Costa Rica was something I agreed to do in a weak moment. I had no intention of making it permanent. Besides, the study grant my entomologist brother-in-law got from Cornell's Experiment Station was only supposed to be for a year. Even though I had heard a nasty rumor from Godfrey Klein, who worked with Jason, that the grant might be extended.

Bite your tongue, Godfrey.

For the past five years I had earned a decent living writing screenplays, and I intended to keep it that way. Overseeing Two Witches Winery was simply a favor. A favor that was due to expire in ten months, at which time I'd be back in Manhattan saying adios to the person who had sublet my apartment.

Catherine gave my wrist another pat and sighed. "I'm so sorry to break this to you, Norrie, but Steven won't be able to make it for Labor Day Weekend as planned. You wouldn't think his law firm would have such a big caseload, but it does. I suppose the state of Maine gets its fair share of crime, too."

"Huh?" All I'd heard were the words "Labor Day Weekend" and "Steven." I kind of pieced together the rest in my mind. Catherine Trobert had grand designs of fixing me up with her son, even though I'd hardly known him in high school. He was a few years older than me and hung out with the jocks and future leaders of America on the student council. I was too busy writing poetry for the literary magazine and articles for the school newspaper to notice him.

"I know. I know," she said. "You haven't seen Steven since high school, but I'm certain the two of you would enjoy getting reunited."

Reunited? We were never united. Never ever. "Um, that's too bad. Send him my regards."

"I will, dear. I most certainly will. On a positive note, Gladys Pipp is back at work from her hip replacement. Moves around as if she were sixteen and not sixty."

"Um, is that one of your workers?"

"Oh heavens no. Gladys is the secretary for the

Yates County Department of Public Safety. Unlike those dour deputies over there who can barely utter a single syllable, Gladys is a wealth of information, if you need her. Shh! Don't tell anyone, but she gave me the heads-up about that nasty little speed trap just past Snell Road."

"I'll keep that in mind."

Just then, Stephanie Ipswich from Gable Hill Winery and Rosalee Marbleton from Terrace Wineries came into the room. I immediately greeted them. Anything to stop Catherine from lamenting about Steven or bringing up people I didn't know. Speed traps or not.

Madeline Martinez followed and placed a tray of scones, chocolate filled croissants, and butter cookies on the large coffee table. "Coffee and tea are on the credenza. Help yourselves, ladies. This should be a really short meeting. We've only got two things on the agenda—the Federweisser Festival and the inclusion of the Grey Egret Winery into our WOW association."

Rosalee moved her wire-rimmed glasses farther up her nose and straightened her shoulders. For a small, stout woman in her early seventies, she looked as if she could command an army. "Let's be honest. If it wasn't for the Grey Egret, our West Side Women of the Wineries, which most of us simply refer to as WOW, abbreviated or not, wouldn't exist. And neither would the 'Sip and Savor' event or the Federweisser. It was Angela Martinelli who got the whole ball rolling."

"True, true," Catherine said, "but Angela no longer owns the Grey Egret. She sold it to Don and Theo a few years ago. They're the owners now. How can we have a women's winery group if two of the members are men?"

Stephanie selected the tiniest butter cookie from the

tray, God forbid she eat something that would destroy that knockout figure of hers, and took the smallest bite. "Who says we have to be a women's group? Let's face it, the Grey Egret takes part in all our west side functions, and that means we have to call them constantly when we could simply converse with them at our meetings. I say we let them join the group."

"I second that!" I shouted.

"It's not a parliamentary procedure meeting, Norrie," Catherine whispered.

I shrugged. "I still think we should let them in. Don and Theo are great guys and amazingly supportive. When Elsbeth Waters's body was discovered in our Riesling vineyard this past June, it was Don and Theo who helped me get through that whole mess."

"That whole *murder*, you mean," Rosalee said. "I happen to agree with you." Then she turned to the others. "Invite them into our group, for heaven's sake, and let's get on with this meeting."

I'd never known Rosalee to appear so agitated, but I figured she had lots on her plate, so to speak, with the grape harvest starting and the fall tourist rush only weeks away.

Madeline nodded and gazed into her coffee cup. "Hmm, then what do we do about the name? WOW is so catchy."

I did at least three mental eye rolls and one silent scream. "Can't the initials represent something else? Drop the west side part of the title, since no one uses it anyway, except for my sister, and have the WOW stand for Winery Owners of the West. That would work, wouldn't it?"

"Norrie, you're a genius," Stephanie said. "So? Is it agreed, ladies? The Grey Egret joins our group?"

Everyone said, "Yes," and Madeline announced she'd call Don and Theo to let them know the news.

"I hope the Federweisser portion doesn't take too long," Rosalee said. "I've got some pressing business to deal with."

"Everything okay?" Catherine asked.

"Not really, but I don't want to take up all of your time."

Madeline looked at each one of us. "It'll be fine. Go ahead."

Rosalee clasped her hands together and squeezed them tight. She sat up even straighter than before. "It's our water situation. At the winery, not the house. Fortunately, the house is located close enough to the road so we get water from the village waterline. The winery wasn't that lucky, and the village has no intention of expanding its waterline. Anyway, we've been getting the water for our vineyards from the lake, and we truck in potable water for our own use at the winery. Lots of lakeshore wineries use a surface water source as well as a commercial one."

She paused for a moment and none of us said a word.

"We paid for a special waterline that went through the Baxters' property. For years we paid them for the land use. No different than someone owning a mobile home but renting the lot. It was a fair and reasonable price. Then, a few months ago, the Baxters sold their property and moved to Texas. The new owner jacked up the price to an astronomical level. He said if we don't pay, he'll cut off our water access."

"My God!" Madeline put her coffee cup down and covered her mouth.

"How can they do that?" Stephanie asked. "That's highway robbery."

Rosalee's voice sounded shaky. "I'm afraid they can and they will. Without water, our vineyards will be destroyed and our winery gone for good."

My heart began beating faster. "Isn't there anything you can do?"

"There are stopgap measures, like having non-potable water trucked in and placed in huge holding tanks. We've already started to do that, but it's an awfully expensive way to get water. That's why I'm headed into Geneva to see our attorney. Maybe we have legal rights. If not, we're doomed."

Catherine made a strange chortling sound. Something in between clearing her throat and gargling. "What kind of a selfish thug would do a thing like that? Terrace Wineries has been in the Finger Lakes since before I was even born. This isn't right. Clearly, there must be something we can do."

Rosalee gave a halfhearted smile. "Thanks, dear. I'm hoping my attorney will have an answer. Or even a decent idea. Anyway, I really must go. I'm sure you'll all get on fine with the rest of the meeting. Thank goodness the Federweisser event is at Two Witches this year and not my place. I'm sure Norrie will do a splendid job."

With that, Rosalee picked up her floral pocketbook, which looked as if it could double as a carpetbag, and headed out of the room. The rest of us sat there in silence for a few seconds before Madeline spoke.

"My husband's a county board representative. I'm going to see what he has to say about this. Rosalee was right, you know. About the wineries on the lake having to get their water from the lake. What if some of them are in the same predicament she is? Putting in pipelines and paying for land use because they don't own the property rights. A greedy land owner could really put the screws to them."

"I think we should call Henry Speltmore. He's in charge of the wine association. Maybe he has an idea or two floating around in his head," Stephanie said.

Madeline laughed. "If he does, that would be a first. But yeah, give him a call. He's a nice enough guy, and it couldn't hurt. Well, I suppose we should get on with the last piece of business—the Federweisser."

I squirmed around in my seat, certain they were going to ask me what we had planned for the event. I knew I should've paid more attention to Cammy, our tasting room manager, when she went over the food menu for the Federweisser, but I didn't. I was too busy trying to get a dialogue straight in my mind for a scene that had to be worked out for my screenplay.

Same thing with Franz, our winemaker. He must've explained the process for making Federweisser to me at least three times, but I still wasn't a hundred percent sure I understood. Something about adding yeast to grapes so they fermented quickly. Oh, and the sugar. I remembered that part. The sugar in the grapes turns into alcohol and carbon dioxide, and when it reaches four percent, it becomes Federweisser, a really cool drink that tastes like a champagne soda. The thing is, the alcohol percentage keeps growing, so the Federweisser has to be consumed within a few days. Otherwise, the stuff just becomes regular wine.

"Entertainment. Didn't you hear me, Norrie?"

"Huh?" I looked at Madeline and knew she had asked me a question, but I was too busy trying to recall the last two conversations I'd had that I didn't pay attention to.

"Um, can you repeat that?"

Stephanie jumped in before Madeline could reply.

"She asked if you were having any entertainment at the Federweisser. Last year, when it was held at Rosalee's, they hired a polka band."

I don't suppose watching Alvin, our Nigerian Dwarf Goat, spit at people constitutes entertainment. "Uh, yeah. We're working on that. But everything else is all set." And if it's not, it will be.

Madeline nodded and gave me a thumbs-up. "That sounds fine. Let us know if there's anything you need. We'll all make it a point to advertise for you, and we'll be sure to drop by for the festivities. Goodness. That's only three weeks away. My, how time goes by."

Not fast enough, judging by the length of this meeting.

"Well, ladies," Madeline said. "That about concludes the meeting for me, unless anyone else wants to bring up something."

My eyes widened, and I held my breath.

Madeline clapped her hands together, startling us. "Okay then. We'll meet again right before the Federweisser. And if my husband has any bright ideas about how the county can help Rosalee, I'll let you know."

The next few minutes were spent commiserating about the mess Terrace Wineries was in, and then we all left Madeline's place. Stephanie motioned for me to chat with her once we got to the parking lot. I walked over to her car as she clicked the door open.

"You're a good sleuth, Norrie. Think you can dig up the dirt on that new landowner who's bilking Rosalee?"

"Me? I'm not an investigator."

"No. You're better. You get answers. They get red tape. Look, I'd be willing to do some checking, too, as long it's on the Internet. Between the winery and two first graders, I'm lucky I can get through the day with a coherent thought. Not to mention, we'll be closing on the Waters property in a few weeks."

"That's right. I'm glad it worked out for you."

"Me, too. Elsbeth's niece, Yvonne, couldn't sell that B & B fast enough, but she knew it would be a tough sale with all that land. Fortunately, she was able to have it divided up so we could buy the property for vineyards and someone else could buy the B & B."

"Did she find a buyer for the business?"

"Uh-huh. I'm not sure who, but she said they were thrilled to run a bed and breakfast in the Finger Lakes."

"Did she say anything else? Like what she plans to do?"

"Not really. She was kind of tight-lipped about it. Can you blame her?"

"No, I suppose not."

"Anyway, let me know if you decide to poke around regarding that crummy water hog of Rosalee's."

"Sure thing."

"At least you don't have to find a murderer this time."

"Don't say that out loud!"

"You're not superstitious are you?"

"No, just careful."

I waved good-bye to the other ladies in the parking lot and drove home. Maybe I was just a tad superstitious, but at least I wasn't downright loony, like Glenda from our tasting room. I still couldn't believe I let her hold that ridiculous séance to contact Elsbeth's restless spirit. Stephanie was right. This time I'd be snooping around to dig up dirt, not a dead body.